W9-CJO-678

VICTOR HUGO
and the
Romantic Drama

Albert W. Halsall

UNIVERSITY OF TORONTO PRESS
Toronto Buffalo London

© University of Toronto Press Incorporated 1998
Toronto Buffalo London
Printed in Canada

ISBN 0-8020-4322-4

Printed on acid-free paper

University of Toronto Romance Series

Canadian Cataloguing in Publication Data

Halsall, Albert W.
  Victor Hugo and the romantic drama

  Includes bibliographical references and index.
  ISBN 0-8020-4322-4

  1. Hugo, Victor, 1802–1885 – Dramatic works.   I. Title.

  PQ2301.H3 1998   842 .7   C98-930487-6

University of Toronto Press acknowledges the financial assistance to its
publishing program of the Canada Council for the Arts and the Ontario
Arts Council.

This book has been published with the help of a grant from the Canadian Federation for the Humanities, using funds provided by the Social
Sciences and Humanities Research Council of Canada.

For Mary, as always

Contents

viii   Contents

Introduction

> That play [*The Merchant of Venice*] is a drama. I think that to a certain extent
> that is true of all Shakespeare's plays: they are all dramas and any attempt to
> call them histories, tragedies, or comedies is not helpful to theatre practi-
> tioners – a director and a group of actors.[1]

Victor Hugo's Romantic dramas have remained the most controversial part
of his work ever since he overturned the neo-classical canons accepted by
the French theatre-going public in the 1830s. Even friendly modern commentators as diverse as Michel Butor and Ruth Doyle have pointed to the
disagreements among critics of his dramas, disagreements much more
marked than those separating readers of his poetry or novels. Doyle, for
instance, opens her 1981 annotated bibliography of Hugo's theatre by calling his plays the 'weakest part of his total work.'[2] Oddly enough, however,
among the 826 items she collected, she lists not a single study in English
devoted entirely to his plays. And yet, by 1981, New French Critics and
'Hugologists' like Ubersfeld, Gaudon, Laster, Leuilliot, and Seebacher had
all but completed their reinterpretations and reappraisals of Hugo's theatre. One recent English biographer, Joanna Richardson, also neglects to
mention, in her hypercritical, sensationalistic, and inaccurate account of
Hugo's life and work, a single post-Structuralist analysis of his dramatic
output or of its reception, contemporary or modern.[3] This is the first study
in English, then, to benefit from the formal discoveries made by recent
French critics of Victor Hugo's theatre; it will supplement them by offering
rhetorical analyses of both his dramatic theory and practice.

   Ignorance about and latent hostility to Hugo's theatre in the Anglo-

Saxon world are easily understood, springing, as they do, partly from the dearth of productions of his dramas in English. Outside France, Hugo the 'dramatist' remained, until 1996, best known as the writer of the work from which the musical *Les Misérables* was taken, and of *Notre-Dame de Paris*, from which Disney produced an edulcorated cartoon version involving the 'Hunchback of Notre Dame.' However, the 1996 production by England's Royal National Theatre of Hugo's *Le Roi s'amuse* (re-entitled *The Prince's Play*)[4] gave English-speaking theatre-goers the opportunity to see a drama banned in Paris after its premiere in 1832 and only rarely staged since in France.

Even in some of the scholarly works listed by Doyle, ignorance of Hugo's dramas extends to the meaning of the word he used to designate the genre which they exemplify. While he may not have invented the French Romantic drama, he certainly produced its most successful definition and created as well almost all of its most lasting paradigms (the exception being Musset's *Lorenzaccio*). Before Hugo revolutionized French canons of theatrical taste, the French word 'drame' corresponded in meaning with the English word 'drama.' In its generic sense, 'drama' designates, according to the *Oxford English Dictionary*, any 'composition in prose or verse, adapted to be acted on a stage, in which a story is related by means of dialogue and action, and is represented with accompanying gesture, costume and scenery, as in real life: a play.' (Incidentally, this definition seems to confuse dramatic and narrative modes, separated since Plato into mimetic, or direct, speech and diegetic, or indirect, speech respectively.) Thus the expression, the 'French drama,' may well be seen as designating originally a specific, national species of the genus, 'the drama,' which the same dictionary defines as 'the dramatic branch of literature; the dramatic art.' As its etymological notes show, the *OED* bases its own definition on the Greek word δρᾶμα, 'deed, action, play, esp. tragedy.' To support this English usage of the term, one could invoke, among one's authorities, Aristotle himself who in Chapter 3 of the *Poetics*, speaking of both tragic and comic writers, Sophocles and Aristophanes in the event, adds that 'they both represent men in action, men actually doing things. And this, some say, is why their works are called dramas, from their representing men doing things.'[5] This generic sense clearly survived into English, subsuming and mingling the various specific forms: tragedy, comedy, farce, indeed all of Polonius' dramatic sub-genres in all of their logical combinations: 'tragedy, comedy, history, pastoral, pastoral-comical, historical-pastoral, tragical-historical, tragical-comical-historical-pastoral.'[6] Before the rise of the 'Romantic drama' in France in the late 1820s, 'drame' retained its generic sense.

So, when Michel Lioure proposed, in 1963, the use of the French word 'drame' to cover stage plays produced in the period stretching from the eighteenth to the twentieth centuries, 'from Diderot to Ionesco,'[7] in his words, he both overturned a linguistic usage going back to the word's first appearance in France, which the *Dictionnaire Robert* lists as occurring in 1657, and extended the term's Romantic usage. Lioure quite rightly asserts the word's lack of currency in the seventeenth century, adding that the great French neo-classical writers Corneille, Racine, and Molière wrote tragedies and comedies, not dramas. Lioure goes on: 'In the French dramatic context, the drama seems, next to proud Tragedy and free-speaking Comedy, as only one – frequently mediocre – moment or form of our dramatic history ... [E]ighteenth-century theoretical assertions about drama attest nonetheless to the actual creation of a genre. By defining itself generically as existing on the margins of tragedy and comedy, the drama made no reference to any earlier form of the dramatic art: *it defined itself in opposition to what existed and invented itself as it went along.*'[8]

As we shall see when discussing in greater detail the dramatic theories and works of its chief practitioner, Victor Hugo, French drama thus made room for itself by opposing the generic distinctions going back to Aristotle, and upon which Boileau, codifier of the seventeenth-century French neo-classical canon, based an absolute preference for 'purity' of tone and temper, tragedy being totally 'serious' and comedy excluding catharsis and offering at best, in Molière's bourgeois comedies, a 'useful lesson.' By combining comedy and tragedy, Romantic drama refused the French model offered by Racine, affirming instead its desire to imitate the universally recognized dramatists of the past, most notably Shakespeare.

The expression 'Romantic drama' describes a form practised in France by Hugo, Dumas, Vigny, Musset, and a few minor authors who wrote a corpus of plays produced for the most part (Hugo's *Torquemada* is an obvious exception) between 1827 and 1843. More recently, Michel Lioure, by combining with 'drama' the adjectives, 'bourgeois,' 'symbolist,' and 'contemporary,' was able to posit a wider genre, one which, since Diderot, has dominated the French stage at least at the pragmatic level. So much so, that nowadays, dramatic conventions in France favour the mixture of tragic and comic action prevalent elsewhere in the West.

This generic use of the word 'drama' is not the only one found, of course. When modern Hugologists or their ideological opponents use the term *drame,* as an evaluative tag, designed to confer value on (or withdraw it from) Hugo's dramatic production, they do so in the context of a logic dependent upon a literary historical view that seeks to place (or omit) him from the 'Pantheon' of the world's 'great' dramatists. When Anne Ubersfeld, for instance, certainly the principal Hugologist to specialize in the study of his theatre, defines the Romantic drama, she does so in this way: 'The drama is a literary genre which originates neither in France in 1830, nor even in Germany in 1790–1800. The "drama" is much older, and when becoming conscious of itself, looks for guarantors and precedents in the England of Shakespeare and in Spain's Golden Age. Nor does it stop at the end of the 1830s, but continues to return to its Romantic sources, seeing its posterity not so much in Northern Naturalist drama (Ibsen, Strindberg) as in the theatre of Symbolist authors like Villiers de l'Isle-Adam, Maeterlinck and Claudel' (*DR*, 7). And she is right to point out that in *William Shakespeare* Hugo demonstrates drama's 'almost infinite range': 'Drama, [Hugo writes], is a strange artistic form. Its diameter encompasses [Aeschylus'] *Seven against Thebes* and [Sedaine's] *A Philosopher without Knowing It*, Brid'oison [in Beaumarchais' *Marriage of Figaro*] and Oedipus; [Seneca's] *Thyestes* belongs in it, as well as [Lesage's] *Turcaret*. If you wish to define drama, include both [Aeschylus' and Sophocles'] *Electra* and [Marivaux's] *Marton* in your definition' (*OC*, 12, 204).

Encouraged, seemingly, by Hugo's breadth of vision, Ubersfeld goes on to propose a definition of drama encompassing all performed works, irrespective of genre but characterized by 'freedom': 'Even when limited to its Romantic form, the drama has a history whose limits are ill-defined. Any work may be defined as a drama which, without consideration of form or code, pathetic or comic effect, presents a story, a *fable* implying both individual destinies and a 'social' universe. This extremely broad definition excludes, however, 'traditional' forms like tragedy and comedy or 'new' ones such as melodrama or comic opera [*vaudeville*], since all of them are linked to a pre-existing structure or 'code.' Drama's essential characteristic is its *freedom*. But all freedom is a battle against constraints: so no one will be surprised that drama is a perpetual battlefield' (*DR* 7). Ubersfeld's definition is indeed broad. It will be part of our task in the following pages to examine to what extent and in which ways it may be said to coincide with Victor Hugo's theoretical vision and dramatic practice.

Aiming to analyse the rhetoric of his dramas, the following study carefully distinguishes the generic characteristics of the Romantic drama that separate it from French neo-classical tragedy and popular melodrama. As well as studying the pre-eminently rhetorical notion of *genre*, we shall examine also, among other discursive techniques, Hugo's use of dramatic irony, and his construction of paradoxical characters, composed of conflicting emotions, antithetical moral impulses, and personifying conflicts between social status and meritocratic or erotic aspirations. Hugo's use of *anagnorisis* in plots based on mistaken identity and subsequent recognition shows him exploiting one of the dramatic devices Aristotle discussed in the *Poetics*, one which also, when productive of catharsis, makes a decidedly rhetorical appeal to an audience's emotions. We shall see that Hugo used plot-logic in order to persuade the French theatre-going public of the validity of his anti-royalist and unfashionable ideas concerning social justice in nineteenth-century France. The Romantic theory of drama he conceived permitted the creation of dramas certain to launch strong emotional appeals to audiences by invoking their sense of historical verisimilitude and ideological beliefs. His plots, by showing virtue despised and destroyed, aim to arouse indignation against social injustice, religious fanaticism, and the exploitation of women by egotistical husbands and lovers.

In discussing Hugo's dramatic rhetoric, we shall foreground Hugo's theatrical practice: his remarks on the staging of his dramas and the detailed stage directions he included in them reveal most clearly how he envisaged the dramatization of his aesthetic ideas and socio-political concerns. Although many of his ideas appear in the prefaces he wrote for his dramas, he was no mere writer of theatrical tracts: ideologically speaking, Hugo fleshed out his value judgments by producing heroes and villains who personify both his ideals and the objects of his contempt. If his characters share with the orator a skilful use of language and gesture, it is because Hugo endowed them with a delivery, or *actio*, whose procedures and function have been discussed since it was codified by Aristotle, Cicero, Quintilian and their epigones. Rhetorical analysis, which exposes the 'logic of value judgements,'[9] will permit us to clarify Hugo's positions on aesthetic and socio-political matters, just as it will empower our discussion of the generic characteristics distinguishing the Romantic drama from neoclassical tragedy or Revolutionary melodrama. Rhetorical analysis also provides the tool best designed, since the ancient rhetors first studied the precise reactions of the specific audiences they addressed, for the discussion of the different kinds of receptions accorded a performance by particular audiences. The history of the reception of Hugo's dramas between his day and ours allows us to chart their persuasiveness as vehicles exemplifying, and promoting, his ideas both aesthetic and social.

In order to follow Hugo's development as a dramatist, we shall trace his progress from his first experience of melodrama to the experiments he conducted, late in his career, with epic or bourgeois drama. It is to his first exposure to the melodrama, both as he and his family lived it in Napoleonic France, and as he first saw it in Pixérécourt's popular plays that we shall turn first.

ACKNOWLEDGMENTS

I should like to thank Stuart Adam, who, when Dean of Arts at Carleton University, granted me the funds necessary to obtain from the copyright holders the permission to reproduce the illustrations presented here. Also at Carleton University, my appreciation goes to Callista Kelly and her team of researchers in the Interlibrary Loan Department of the Maxwell MacOdrum Library. I should also like to thank Ron Shoeffel, Editor-in-Chief at the University of Toronto Press, and Marion Filipiuk, the copy editor.

A Note on Sources and Abbreviations

I have used the standard edition of Hugo's *Oeuvres complètes,* directed by Jean Massin, in 18 volumes (Paris: Le Club Français du Livre, 1967–70), for all Hugo quotations. In references it is abbreviated to *OC*.

Passages from the plays are cited conventionally by act and scene, or by 'part,' 'day,' and 'scene,' when Hugo uses the latter terms. *Lucrèce Borgia* is divided into acts, parts, and scenes; so the references contain three elements (e.g., 1, 1, 3). *Marie Tudor* and *Angelo* each comprise three 'Days,' with each 'Day' divided into scenes, and in both plays 'Day 3' also contains 'parts.' In *Marie Tudor,* therefore, (3, 1, 4) refers to Day 3, part 1, scene 4; in *Angelo* (3, 2, 1) to Day 3, part 2, scene 1. *Les Burgraves* is made up of 'Parts' and scenes only (e.g., 2, 1), whereas *Torquemada's* two 'Parts' contain both acts and scenes. In the latter case (1, 1, 7) refers to Part 1, Act 1, scene 7.

A complete list of works consulted precedes the index. The following list identifies abbreviations appearing in the text which refer to the principal critical sources cited more than once.

List of Abbreviations

CI	D.C. Muecke, *The Compass of Irony* (1969)
DR	Anne Ubersfeld, *Le Drame romantique* (1993)
DRGC	Descotes, *Le Drame romantique et ses grands créateurs* (1955)
FS	M. Carlson, *The French Stage in the Nineteenth Century* (1971)
HADF	T. Gautier, *Histoire de l'art dramatique en France,* 6 vols. (1858–9)
HR	M. Carlson, '*Hernani*'s Revolt from the Tradition of French Stage Composition' (1972)

MSF	M.-A. Allévy. *La Mise en scène en France* (1938)
PF	A. Laster, *Pleins Feux sur Victor Hugo* (1981)
PVH	H. Lyonnet, *Les 'Premières' de Victor Hugo* (1930)
RB	Anne Ubersfeld, *Le Roi et le bouffon* (1974)
RBL	Anne Ubersfeld, *Ruy Blas*, critical edition, 2 vols. (1971–2)
RH	Anne Ubersfeld, *Le Roman d''Hermani'* (1985)
RS	Stendhal, *Racine et Shakespeare* (1965)
SG	W.D. Howarth, *Sublime and Grotesque* (1975)
TF	J. de Jomaron (ed.), *Le Théâtre en France* (1992)
VHR	*Victor Hugo raconté par Adèle Hugo* (1985)
VHT	J. Gaudon, *Victor Hugo et le théâtre* (1985)
VHTL	*V. Hugo, Théâtre* (Laffont edition), 2 vols. (1985)

Photo-montage: 9 portraits of Victor Hugo between the ages of 18 and 55.
Victor Hugo Museum, Paris.

Lucrèce Borgia: Christine Fersen, Comédie-Française, 1994. Emmanuel Robert.

Hernani: Sarah Bernhardt as Doña Sol. Musées de la ville de Paris © SPADEM 1995.

Gillot Saint-Evre, *Inès de Castro*. Victor Hugo Museum, Paris.

Marie Tudor: Porte-Saint-Martin Theatre, 1873. xvii Musées de la ville de Paris © SPADEM 1995.

Marie Tudor: Maria Casarès, production by Jean Vilar, Théâtre National Populaire, 1955. Agence de Presse Bernand, Paris.

Angelo, tyran de Padoue: Portrait by Célestin Nanteuil of Marie Dorval as Catarina. Musées de la ville de Paris © SPADEM 1995.

Angelo: Sarah Bernhardt as La Tisbe and Deneubourg as Rodolfo, 1905.
Victor Hugo Museum, Paris.

Angelo: Pierre Tabard and Geneviève Page, production by Jean-Louis Barrault, January 1984. Agence Roger-Viollet, Paris.

Ruy Blas: Gaby Silva and Gérard Philippe, production by Jean Vilar, Théâtre National Populaire, 1954. Agence de Presse Bernand, Paris.

Les Burgraves: Caroline Segond-Weber as Guanhumara, 1902. Musées de la ville de Paris © SPADEM 1995.

Torquemada: frontispiece by Maillard from the Hugues edition of the text.
Victor Hugo Museum, Paris.

Victor Hugo and the Romantic Drama

1. Youth and Dramatic Juvenilia

> Despite a few attempts by Freud and some of his successors, the psychoanalysis of literature that respects the *literary signifier's originality* has not yet begun, and that is probably not an accident. Up to the present, only the *signifieds* of literature have been analysed, which is to say literature's non-literary *signifieds*. Such questions refer to the whole history of literary forms themselves, and to everything in them that was specifically intended to authorize this misunderstanding.[1]

If we take Anne Ubersfeld's definition of the drama, namely 'a story, a *fable* implying both individual destinies and a "social universe"' as the basis for studying Victor Hugo's career in the theatre, then we encounter a precise theoretical problem. As many of his biographers and critics have pointed out, his plays frequently dramatize the problems occurring among and between members of a family: incest, sibling rivalry, ancestor worship, are only some of the most obvious of such subjects. Formalists would argue that, in constructing his dramas around family strife, Hugo the pragmatic dramatist was merely following Aristotle's remark in Chapter 13 of the *Poetics* that 'the best tragedies are written about a handful of families.' Because the close relationships existing among family members are complicated and multi-directional (maternity clashing with incest, filial respect with sexual or political rivalry, etc.), such subjects sharpen the focus on internal strife and dramatic confrontation. Or should we, like the recent school of Hugo specialists at the University of Paris VII, editors and contributors to the monumental 'Chronological Edition' of Hugo's complete works (1967–70), use the plays as documents permitting a psycho-analytical examination of their author? Should we then see his plays as Romantic dramas of personal identity and (mainly) fraternal guilt, as these and other biographers have done? It seems to us that our task should be to adduce the relevant biographical evidence for both kinds of interpretation of his plays, the formally pragmatic and the allegorically confessional. Readers will, of course, decide which interpretation they prefer. It should be noted, however, that the biographical account in the following pages aims principally to show the importance which the Romantic drama occupied in Hugo's life.

Victor-Marie Hugo was born in Besançon on 26 February 1802. The date is significant: it is the year when Napoleon Bonaparte became Consul for life, thus preparing for his proclamation as Emperor of the French two years later. It is doubly significant because the child's father was to rise to prominence in Napoleon's armies, even being admitted to membership of the imperial nobility. His mother, however, Sophie Hugo, née Trébuchet, from a royalist Breton family, was so far from sharing her husband's Napoleonic sentiments that she even sheltered one of the many plotters against the Emperor's life. From this disunited home, forced as a child to follow his father in his postings as a serving officer and, presumably, with less need of obligation, to bask in his professional achievements, Victor was to learn much that he later put to good use in his dramas, as we shall see.

The boy's father, Joseph Leopold Sigisbert Hugo, belonged to the heroic generation which, by following Napoleon, rose to glorious heights. Their Romantic sons, in the person of Alfred de Musset,[2] were to protest that fate, by delaying their births, had forever denied them access to a similar glory. Leopold, born in Nancy, was fifteen when he first enlisted in the citizens' army in 1789. He served with distinction on the Rhine and in the Vendée, where, as a loyal republican, he fought against royalist French officers who had emigrated after the Revolution. While thus engaged, he met in Châteaubriant Sophie Trébuchet whom he married in Paris in November 1797.

Sophie was originally from Nantes and although in her youth she expressed Voltairean, even republican, opinions, she later moved politically to the right, and was, as a confirmed monarchist, delighted by Louis XVIII's Restoration in 1814. Never a Catholic – her marriage to Leopold was a purely civil affair – she never had Victor or his two elder brothers Abel and Eugène, born in 1798 and 1800 respectively, baptized. The marriage, between a violent-tempered serving officer of Napoleon and a stubborn, unforgiving supporter of the Bourbon monarchy, soon went wrong. Sophie's affair with General Lahorie began the year of Victor's birth; and Leopold's liaison with Catherine Thomas followed the year after. Sophie learned of her husband's infidelities long before Leopold discovered, in 1811, her relationship with Lahorie, one of his own superior officers. The family lived in an atmosphere of mutual reproaches and quarrels until the official divorce in 1815, which Leopold successfully sought on the grounds of his wife's adultery. The boys, who were placed in the care of their father, supported their mother's cause throughout the marital disputes, gladly accepting the final legal settlement which, in 1818, returned them to their mother's care.

As his marital life was falling apart, Leopold continued to advance in rank at the extraordinary rate made possible by Napoleon's almost continuous military campaigns. In 1800, after distinguishing himself at the battle of Marengo, he was promoted battalion commander. This triumph brought him to the notice of his future protector, Joseph Bonaparte. After the birth of his third son, Victor, however, he was sent in semi-disgrace because of his republican opinions and his unsuspecting friendship with Lahorie, who was known for his anti-Bonapartist sentiments, on garrison duty first to Marseilles, then to Bastia, and finally to Elba. While Sophie pleaded on his behalf in Paris, Leopold, alone in Elba with his three sons in December 1803, met Catherine Thomas, the mistress he would marry in 1821. Even in disgrace, his star continued to rise, however, bringing him the Legion of Honour in 1804. Recalled to the colours, Leopold once again distinguished himself in battle, this time serving in Massena's victory over the Archduke Charles at Caldiero, in Venetia. In 1806, after helping Joseph conquer and so become King of Naples, Leopold, now a major, captured after a long and difficult campaign the bandit Fra Diavolo, gaining as reward the military governorship of the province of Avellino. Once again Sophie and her three sons journeyed to share his military quarters, this time to Naples where, however, no lasting marital reconciliation ensued. In February 1808, Colonel Hugo followed Joseph to Spain where, in July of the following year, he again won promotion in battle, this time at Talavera. Appointed Brigadier-General, Governor of the province of Avila and Inspector-General of Spanish troops, Leopold, in 1810, defeated at Sigüenza the guerrilla chief Martin Diaz. Raised to the Imperial nobility as Count of Sigüenza, governor of several Spanish provinces and assured of a glorious career while the Emperor reigned, Leopold suddenly found himself called to order by Joseph Bonaparte, who professed himself scandalized by his protégé's irregular liaison with Catherine Thomas. Joseph ordered him to send for Sophie and the family, a decision which explains indirectly why Victor at an early age came to learn Spanish and to get to know and love Spain, the country that was to become a principal setting for the action of his dramas. He also discovered, in the toponyms of two small Spanish towns passed through on his way to Madrid with Sophie and his brothers, the names he would give to his bandit chief, Hernani, as well as that of his Grand Inquisitor, Torquemada.

On the journey to Madrid Victor also experienced the pleasures of theatrical, as opposed to existential, melodrama. This event, not without importance for Hugo's theory and practice of the Romantic drama, as we shall see, was recounted many years later by Victor's wife, Adèle, in the account she left as a 'witness' of the life of her husband, who by that time was the most famous writer alive. As she explains, Victor, his mother, and brothers Abel and Eugène arrived in the border town of Bayonne on their way to Madrid. There they discovered that the military escort necessary to protect French travellers from Spanish guerrillas would not leave for a month. Compelled to stay in Bayonne, Sophie reserved a box in the local theatre for the entire period. The reservation delighted the boys who looked forward to the prospect of a whole month of nightly visits to the theatre. The first night they rushed off to see Guilbert de Pixérécourt's melodrama, *The Ruins of Babylon*. Hugo's wife continues:

> The children stared wide-eyed, dancing with joy at the spectacle. Jiaffar's apricot-coloured costume made a particularly vivid impression upon them.
>
> The next evening, still full of the previous performance, they rushed, as if drunk, to the theatre. *The Ruins of Babylon* was again on the bill. The play was so enjoyable that they were happy to see it again.
>
> The third day, they entered their box at the usual time. The curtain went up. On *The Ruins of Babylon*. They took some pleasure in looking out for a few of their favourite places in the play. Eventually, they fell asleep. (*VHR*, 178–9)

Another two visits were necessary to convince them that Pixérécourt's play was going to be the only show in town during their stay.

The incident's significance derives from the influence Pixérécourt-style melodrama was to have on one of the very first written works by Hugo that survive. *Hell on Earth* (*L'Enfer sur terre*) and *The Devil's Castle* (*Le Château du diable*), both dramatic texts, were apparently written in 1812 when he was only ten years old.[3] Little of Pixérécourt's melodramatic style appears, however, in *Hell on Earth*, which at this distance seems more like a child's view of a medieval peasant *fabliau* or Molièresque farce.[4] In the twelve completed scenes, four characters, the Norman peasant Cassandre, his wife, her would-be lover Sylvain, and the Devil, contrive a reversal of the initial action in which the evil-tempered Cassandre slaps his wife. He later confides to Sylvain that he would prefer his 'reasonable' wife to be unreasonable and difficult, adding that she should even beat him. In scene 8, the Devil, having assumed the appearance of Mme Cassandre, returns with interest to her husband the slap he had given his wife in scene 1. In the same guise, the Devil, in scene 9, offers to Sylvain's lecherous advances the warm encouragement that Mme Cassandre had refused him in scene 4. Sylvain and the Devil, in three soliloquies (scenes 3, 5 and 7), explain the changes they would like to see or intend to make in the present situation. This use of the soliloquy as an expositional or explanatory device making possible dramatic irony (the public is better informed as a result than one or other of the characters) is interesting because it is a device used frequently by Hugo in subsequent plot construction. The scenes completed contain no sign of the happy ending proposed by the Devil in scene 5, where he claims to wish to restore harmony to the disunited husband and wife. This is typically Hugolian: unlike traditional melodrama, none of his dramas end happily for the protagonists.

More influenced by the melodrama is *The Devil's Castle* which, unlike Hugo's dramas, does have a happy ending. The convention conforms in part to Ubersfeld's view of melodrama whose sentimentally optimistic *dénouements* Hugo's Romantic dramas were to overturn: 'Melodrama is highly coded, and rigidly systematic [she writes]: its characters are prefabricated "types." First, the Traitor, greedy and hypocritical ... His adversary, the disinterested Hero (rarely a woman): acting out of pure virtue, he is not the lover, and receives no other reward than a clear conscience. His helper is a man of the people, a Simpleton, whose linguistic malapropisms and behavioural *faux-pas* provoke good-natured laughter. The Young Girl is the designated victim, coveted by the Traitor along with her fortune; frequently kidnapped, she remains virgin pure. Finally, the Father, persecuted in the past, rediscovers at the end, thanks to the Hero, his family and place in society' (*DR*, 90). The influence of some of these melodramic conventions is clear in *The Devil's Castle*, but so too are young Victor's departures from the generic model.

The *dramatis personae* comprise Raoul, the disinterested hero; Robert, his comic henchman, a simple-minded, cowardly boaster, who is beaten onstage by an imp from hell; Adélaïde, Raoul's love object who, like Doña Sol in *Hernani*, joins her lover in death; the Brigand, who tempts the Hero with money and panders for his mistress, the Brigand-Queen; and two utility roles, Martha, Robert's wife and confidant (useful for expositional purposes), and a slave who claims to be able to offer the Hero a means of escaping his fate (a false peripeteia, as things turn out). But, like Hernani and Doña Sol in Hugo's later drama, both Robert and Adélaïde commit suicide. How then can *The Devil's Castle* conform to the melodrama's demand for a conventional happy ending? The answer is by a final reversal which abandons the dramatic logic of the previous scenes. The final scene takes place in the Castle's throne room in an atmosphere appropriate to a Christmas pantomime, as the young Hugo's stage direction makes clear: '*The stage represents the throne room; the throne, supported by four magnificent col-*

umns, is raised up at the back of the stage, with the old Count of Richaumont seated upon it. Around him are ranged all the actors in the play.' Here the father-figure, the Count, Adélaïde's uncle, effects the magical reversal, bringing back to life the dead lovers, adding the final gesture of reconciliation, and the apparent guarantee of future happiness: 'Raoul, Adélaïde, come to my arms, my children. What I have done was merely to test you; it was only a ceremony played out by my men-at-arms and my vassals. Raoul, you are worthy of my niece; Adélaïde, you have a husband who deserves you. My children, I give you all my wealth. Be happy (*OC*, 1, 21).

Before taxing Hugo, whether he was ten or fourteen years old at the time, with having created a phantasmagoria fatal to the suspension of disbelief, it is worthwhile remembering that he did not in fact invent the plot. Éliette Vasseur points out that almost all the elements of Hugo's play, title, subject, peripeteia, ending, even the characters' names derive from the 'heroic comedy of one Loaisel de Tréogate, a Breton pre-Romantic writer' (*OC*, 1, ii). Rather than charging Hugo the young dramatist with a lack of stage technique should we then tax him with plagiarism? It seems more productive, given the author's youth, to point to the mixture in *The Devil's Castle* of some of the conventional characters of melodrama with, already, some still timid departures from the genre.

Mention of such intertextual problems as influence, sources, and plagiarism inevitably raises the question of Hugo's first exposure to the plays which were to inspire his own first written works. Adèle Hugo recounts that among her husband's earliest memories was a play, *Geneviève de Brabant*, put on at the school which the three-year-old attended and in which he played Geneviève's child, disguised in a sheepskin equipped, bizarrely enough, with an iron claw. He seized the opportunity during her speeches to prick her legs with the implement, so that she was forced into some very audible out-of-character vituperative asides to her offspring (*VHR*, 102). The same source recounts that after the experience of seeing Molière's *Comtesse d'Escarbagnas* and Pixérécourt's *The Ruins of Babylon*, Hugo saw in Valladolid his first Spanish play. The account is interesting from several points of view, not least because it illustrates the perils of reading biographical events as the direct source of an author's literary works or theories: 'In the play performed, there was a character who died from a dagger thrust. Real blood, or at least what created the illusion of blood, spilled from the wound and covered the stage. Until that time, young Victor had seen, among tragic works, only plays in which everything was fake, emotions as well as production values. He was extremely struck by the dying man whose blood was spilled because such a thing must happen if one is stabbed. This scene gave him, for the first time, the idea of reality in art' (ibid., 206). One can only agree with the annotator (ibid., 722, n10) of this passage that its glib character as a description of Hugo's much later dramatic practice represents a case of *post hoc ergo propter hoc*, of sequence being taken for consequence. Just as likely is the reverse: later practice may well have served to reconstruct the 'memory' and its 'effect.'

The next event in Hugo's education as a dramatist occurred after his return from Spain to Paris and concerns a passing fascination with Bobino and Jocrisse, French avatars of Mr Punch and his wretched wife. The French version was played by two human actors: Bobino, the master, beats his loudly protesting valet, Jocrisse, to the delight of the French children forming the audience. In 1814 when the brothers Hugo saw it, the scene was played to attract patrons outside the Bobino theatre, near the Luxembourg gardens. Once inside the theatre, the Hugos were introduced to the puppets, almost half life-size, moved by wires and wooden batons, but they were so lacking in life that the boys preferred the human attraction outside. Nevertheless, the visits did induce them to procure a puppet theatre, for which Hugo improvised dramatic scenes and dialogues.

He also wrote the texts for a series of dramatic performances which took place at the Cordier boarding school he attended in 1815. For these entertainments, which Mme Hugo later compared to the first circus performances arranged in revolutionary Paris by Antonio Franconi, he also helped with the 'sets' and took an interest in costumes, both of which activities he was to continue during his career as a Romantic dramatist. The plays he wrote for his companions were largely based on the battles of Napoleon; in them, as author, he gave himself the role of Emperor. With the collaboration of his brother Eugène, he staged Imperial triumphs on classroom tables, and according to Mme Hugo, 'The [schoolboy] spectators drawn up on benches in the most orderly fashion applauded' these performances (*VHR*, 280).

His familiarity with classical tragedy coincides in part with his Philosophy year at Louis-le-Grand, one of the most highly reputed schools in France. The Jesuits who ran it specialized in theatrical presentations in Hugo's time, just as they had when among their pupils they counted Donatien, later the Marquis, de Sade. Maurice Lever, Sade's most recent biographer, writes: '[T]heatre occupied a central role in the life of the school. They organized dramatic presentations and staged tragedies, comedies, pastorals, and even oratorios and operas, which the good fathers generally wrote themselves on edifying subjects and assigned their students to interpret with the aid of professional dancers from the Opera ... The school's productions were notable for their sumptuous scenery and complex machinery, which served to evoke splendid palaces, grand perspectives, colonnades, and fantastic landscapes. Formal performances were held every year in August, at the school prize-giving in the main courtyard.'[5] As dramatists, both Sade and Hugo benefited from the good fathers' enthusiasm.

In 1816, when he was fourteen, Victor Hugo decided to write a tragedy. His decision derived in part from his voracious reading: in the summer of 1815, for instance, confined to bed with a knee injury sustained in a schoolboy fight, he read, among several other works listed later by his wife Adèle, all the tragedies of Voltaire. *Irtamène*, the promised tragedy, 1,508 lines in five acts, written between 17 July and 14 December 1816, became his mother's New Year's gift on 1 January 1817. *Irtamène* certainly conforms to many, but not all, of the conventions of French neo-classical tragedy of the seventeenth century, as codified by Boileau in his 1674 *Art poétique*. Boileau's canonization of French neo-classical dramatic authors, most notably Corneille and Racine, takes remarks by Aristotle and Horace and hardens them into a set of 'rules.' Thus, an author of tragedies should, he believed, respect the unities of time, place and action ('a single thing done, in one place, in one day'), avoid the resolution of a complicated action by a final, surprising peripeteia, and display judgment in the choice and treatment of subject ('see that love appears as a weakness, not a virtue').[6] Boileau adds to these prescriptions the doctrine of *bienséance*, which decrees that onstage action must observe the contemporary proprieties, (i.e., the rigid social code of Louis XIV's Versailles): for this reason no violence may be shown. Finally, the dramatic author, says Boileau, must respect his audience's view of what is believable, the criterion being their sense of verisimilitude. This is the Aristotelian notion of *doxa*, a rhetorical criterion of plausibility aimed at persuasion. How does *Irtamène* conform to Boileau's model for French neo-classical tragedy?

The action concerns Irtamène's refusal to accept usurpation of the throne of Egypt by Cambyse who has deposed the young Zobéir's father. Irtamène, an officer in the former king's guards, opposes Cambyse's minister, Actor, who is only deterred from putting the former guardsman to death by his own passion for Phalérie, Irtamène's loving wife. Several complications result from this initial motivational tangle: Irtamène is happy to die, is even ready to commit suicide, while Actor is ready to free him in exchange for Phalérie. She prefers to die with her husband who, while attempting to dissuade her, cannot contemplate her union with his hated rival, Actor. As in neo-classical dramas, discussions, lyrical and rhetorical, by all the characters, including the confidants, form the development of the subject. It is by inviting spectators to participate imaginatively in such (monological and dialogical) discussions that neo-classical dramatists achieved what is still recognized by many as their greatest strength, the illusion of psychological 'depth' in the characters. In fact, such plays present the characters with one or a number of difficult choices, placing them in situations where they face a series of what seem to be unsolvable dilemmas. Their choices involve the primary emotions and threats to their personal security or that of their families: love or death, honour or loss of reputation, patriotism or imprisonment and execution, marital or incestuous love, enforced adultery or the loss of one's child, and so on. Such virtually impossible choices produce characters of great moral intensity, but onstage action becomes purely verbal, being reduced to a succession of tirades, dialogues, and soliloquies. All events like deaths, duels, battles, etc. take place in the wings, as it were, and they and their results are communicated by messengers to public and actors alike.

The complications inherent in the initial situation of *Irtamène* would be ample for a conventional neo-classical tragedy bound by the unities and dramatic proprieties. But Hugo shows his lack of sympathy with such conventions in several ways. First, he violates the unity of space. The action takes place in three different sets: Actor's palace in Acts 1–3; Irtamène's dungeon, which comes equipped with a secret door, in Act 4; and in a 'vast space surrounded by columns' in Act 5. The unity of action, which the plot summary just given seems to guarantee, accounts for six characters: Irtamène, Actor, and Phalérie, and their three confidants, Phorcys, Mégabise, and Cirma, respectively. Hugo exploits the confidant's traditional roles in neo-classical tragedy, those of expositional aid and messenger: Cirma's misunderstanding of her mistress's motivation allows Phalérie to explain her real feelings, and it is Phorcys who recounts, in a monologue of some 96 lines, Irtamène's escape from the scaffold and the final battle in which he kills Actor.

Fatal to both the unity of action and to the tragic quality of the play is the presence of a seventh character who has only a secondary, or derived role in the Irtamène-Actor confrontation, but whose presence guarantees that tragic despair will be resolved by a happy ending. This seventh character is the son of the deposed king, the youthful Zobéir, for whom Irtamène declares his readiness to die. Phalérie too decides to die out of love for her husband, going so far as to draw a knife onstage preparatory to plunging it in her bosom. A contemporary audience would not have been impressed by such a gesture, confident that no violence could be shown to happen. This miscalculation of effect by the young author demonstrates his uneasy grasp of neo-classical conventions. Zobéir's presence in Act 4 is only made possible by another 'Romantic' addition to the neo-classical model: the already mentioned secret door. Such devices were condemned by the doctrine of verisimilitude, which seventeenth-century audiences interpreted more severely than either the popular audiences that Hugo was later to address, or modern audiences brought up on the cinema's 'special effects.'

Two other principal features of neo-classical tragedy respected by the young author of *Irtamène*, the alexandrine verse and the 'high style' (*le style noble*) are more difficult to illustrate in translation, a problem which will recur throughout this study. The verse itself is, in any case, untranslatable without the loss of its poetic qualities, and although poetry is often regarded by French-speaking critics as the most successful characteristic of Hugo's dramas, I shall in my translations give only the meaning of the passages relevant to the discussion. As for the *style noble*, it consists of a literary dialect from which, because of the respect reigning at Louis xiv's Versailles for 'propriety' (*bienséance*) all 'low' words, i.e., popular, practical or technical terms, were banished, their place being frequently taken by more abstract, figurative terms, by vague but unexceptionable synonyms, metonyms, synecdoches, etc., and by loose, euphemistic, periphrastic structures. A good example of the differences between French and English notions of what should form the 'politically correct' kind of language in tragedy is Voltaire's translation into the linguistic code acceptable in eighteenth-century France, of Hamlet's famous soliloquy on suicide. Voltaire replaced Hamlet's 'When he himself might his quietus make / With a bare bodkin,' for example, by what he judged the more courtly 'Death would be too sweet in these extremities.'[7]

It is perhaps natural that in his despair, Irtamène, for example, should employ courtly language, using, among other rhetorical figures of the high style, appropriate emotional appeals like apostrophe and *exclamatio*:

> I see myself in irons, and in this palace itself
> In which my king from my hand received the diadem,
> In this palace which saw my happiness,
> And [is] now witness to my dark grief ...
> Unfortunate one! what have I said? Alas is it for the earth
> To raise its eyes to the seat of the thunder?   (4,1)

Similarly during Irtamène's interview with Zobéir, whom he considers to be his real king, both men, in seeking to outdo each other in generosity of soul, use the heightened language conventional in neo-classical tragedy:

IRTAMÈNE
What? my Lord, in this place you expose your life!
Ah! Have you forgotten that Actor still commands here?
Have you considered that his hand can ...

ZOBÉIR
What dare you say to me?
When it is to serve me that you spill your blood,

> I should fear decease when Irtamène expires!
> I should fear the iron of a vile Persian!   (4, 2)

But such high-flown language may well appear strange in the mouth of a furious Actor, determined to murder his rival, as he explains to his equally unscrupulous henchman, Mégabise:

> The traitor will experience all that my rage may do!
> He is the too happy husband of Phalérie ...
> May he curse the fate which seems to him so sweet!
> But think not, friend, that my vain anger
> Will be limited to giving him the death he craves ...
> Could poison, or the dagger worthily
> Serve the just transport of my wrath?   (3, 6)

Boileau's advice to authors that they 'Enliven [their] work with a world of verbal figures.'[8] is here followed to the letter, down to the final rhetorical question. The language in the original, further complicated by the demands of versification (despite several cases of *enjambement* or run-on lines), abounds in inversions of subject and verb, of verb and object, of verb and adverbial phrase, etc. But the 'noble' or 'high' style is used throughout, at the expense, perhaps, of one of Boileau's equally imperative criteria, verisimilitude. In his dramas, however, Hugo will show no fear of either popular expressions or technical terms.

And what of *Irtamène*'s possible meanings? The play can be interpreted as a political allegory, as Éliette Vasseur chooses to do (*OC*, 1, ii). This is only possible, however, if the play is taken to represent a world other than that of post-Restoration France. Briefly, according to Vasseur's reading, Irtamène represents the royalists who fought successfully in 1814–15 against Bonaparte, the usurper, in order to restore the Bourbon monarchy in the person of Louis XVIII. The problem here, as she admits, is the process of idealization Hugo's king seems to have undergone. Instead of being, like the historical Louis XVIII, old, fat, and lethargic, Zobéir is young, handsome, and energetic.[9] Myth has always been able to improve upon history, as Aristotle pointed out. And Hugo did, after all, give *Irtamène* to his royalist mother as a present. Maybe wishful thinking does explain why he chose this subject for utopian treatment.

Later in the same year, 1817, the studious, and ambitious young Hugo once again attempted, in *Athélie ou les Scandinaves*, to do homage to Racine and Voltaire, the two 'demigods of the French theatre' he had mentioned in the poem he sent to his mother to accompany *Irtamène*. This time he was less successful, and though he spent a month, from 15 September to

15 October, on the tragedy, he managed to complete only two acts along with an outline of the whole five-act play. Vasseur suggests that Hugo was unable to complete *Athélie* because, although in the two acts completed he respected the unities, the plan shows that in the rest of the play such obedience to neo-classical convention would prove impossible. The heroine's name, at least, recalls that of Athalie, heroine of Racine's final tragedy, whose action is also set in a temple. The Nordic element, evident in the names of the other characters and in the choice of setting of *Athélie* suggests, rather, Voltaire's attempts to renew French tragedy by situating the action in places other than classical Greece or Rome, or Biblical Israel. Hugo's opening stage direction indicates the cultural specificity the set should attempt to represent: *'The action takes place in the sacred wood of Torston, inside the temple of Odin. On the right stands a black, marble tomb bearing Duncar's name; in the background is the altar covered with a veil'* (*OC*, 1, 193). This already Romantic decor, if considered along with the props necessary for the projected final act, a poisoned chalice and a black shroud covering a corpse revealed onstage in the final scene, indicates how far from neo-classical tragedy's conventional anteroom between royal apartments is the setting of *Athélie*.

The complicated plot also departs from the neo-classical doctrine stipulating unity of action. *Athélie* involves both a conflict between love and dynastic marriage and a revenge drama. Athélie, Queen of Scandinavia was married by her father to Duncar, whom Althur, her ex-suitor, has killed, tricked by the treacherous Morler. Having sworn to avenge her husband by executing his killer, Athélie learns from Duncar's ghost that Althur, whom she has chosen to be her second husband, is the guilty party. He, however, feels no guilt, believing that although Duncar died at his hands, Morler's treachery made *him* the real murderer, and Althur hopes to expiate his crime by offering to Athélie, whom he now expects confidently to marry, Morler's death. The existing two acts present the exposition of the subject and show Athélie's first hesitations.

One reason Hugo did not complete the play seems clear from the exposition. The subject, as stated, is impossible according to the dictates of Aristotelian and French neo-classical tragedy. Honour, a principal tragic motivation, dictates that Althur, the murderer of Athélie's husband, must not profit from his act by marrying her, since such an arrangement smacks of cynical self-interest. The promised expiation in no way exculpates Althur, since he will not suffer in the process of winning his reward, the hand of his beloved. Corneille, in *Le Cid* (1637), had attempted a similar subject, but in his case, Rodrigo had 'only' killed in a duel Don Diego, Chimène's father. Nonetheless, the resolution of such a highly charged subject did not convince the play's many critics: at the end, Rodrigo is sent off to war so that in time, perhaps, Chimène will see in him something other than her father's murderer. In fact, Corneille's play produced one of the great controversies in the history of seventeenth-century theatre in France, and it is even now frequently identified as a tragi-comedy because of its potentially happy ending.

It would be unreasonable to expect Hugo, at fifteen, to resolve a problem even more highly charged than the one Corneille faced in *Le Cid*. The projected ending of *Athélie* shows how far his practice of 'tragedy' had already led him towards the Romantic drama. Philippe van Tieghem quite rightly sees in the projected ending 'a grandiose spectacle, one of those that Voltaire dreamed of in order to increase tragedy's visual appeal.'[10] Hugo's outline for the setting and action of the final climactic scene presents many of the effects that he would use again in his Romantic dramas:

> *The great veil of the temple is raised, the altar appears brilliant with light and orna-ment; the temple's interior is similarly decorated, with priests and bards placed to the right and left of the altar. Althur, eyes blazing, dressed in a king's armour, followed by a litter covered by a black sheet and carried by his warriors, enters from one side of the stage; from the other side, Athélie advances, pale, trembling, hardly breathing and supported by her women. Althur, raising his sword towards the altar, swears to love and protect his wife; then the high priest presents him with the sacred chalice. Athélie, seeing her lover about to drink from the poisoned cup, cries out, gathers her strength, seizes it and gulps down the poison; then she explains everything to Althur, urging him to live because her husband is avenged [by her death]. Petrified with horror, Althur explains in his turn to Athélie Morler's treacheries and, raising the black sheet shows his dying wife the corpse of the traitor he has just sacrificed to his vengeance, adding that he had intended to admit everything to Athélie immediately after their marriage and to pacify Duncar's ghost by killing the real murderer. But, he adds, since the gods have ordered things differently, I will follow you, as is only just; with these words, he draws his sword and falls upon it over the body of his dying wife.*
> (*OC*, 1, 223)

The *Liebestod* immediately suggests the ending of *Hernani*, while the use of stage props like the poisoned chalice, the (chivalric) costume indicating a medieval, rather than a Graeco-Roman subject, characterize Romantic drama rather than seventeenth-century tragedy. *Athélie ou les Scandinaves* is the last time Hugo will court neo-classical prestige by calling one of his plays a 'tragedy.'

It should not be thought, however, that Hugo's dramatic writing in 1817 was uniformly tragic or melodramatic. As a New Year's gift to his mother in 1818, he gave her the enigmatically titled *A.Q.C.H.E.B.*, initials which stand for *À Quelque Chose Hasard Est Bon* (*Chance Is Good for Something*) and which he identifies generically as a 'comic opera' in 24 scenes not divided into acts. The 'operatic' part is composed of fifteen songs, in several metres: octosyllables dominate but lines of six and ten syllables also appear. The tone differs sharply from song to song, although all of them serve to reveal the character of the singer: Armand's epic account and expression of gratitude for Saint-Léger's exploit which saved his life in battle, contrasts, for example, with the comic political song of Maître Jacques whose versification is as faulty as his grammar. A sung finale in which each of the main characters explains the meaning of the title as it applies to his or her role in the play offers both a joyful summary of events and an appeal to the audience to forgive a young author's lack of art. Although these poems are called songs, and although Hugo did hope to have the play performed at the Feydeau Theatre, no record remains of the music necessary to turn a comedy in prose and verse into a comic opera or musical comedy.

Vasseur suggests that the enigmatic quality of the title reflects the formulas, random numbers, and logarithms studied by Victor and Eugène in 1817–18, their Mathematics year at Louis-le-Grand. The apparently random nature of the crucial events of his life is well summarized by Saint-Léger: 'Born by chance I don't know where, entrusted by chance to the care of a notary, condemned by chance ... to pay I don't know what debt, a duellist by chance, in love by chance, you will admit that I can't share the opinion of those who claim that chance is unimportant' (*OC*, 1, 234). Once his problems are resolved – his identity established, his long-lost brother found, his debts and the legal charges against him dismissed, and his marriage to Céline assured – Saint-Léger can well afford to sing in scene 24: 'Chance tangled up my fate's mysterious thread. Chance's stubborn rage has long darkened my wretched life. But today mends all. Although I have been a poor vagabond, my happiness is being prepared. Chance is good for something' (*OC*, 1, 273).

The fortuitous means which unite the lovers and defeat the swindler, Coinclipper (*Rognespèce*) include many of the props and dramatic tricks of melodrama, among them, disguises and coincidences. The discovery of the truth about Saint-Léger's birth, for example, which forms the final reversal resolving the drama, is made possible by a snuffbox containing a portrait of his mother recognized by Count Dorval, who turns out to be not only his long-lost brother, and the Colonel he wounded in a duel, but also his rival for Céline's hand, a rival happy to yield his place to his new-found brother. If we can allow the snuffbox and portrait to be conventional agents of the type of recognition that Aristotle calls '*anagnorisis* by signs,'[11] the dramatic multifunctionality of the Count may well appear hyperbolic. Such functional over-motivation rarely produces verisimilitude, as Genette points out.[12]

New in Hugo's juvenile theatre are the pieces of comic business which show the swindler and his Latin-spouting clerk, Polygraph, receiving their come-uppance from both brothers. Of even greater interest to our post-modern age is Hugo's foregrounding of the work's literary devices. Thus Saint-Léger, Hugo's chance-led hero, is writing a comic opera about his own life, he tells Armand in scene 4, so that art can improve upon reality: 'On earth, where everything follows Chance's chariot, let Chance command me; there [in my work], I command Chance. There I am loved and I am to be married; here, I'm only in love. Here, fate thwarts me, but there, I know how to achieve happiness ... You see, my dear friend, that I have found an excellent remedy against boredom and grief; unhappy in reality, I'm happy in my head, and that's all I need' (*OC*, 1, 236–7). It is possible to see in this declaration by Saint-Léger of the artist's almost absolute right to rearrange reality by the power of imagination an attempt by Hugo to excuse the play's lack of verisimilitude on the grounds that the pleasure art offers is of greater value than mere plausibility. This is the type of pleasure comic opera proposes. The lines just quoted have also been taken, by Vasseur for instance, to relate to Hugo himself who, still confined in the Cordier Pension in 1817 and separated from his mother, was deeply unhappy.

Art's self-reflexivity appears at least once more in the play's finale where, Prospero-like, M. d'Escour, Céline's father, draws an analogy between his indulgent treatment of the lovers and the good-natured reception authors, particularly young ones, need to receive from the public: 'Yes, like any loving father, I do want to make the lovers happy. (*Addresses the stalls.*) Gentlemen, can authors expect a similar kindness from you? If, by chance, you pardon them their youth, they will joyfully repeat "Chance is good for something"' (*OC*, 1, 273). Hugo was not here abandoning his 'rough magic,' but he certainly put aside comedy after *A.Q.C.H.E.B.* Not until *Le Théâtre en liberté* would he write another play that ends well for all the protagonists.

A.Q.C.H.E.B. is also the last of Hugo's plays, until his exile in the 1850s, not expressly written for public performance. The reason is simple enough: if he was to make his living as a professional writer, his works would need to make money. But in 1818 he had not yet decided on a final choice of career. In that year, as well as entitling one of his poems 'Mes Adieux à l'enfance,' Hugo received permission from his father to study law, studies he continued until 1821. Victor and Eugène also left the Cordier boarding school to live again with Mme Hugo, where Victor wrote in two weeks the first version of his novel, *Bug-Jargal* to win a bet. One event that did incline him towards a literary career was his 1820 meeting with Chateaubriand: the sight of the old writer at the peak of his fame fuelled the boy's ambition to be a great author.

In 1819 Hugo's ode on the restoration of Henri IV's statue in Paris won the grand prize, the 'Golden Lily,' in the poetry competion called the 'Floral Games,' organized by the Academy of Toulouse. In April, Victor and Adèle Foucher, daughter of a family long friendly with the Hugos, declared their love for each other, and Victor made many visits to the Fouchers in Issy that summer. A secret correspondence between the lovers, begun in January 1820, was discovered by Mme Hugo in April. Despite the friendship between the two families, she refused to contemplate the marriage, and broke off relations with the Fouchers. Until her death on 27 June 1821, Adèle and Victor were forbidden to see one another. In July 1821 Adèle's father allowed their betrothal, making clear that marriage was out of the question unless Victor could prove his ability to support a wife. The lovers were forced once again into a clandestine correspondence, and family disputes followed, during one of which on 11 April 1822, Adèle threatened suicide in an attempt to break her father's opposition to the marriage.

M. Foucher may well have found more persuasive the signs that Victor's name was becoming known in literary and even in court circles. In March 1820, Hugo received 500 francs from Louis XVIII for his 'Ode on the Death of the Duc de Berry,' and in June 1822 he was awarded an annual royal pension of 1200 francs on the publication of his *Odes et poésies diverses*. The marriage was approved by both fathers, but a problem remained, preventing the couple from being married in church: Victor had never been baptized. Armed with a false declaration, signed by his father, that the baptism had taken place abroad, Hugo and Adèle were finally able to marry at Saint-Sulpice on 12 October 1822.

Much more disturbing than the bureaucratic irregularity was the change in the character of Eugène, Hugo's elder brother and friendly rival in the various literary competitions they both entered. Rivalry had turned into envy on Eugène's part, as he saw his brother's greater success, and into sexual jealousy, when he saw that Adèle preferred Victor to himself. The first sign that all was not well was a letter to Victor on 14 July 1818 from Félix Biscarrat, the boys' friend and tutor at the Cordier boarding school, who wrote of his fears concerning Eugène's sanity. His parents' separation and the resulting division of loyalties and frequent changes of residence cannot have added, during his eighteen years, to Eugène's mental stability. In March 1820 Eugène withdrew from the editorial board of the review, *Le Conservateur Littéraire*, which the three Hugo brothers had founded in 1819. Then in April 1822 Eugène suddenly disappeared, having apparently set off towards Blois to convince himself that Leopold, his father, really had married again. Arrested in Chartres without papers, Eugène had to write for his father's help to obtain his release from jail. But the climax came during the night following Victor's marriage to Adèle. She gives the following account, in which her presence as eyewitness to some of the events in question should be noted: 'During the night, Eugène had become violent and Abel had called to him [Biscarrat] to help care for his brother. For some time now, Eugène had been a cause for concern, as the strangeness of his mind became more apparent ... All our strength and love were needed to control the fit. Victor rushed to his brother. Medication and good nursing pacified the sick man, but he was never to regain his reason.'[13] In fact, after attempting to care for Eugène themselves, the family were forced, after another violent outburst, to have him permanently committed in June 1823 to the asylum at Charenton. Not allowed vistors because of the violent nature of his condition, he died there in 1837.

By the end of his period as a juvenile or adolescent dramatist, Victor Hugo had tried all the genres then prevalent in the French theatre, from neo-classical tragedy to melodrama, and even comic opera. But, not unnaturally, none of these youthful efforts gained more than a general reading by a troupe of actors. His next plays would encounter all the practical problems that timid or dictatorial theatre managers, recalcitrant actors, incompetent theatrical costumiers and set designers, the official censor, and the notoriously flighty Parisian theatre-going public placed in the way of a young and productive dramatist. It is time to examine the conditions under which plays were produced in France, particularly in Paris, in the 1820s.

2. Theatre in France 1800–1830

After the Revolution, the number of theatres in Paris and the provinces rose considerably. In 1791 the National Assembly proclaimed the freedom of theatres by a decree which authorized 'any citizen to open a public theatre and to play there dramatic works of any genre.' This latter stipulation replaced the monopoly to present classical tragedy or comedy that state-funded theatres like the Comédie-Française had enjoyed before the Revolution. In 1792 the Assembly made Schiller, one of the foreign authors most admired by theorists and practitioners of Romantic drama, an honorary Citizen of the French Republic. In 1793 the Convention established free performances 'for and by the people,' an act which extended the pleasure of theatre-going to the popular classes. The aim was to promote theatre as a means of educating the people in civic virtue, a role the melodrama filled admirably, with its fables involving the poetic justice which rewarded virtuous characters after their struggles against antisocial evil-doers.

The result of such liberalizing acts was disastrous for the state-subsidized theatres which lost their bourgeois audience to the almost two hundred popular theatres which sprang up between 1791 and the end of the century. But the liberalizing trend ended when Napoleon became Emperor. Anxious to establish a national theatre which would both reflect France's recently acquired glory and good taste and provide a link between his new institutions and those of the Ancien Régime, he immediately took steps to rebuild the prestige and increase the subsidy of the Comédie-Française.

In so doing he built upon a policy begun in 1799 by the Directory which, on 25 Floréal an VII (14 May 1799) signed into law an agreement with twenty-seven actors of the troupe that was to occupy the new theatre on the rue de Richelieu. The government gave the troupe the right to occupy the theatre, and to exploit the necessary furniture and sets it contained. The government also paid the Society's debts and re-established members' pensions. In return the 'citizen artists' undertook to open the new 'Theatre of the French Republic,' which they did on 11 Prairial an VII (30 May 1799), with Corneille's *Le Cid* and Molière's *L'École des maris*.[1]

In return for financial support for the new theatre, which became from 1804 to 1814 the 'Emperor's Theatre,' Napoleon made full use of its dramatic and propagandistic possibilities. He frequently ordered command performances both at home in his various palaces and abroad on the occasion of his diplomatic visits to foreign cities. In all, Napoleon commanded performances of some 45 tragedies and 79 comedies from the actors of his theatre in cities as widely apart as Brussels (1803), Mayence (1804), Erfurt (1808), and Dresden (1813). He stipulated the presence either of his favourite actors, including the great tragedian Talma, whom we will meet later, or of the whole company, as was the case during his meeting with Czar Alexander at Erfurt in 1808.

In 1806 an Imperial decree named as the four 'major theatres' of Paris the Opéra, the Empereur (or Comédie-Française), the Empress (or Odéon), and the Opéra-Comique. The repertoire for each was carefully defined, with each reacquiring its pre-Revolution monopoly. The Emperor's Theatre gained the right to the repertoire of the old Comédie-Française. The Empress Theatre acquired the exclusive right to any new play premiered there, and the Opéra and Opéra-Comique had exclusive rights in their respective genres. Another Imperial decree of 1807 limited the 'minor theatres' of Paris to four. Melodramas, farces and pantomimes were to be played at the Gaîté and Abigu-Comique Theatres. At the Variétés and the Vaudeville, popular audiences could see parodies, peasant plays, and popular musical shows. The only 'minor' theatre to contest this restriction was the Porte-Saint-Martin, the most popular of the 'boulevard' theatres, called also the 'people's opera,' and the venue to which Hugo and Alexandre Dumas père were to bring their Romantic dramas after breaking with the Comédie-Française. An 1809 decree authorized the re-opening of the Porte-Saint-Martin theatre which, thanks to astute management and the popularity of melodrama, was soon the most financially successful theatre in Paris.

The 'boulevard' theatres were so called because they occupied neighbouring sites along the boulevard du Temple in northeastern Paris. The section of the grand boulevard they occupied became known also as the 'boulevard du Crime,' celebrated in our century in Marcel Carné's 1945 film, *Les Enfants du paradis*, in which Pierre Brasseur offers a sympathetic portrait of the greatest of Romantic actors, one whom Hugo called upon whenever he was available, Frédérick Lemaître. In 1823 a proposal came forward to substitute the boulevard's nickname for its official name, and the *Almanach des Spectacles* explained why:

> We have counted up the crimes that have been committed on the boulevard in the last twenty years. This is what we discovered: Tautin has been stabbed 16,302 times, Marty has been poisoned in one way or another 11,000 times, Fresnoy has been killed in various ways 27,000 times, Mlle Adèle Dupuis has in her innocence been seduced, abducted or drowned 75,000 times, 6,400 capital charges have tested Mlle Levesque's virtue, while Mlle Olivier, who has only recently begun her career, has already drunk 16,000 times from the cup of crime and vengeance. Unless we are mistaken, that makes 151,702 crimes to be shared among six individuals who none the less appear to enjoy excellent health and widespread esteem.[2]

The article attests both to the violent onstage action that melodrama used to such spectacular effect, and to the genre's enormous popularity: even allowing for comic hyperbole on the reporter's part, the figures imply a considerable number of separate performances. Evidently the centre of theatrical life had shifted from the Palais-Royal district to the boulevard du Crime.

Nothing confirms this shift better than Napoleon's unsuccessful attempts to impose a neo-classical repertoire on his official state theatre. Theatre receipts of the time show that the plays written by imitators of Corneille, Racine, and Voltaire simply did not draw the public, despite all of the great Talma's skill and popularity. Even productions of tragedies or comedies by the three great classics themselves, Corneille, Racine, and Molière barely recovered the minimal costs expended on the (threadbare) sets and costumes necessary to produce them. Maurice Descotes explains that when actors' annual salaries were paid (6,000 francs for a principal role, male or female, down to 2,000 francs or 1,200 francs for a Chief or Second Confidant, respectively), along with a system of free passes which saw up to a third of the total house handed out to courtiers, the press, the claque, friends of authors, actors, administrators etc. (many of whom then sold the free tickets for their own profit), even the high ticket prices charged at the Emperor's Theatre could not begin to meet expenses (*DRGC*, 15). The financial débâcle meant not only that scenery, sets and period costumes (actors paid for their own contemporary costumes at the time) were used over and over again, thus confirming the Comédie as a theatre of almost pure declamation without visual spectacle, it made the state subsidy not just attractive but absolutely vital to the theatre's survival.

Along with financial help, however, came interference and censorship, both before and after the Restoration. Since the public censor will play so central a role in preventing the performance of Victor Hugo's Romantic dramas, the institution deserves examination.[3] The new ideal of freedom from the censorship of public performances introduced by the Revolution did not last long. Napoleon instituted state censorship of plays in 1800 and enforced it rigorously until his abdication in 1815. Even plays by great literary figures were forbidden in his reign: Voltaire's *Mérope* and *Tancrède*, for instance, were refused a place in the Emperor Theatre's repertoire. Especially open to charges of political sedition were plays on modern subjects and such plays, even when successful outside France, were banned in Paris: a case in point is Duval's *Édouard en Écosse*, banned by the Imperial censor for its supposed royalist leanings.

Perhaps nothing displays more clearly Napoleon's determination to dominate his state theatre than the decrees he dictated in 1812 from Moscow with the city virtually in flames about his ears. (The only contender for most exemplary incident in this context occurred during the Hundred Days, when he attended a performance of *Hector*, a neo-classical tragedy by the now forgotten Lance de Lancival at the [hastily renamed] Emperor's Theatre on 21 April 1815, less than two months before Waterloo.) In Moscow Napoleon somehow found time not only to thwart the financial demands of the Theatre's then female star, Mlle Mars, he also signed a decree, on 15 October 1812, laying down 101 articles relating to the operation of the Theatre, many of which are still in force today. The Emperor's Commissioner (who became the Royal Commissioner after the Restoration) was to superintend the plays presented and organize the day-to-day and long-term running of the house. The decree also defined the duties of the cashier, the budgetary arrangements, including actors' salaries, pensions and the sharing of profits. It outlined the procedure for broadening the repertoire by accepting new plays, clarified the rights of authors and the responsibilities of actors, particularly with regard to casting and leaves of absence, both sources of dispute in the preceding years. The decree also set rules for the Theatre's 'School of Declamation,' where young actors received their training.

After the Restoration Napoleon's decrees continued to regulate the renamed Comédie-Française with minimal cosmetic changes imposed by the new political regime. Conflicting political loyalties, as shown by riots in the theatre in 1818, caused the censorship of plays to continue, with the difference that the ban now affected plays judged to be Bonapartist in tenor. Censorship would continue until after the 1830 Revolution, when Louis-Philippe abolished it for a few months only, as Hugo was to find to his cost. Neo-classical plays continued at the Comédie-Française, but despite Talma's magic they failed to cover expenses. Not until the arrival in 1825 of Baron Taylor as Commissioner did the Comédie-Française turn towards young Romantic dramatists like Vigny, Dumas, and Hugo as a possible means of warding off bankruptcy. But even Taylor, partly because of the extra expenses on set-construction and on the authentic costumes demanded by the historically minded new dramatists, and because of his frequent absences from Paris on archeological expeditions, failed to change the financial situation of the theatre. Cushioned by the subsidy, flattered by their status as the premier troupe of France, the actors at the Comédie were prepared to accept a situation that Ubersfeld qualifies as 'catastrophic.' She bases her judgment on the theatre's receipts in the fall of 1830, which is eight months after the premiere, and eventual financial success, of Hugo's *Hernani*: 'The balance sheet for September and October 1830 at the Comédie-Française is particularly edifying ... [S]ince we know that costs amounted to about 1,400 francs for each performance, and that receipts went as low as 241 francs on 22 October, and 270 francs on 8 September (there are 21 performances with receipts of less than 700 francs in the two months), we have some idea of the size of the catastrophe' (*RB*, 48–9). If subsidized theatre's condition was virtually inoperable, how was it that the boulevard theatres were thriving? The answer involves looking at several aspects of Parisian theatre between 1800 and 1830.

PARIS THEATRE BEFORE THE ROMANTIC DRAMA

First, ticket prices were lower at the popular theatres, so that while bourgeois patrons of the Comédie-Française could easily afford to patronize the Porte-Saint-Martin theatre if they so chose, the more numerous working-class audience that occupied the 'Paradise' or 'Gods' at the theatres on the 'boulevard du Crime' could not so easily afford the Comédie-Française. Maurice Descotes lists differences in ticket prices ranging from between 30 per cent for the most expensive seats in the two theatres (C.-F. 6fr.60, P.-S.-M. 4fr.) to up to 60 per cent for the cheapest seats (C.-F. 1fr.80, P.-S.-M. 0fr.60; *DRGC*, 9). Obviously, the social and intellectual differences between, and expectations of, the two audiences would also show themselves in any theatre they patronized. It is difficult to imagine the young, penniless artists who would form part of Hugo's supporting claque at the 'battle' of *Hernani* behaving as the following remark claims was typical of patrons of the Comédie: '"Fashionable Society," the "elite" returned to the Comédie Française [after the Restoration]; it was the official stage on which the classical masterpieces were acted, and it was good taste to come along for some noble boredom. Right from the time of the Empire, middle-class ladies had their boxes where they spent an hour or so showing off their diamonds.' M. Descotes also cites an amusing article from the *Globe* (1 January 1825): 'Go, if you dare, and find a seat once a week in the stalls at the Comédie-Française, in the midst of the group of experts whose formal demeanour and dignified pose betray their claim to be there to judge the play, much more than their desire to enjoy it ... in their view the theatre is a kind of academy where pompous declaimers methodically recite long speeches' (*RB*, 45). As well as being useful in characterizing attitudes in the audience at the Comédie-Française, once satiric hyperbole is discounted, this passage also touches on the antiquated style of acting which separated the official troupe, still the best in Paris at declaiming plays written in alexandrine verse, from popular boulevard actors like Lemaître, Marie Dorval, or Bocage.

Despite its stars, Talma and Mlle Mars, to whom we shall return, acting at the Comédie-Française still reflected the lessons in declamation taught in its school by former members of the troupe like the great Voltairean actor, Henri Lekain.[4] Accounts of the day speak of the actors' habit of standing in a bunch around the prompter's box,[5] declaiming their tirades to the public without so much as looking at each other, even during dramatic climaxes. One commentator even added that 'too often, the actor who is not speaking, stares off into the boxes, to see who is in them, which totally destroys the illusion.'[6] Critical judgments of such a performance can do no more, logically, than commend or criticize the physical attributes of performers, their skill at memorization, at vocal mellifluousness and rhythmic recitation of the twelve-syllable lines. Before Talma's innovations, little attempt was made to suggest violent emotion other than by the conventional 'sob' which frequently marked the caesura, the slight pause at the hemistich. Talma's greatness as premier tragic actor at the Comédie until his death in 1826 which prevented Hugo's offering him the title role in *Cromwell*, a play in which he had apparently shown great interest,[7] saved for a time the neo-classical tragedies still being performed there. His death signalled their demise.

Some of Talma's innovations directly anticipated Hugo's remarks in the Preface to *Cromwell*. Talma's study of the classical statuary produced by the official Imperial sculptor David, his seeking out in museums, art galleries, and libraries authentic historical models and adopting them for his costumes, rather than relying on the anachronistic, fashionable dress actors continued to wear even when playing Roman or Greek characters, form one of his innovations. He also preferred the violent stage effects that English dramatists, Shakespeare particularly, offered the actors and that French classical tragedy denied them. According to Maurice Descotes' reading of contemporary reviews, Talma played Hamlet as a 'man possessed, at once lucid and terrifying ... Right from his first entry, his disorder and inarticulate cries, the terror on his face made visible to the public the ghost of his father following on his heel; and during the recounting of the murder, his eye, going in turn to his mother and then to Claudius, expressed "his various impressions by admirably diverse means," which the narration concerning the two characters produced upon him' (*DRGC*, 29). Shakespeare was to influence French actors in other ways, as we shall see.

Marvin Carlson, a specialist in the drama of the Revolutionary period and after, points to other ways in which Talma, out of his concern to save classical tragedy from oblivion, sought to increase its emotional appeal to contemporary audiences: 'In the fourth act of [Racine's] *Britannicus*, for example, during Agrippine's lengthy harangue of Néron, tradition kept the young emperor glum and quiet, but Talma wearily adjusted his robe, toyed with the arm of his chair, followed patterns on his garment. Some critics, such as Charles Nodier ... on the *Journal des Débats*, protested against this spreading of the *drame* into tragedy, but the general public was delighted. Even more daring were the innovations in Étienne de Jouy's *Sylla* (1821) ... For the first time a classic tragedy made extensive use of crowd scenes; for the first time a tragic hero lay down in a bed on stage' (*FS*, 29). It is no wonder that Talma was harshly criticized by his own colleagues at the Comédie, as unused to being upstaged as were conventionally trained actors in the 1950s by their colleagues of the 'Method' school of acting.

The Comédie's female star, Mlle Mars, was not as interested in innovation as Talma. She was famous for her roles as coquette in classical comedies. Beginning in 1810 with *ingénue* roles like Agnès in Molière's *L'École des femmes*, she went on to play all the *grandes coquettes* in the comedies of Molière and Marivaux: Célimène, Elmire, Araminte, Suzanne, adding to them some of the great lovers in these plays: Sylvia, Rosine, Henriette, and Isabelle. Beautiful, elegant, and imperious, she ruled at the Comédie-Française after Talma's death, demanding (and getting) unheard-of salaries, permitting herself illicit leaves of absence and lengthy provincial or foreign tours, and exercising her absolute right to pick and choose among the leading roles in old and new plays. This right explains why Mars, primarily a comedienne, was to play the ultimately tragic Doña Sol in Hugo's *Hernani*. Although she disliked Romantic rhetoric, the play was important; her prestige demanded, therefore, that as the uncontested star of the Comédie, she must play the new heroine, even if at fifty-one she seemed an unlikely candidate for the role of an eighteen-year-old. The reason she was able to dominate the state theatre for so long was, naturally, financial: she could attract an audience to a theatre badly in need of one.

As to her acting itself, Jules Janin described it as follows: 'Mlle Mars's acting was cerebral, well reasoned, most highly intelligent. This is what limited her. She was marvellous at acting out the tricks of a coquette; she could dismiss an importunate lover with inimitable scorn, brush off a bore rudely yet without giving offence. But witty roles suited her better than those demanding feeling; she was good at speaking from the head, not so good at speaking from the heart. / To serve her gifts, Mlle Mars had a voice admired by all her contemporaries. They described it as supple, fresh, cristalline, quite the opposite of Mme Dorval's voice, deep, hoarse, trivial on occasion' (*DRGC*, 74).[8] Mlle Mars' undoubted intelligence enabled her to see in the Romantic drama one means of renewing a moribund theatrical repertoire. And when the occasion presented itself in 1827, it enabled her also to recognize, and imitate, the new style of English acting, a style she was to exploit in her appearances in the dramas of Hugo, Dumas, and Vigny.

In the history of the Romantic drama, nothing shows more clearly the virtue of arriving in the right place at the right time than the second of the three visits to Paris made by English companies between 1822 and 1832. In 1822, which was too soon after Waterloo for the liking of most Parisians, the actors were booed off the stage with cries of 'Down with Shakespeare; he's an aide-de-camp of Wellington' (*RS*, 169). The second English troupe, including among its members such accomplished actors as Kemble, Kean, Macready, and Harriet Smithson, would triumph in Paris in 1827–8, however, leaving behind an influence on Romantic dramatists that, as they admit in their memoirs or theoretical texts, is hard to exaggerate. Mme Hugo, for instance, recounts as follows the effect the performances by the English actors had in 1828 on her husband: 'Victor Hugo attended Miss Smithson's brilliant debut-performances and, for the first time, saw Shakespeare acted. At that moment, he was writing the Preface to *Cromwell* and he was inspired to write this commentary on the English master's dramatic art: "[Shakespeare] this god of the theatre, in whom appear to be united the three great geniuses who characterize our theatre: Corneille, Molière, Beaumarchais"' (*VHR*, 420). Alexandre Dumas was even more emphatic in describing the first night of *Hamlet*, 11 September 1827: 'This was the first time that I saw in the theatre real passions felt by men and women of real flesh and blood.'[9] And by the time that a third English troupe returned in 1832, French dramatists, actors, stage managers, set designers and costume-makers had so well learned their lesson about Shakespearean *mise en scène* that these English performances were compared, to their detriment, to the recent triumphs of Frédérick, Marie Dorval, Bocage, and others.

Since Shakespeare, along with Schiller, is generally regarded as the principal influence on French Romantic drama, it is worth tracing the history of the knowledge and reception of his works in France at this time. Audiences in the late eighteenth century knew his plays in the 1769–92 translations by Jean-François Ducis. But as Carlson explains in recounting an 1804 revival of Ducis' version of *Hamlet*, his 'translations' were in fact adaptations or bowdlerizations of Shakespeare: 'As in all of Ducis' Shakespearean adaptations, great care had been taken to adjust or weed out English irregularities. Ophelia is made the daughter of Claudius to give Hamlet a Cornelian choice between love and duty. Gertrude deserts the king to aid Hamlet, who is not killed but crowned at the end' (*FS*, 24). Ducis had no English, basing his adaptations on Letourneur's 1778–83 translations. France would have to wait for more faithful translations of Shakespeare until Vigny's not entirely successful attempts in 1828–9, and then until François-Victor Hugo, the dramatist's son, produced a complete translation, published between 1859 and 1866.

When Kean played Hamlet in Paris in 1827, however, he did so in English and, if the words were little understood by the young unilingual Romantic enthusiasts, his style of acting bore out everything they were saying against declamatory fossilization at the Comédie-Française. The English troupe stayed in Paris from September 1827 to July 1828 (although the stars came and went as repertoire demanded), time enough for a varied season of Shakespearean offerings which overturned French notions of, among other dramatic conventions, stage propriety. Comment was aroused, for instance, by the *Romeo and Juliet* of Kemble and Miss Smithson. In the balcony scene, the actors remained upstage (where the balcony was), never looking at the audience; in fact, Kemble never once turned his head towards the house, and Miss Smithson's asides were made to the side, rather than to the public. Étienne Delécluze noted the following remarks in his diary after attending a performance of *Richard III* starring Edward Kean, the actor who most impressed Dumas and Hugo: 'Richmond and Richard fight with swords for *five or six minutes*. Richard is finally stabbed by his opponent. Richard-Kean, when he receives the wound, stays on his feet staggering about. He continues to wave his sword, then he drops it and soon with his empty hand, he pretends to continue fencing. Finally Kean falls down, and writhing around in that position, speaks half-a-dozen lines that form no more a part of the play than does any of the pantomime which preceded them' (*DRGC*, 38). Clearly, conservative French spectators like Delécluze preferred the convention whereby such disturbing events as death occurred in the wings, while motionless actors declaimed the author's lines to the public.

Other commentators, the Romantic poet Heinrich Heine, for example, have left their impressions of performances they attended. Even Heine found the English style of Shakespearean acting 'not against nature, but rather nature exaggerated.' He complained about the 'shouting' of both male and female actors, adding that it was possibly explained by the greater size of English popular theatres, as compared to the French houses (*DRGC*, 38–9). Some French actors, on the other hand, were paying careful attention to these new ways of portraying death or madness, believing that such histrionic techniques would enable them better to express emotion or counterfeit physical pain. They also acquired some of the tricks associated with the English stars: Kemble's sardonic, or 'satanic,' laugh made its reappearance in 1831 when Bocage played the title role in Dumas' *Antony*.

Dumas is the best source for comparisons of English and French actors before and after 1827–8. In his *Souvenirs dramatiques*, he compares, for instance, five different interpretations of Othello: 'I saw the Othellos of Talma, Kean, Kemble, Macready, and Joanny [Talma's successor as principal tragedian at the Comédie-Française]. Talma's Othello was a Moor with a veneer of Venetian civilization; Kean's was a wild beast, half tiger, half man; Kemble's was a man in his maturity, hot-headed and violent; Macready's was an Arab from the time of the Moors in Spain, elegant and chivalrous; Joanny's Othello was ... Joanny' (*DRGC*, 41). And on the subject of Othello's suicide Dumas writes: 'Talma used a downward thrust; Joanny followed the tradition established by Talma; Kean and Kemble drove home the dagger horizontally. Macready stabbed himself under the ribs with an upward movement. Then he introduced something that had a great effect on the audience: although wounded, he retained the strength necessary to get to the bed, and, speaking Desdemona's name with his last gasp, fell, kissing in death his victim's hand' (ibid., 41). Unlike Joanny, some French actors learned well, using the English style of acting to hone their own techniques. The most famous boulevard actors, Frédérick Lemaître and Marie Dorval, form a case in point.

By all accounts, Lemaître's acting had the two characteristics most despised at the Comédie-Française: it was instinctive, and it made him a star big enough to ignore their socio-artistic pretentions. He had little dramatic training, except for a few months at the Conservatoire where, encouraged by his teacher Pierre Lafon, he tried and failed the audition to join the Odéon, the Comédie-Française's left-bank house. He began his career in boulevard theatre, achieving stardom in 1824 as Robert Macaire, a vicious bandit who tearfully repents as he dies, in a formula-melodrama, *L'Auberge des Adrets*, written by a 'committee' of three authors, Saint-Amand (with whom Frédérick was to write a sequel, *Robert Macaire*, in 1834), Antier, and Polyanthe. One of Frédérick's biographers continues: 'Frédérick ... shuddered at the threadbare plot, the tearful recognition scenes, the stilted dialogue and the unconvincing ending. / Then he had a sudden inspiration: instead of playing Macaire straight, as a sinister villain, he would turn him into a gay, cynical rascal, quipping as he killed ... / The same evening he told the actor Firmin, who had been cast as Bertrand [Macaire's accomplice] that he intended to guy the part of Macaire, and Firmin readily agreed to follow his example.'[10]

This flash of inspiration made him a star and provided him with as reliable a breadwinner as was to be for Bernhardt her faithful work-horse, *La Dame aux camélias* by Dumas *fils*. The passionate, earthy style of acting necessary for playing principal roles in boulevard theatre served Frédérick well when, among his many successes, he acted Hamlet, Falstaff, Don César de Bazan, Ruy Blas, or Kean. The two latter roles were written for him by Hugo and Dumas, both of whom considered him to be the consummate Romantic actor. The most obvious modern French actor comparable to Frédérick, one also known, among other successes, for his interpretation of the title role in Hugo's *Ruy Blas*, was Gérard Philippe, no more afraid than Lemaître of being criticized on occasion for 'going over the top' in his portrayals, or for 'chewing up the scenery' in the productions in which he starred.

This resemblance between two popular stars brings up an important question: How should these 'larger-than-life' Romantic heroes, heroines, and villains be played? At a revival of *Ruy Blas* at the Comédie-Française in 1938, Colette recorded her doubts concerning the willingness of modern actors to impersonate such characters and also concerning a modern audience's reluctance to accept the Romantic style of acting: 'I don't think that actors can be recruited from any French troupe nowadays willing to play Romantic drama romantically. Victor Hugo's theatre must be acted as its author conceived it, grandiloquently, with fire, great outbursts of wild emotion, contrasts of light and shadow, exaggerated facial expressions. Who at the Comedy will take on, among other risks, that of a ridiculousness so splendid and generous that it commands admiration; who will dare readily to groan, yell, tear out his hair, address (*tutoyer*) the Great Ones of the earth with undue familiarity, summon up the Devil and threaten Heaven itself?'[11] Colette had not seen Gérard Philippe, whose Ruy Blas was in any case, according to contemporary accounts, all the more effective for being understated rather than overacted, but clearly Frédérick's was a hard act to follow even for popular stars. We will have occasion to discuss the ways in which this 'boulevard Talma,' the 'French Kean,' as he was also called, prepared a role during rehearsals of Hugo's *Lucrèce Borgia* and *Ruy Blas*.

If Mlle Mars was the star of comedy at the state-funded Comédie-Française, the queen of melodrama in the popular boulevard theatres was Marie Dorval. The two actresses would play against each other in 1835 in Hugo's *Angelo* at the Porte-Saint-Martin theatre. Like Frédérick's, Dorval's apprenticeship was practical. Before arriving in Paris she acted in touring companies for several years, playing the varied popular repertory that developed her deep, emotional voice later commented upon by all the Parisian critics of her day. She had the same good luck as Frédérick in her lessons at the Conservatoire: not fitting the mould, she was dismissed, thus not having time to acquire the limiting method then taught there by retired members of the Comédie. In 1818, at twenty, she began her career at the Porte-Saint-Martin theatre, playing *ingénues*, victimized virgins (for example in *Le Vampire* [1820], another 'committee' melodrama, this time by Carmouche, Nodier, and Jouffroy), and tearful wives. By 1827 her roles as passionate, frequently heart-broken, sometimes brutalized, heroines had made her the female star equivalent to Frédérick. In that year both actors starred in *Trente Ans ou la Vie d'un joueur* (*The Life of a Gambler*), a popular work by Victor Ducange, writer of melodramas. During her subsequent liaison with Vigny she subsequently played to great acclaim Kitty Bell in his *Chatterton*, a Romantic drama whose success at the time was largely due to a spectacular fall down a staircase she accomplished each night in 'dying.' Théophile Gautier, Hugo's 'lieutenant' at the 'battle' of *Hernani*, and historian of nineteenth-century French theatre, has this to say of her acting: 'Her talent was completely passionate; not that she neglected art, but art came to her from inspiration; she did not calculate her acting gesture by gesture, or mark out her exits and entrances with chalk on the boards; she put herself in the position of the character she was playing and became that character' (*HADF*, 6, 102). As well as being instinctive, her acting effectively communicated emotions audiences found profoundly moving, says Gautier: 'She was able to give meaning to words which had none, and she could change meaningless sentences into heartfelt cries of emotion. Things without worth in any other actor's mouth, when said by her, give a theatre full of people goose-flesh. With words as simple as "What do want me for? My God! I am so miserable!," she knows how to make you weep or shudder' (ibid., 150). By 1829, as great a star as Frédérick, she was the perfect female interpreter of the Romantic heroines in the dramas of Dumas, Vigny, and Hugo. In paying the two actors the following tribute many years later, Jules Janin pointed to their role in making even melodrama an artistically satisfying popular art:

> Between them, these two inspired players effected a total revolution in the art of drama. The audience, used to the shrill tones of melodrama with its din of words and voices, looked at one another in astonishment, moved and charmed by such simplicity and grace. It should be added that Frédérick Lemaître was a handsome young man, admirably fitted for his art, tempestuous, passionate, violent, and proud, while Mme Dorval, with her slightly bowed figure, had all that was required to command the liveliest compassion. She was frail, tearful, humble, and trembling; she wept most movingly;

she excelled in containing her feelings, murmuring: 'Quiet, my heart!' One had only to see them joined in the same dramatic action ... to know that they were made, he to express all the emotions of the human spirit, she to render all its sweet and intimate joys. Together they undoubtedly formed a bold, skilful, and all-powerful combination, the one ready to break everything within reach and magnificent in his fury, the other gracious and humble, fearless, ingenious and sweetly tearful. He had strength, she had grace; he had violence, she had charm.[12]

That the two 'sacred monsters' should gain such praise from Janin, the theatre critic on the *Journal des Débats* after 1836, shows how far critical opinion had moved towards the acting standards set by the melodrama in the popular boulevard theatre in general.

These popular boulevard theatres, as well as the Opéra, provided one more innovation which made the shift from the type and style of production at the Comédie-Française towards Romantic drama more attractive to young playwrights: a revolution in set-design, costume, and special effects. Young dramatists, as Hugo's manifesto, the Preface to *Cromwell*, would state clearly, were no longer willing to accept that the scene of a play's dramatic action should exist almost entirely in the heads of actors and audience. Such a theatre was reduced to static declamation because neo-classical tragedy feared or scorned spectacle. If messengers could report on the events taking place offstage, little need was there for appropriate scenery, elaborate sets, numerous supernumerary players, even stage props. If the action was completed within twenty-four hours, in a single locale, then only one backdrop was necessary, and a few schematic lighting effects could suggest the passage of time from morning to evening. If language and versification were all, then care for authentic costumes and local colour could be dispensed with, not in order, as nowadays, to suggest contemporary relevance, but to allow actors to purchase fashionable clothes that accentuated their attractiveness. Marie-Antoinette Allévy reports the following conversation between Garnerey, the costume designer at the Comédie-Française, and the principal actresses in Lebrun's *Marie Stuart*, played there in 1820:

ACTRESS: A long dress! How horrible! My only beauty is in my legs and feet!
GARNEREY: Well then, how would Madame like to be dressed?
ACTRESS: In the Greek style.
GARNEREY: In the sixteenth century?
ACTRESS: I insist, or I won't go onstage.
GARNEREY: (to Mme George). And you, Madame?

MME GEORGE: I, Oh, half in the Roman style and half in the English. (*MSF*, 78–9)

Clearly, in the power struggle over historical authenticity that was set to take place between actors and costume designers, the latter would have a hard time to get their way.

If, however, none of the old stage rules held good any more, if, for example, the orgy in Act 5 of *Lucrèce Borgia* was to take place onstage, or if spectators were to see 'all of the city of London, splendidly illuminated' in *Marie Tudor* (*OC*, 4, 846), then a serious effort would be needed to create the illusion of such spectacular events and scenes. In fact, new ideas on set design, and on the creation and manipulation of scenery had been coming forward since the century began. To examine them, we must once more look at the boulevard theatres whose successful dramatization of contemporary melodramas had developed the talents of teams of expert set-decorators, architects, and special-effects wizards. Allévy, historian of French techniques of dramatic production in this period, describes thus the change in attitudes wrought by innovations in set design and staging: 'There is no period in which the diverse elements of the spectacle played a greater role than in the first half of the nineteenth century. / Whether at the Théâtre-Français where, before the first Romantic demonstrations, there reigned a scenic poverty maintained by classical tradition, or at the boulevard theatres, long since already won over to magnificent spectacle, or on the stage at the Opéra, set decoration and costumes henceforth were counted among the principal attractions of theatrical production' (*MSF*, 226).

Noting that melodramatic effects like apparitions, thunder and lightning storms, and crowd scenes already figured in Voltaire's plays when staged in the eighteenth century, Allévy points out that heightened interest in spectacle during the Revolutionary period and Empire had produced attempts in the popular theatres to represent historical and natural locales. She cites also melodrama's tendency to substitute spectacular 'tableaux' for acts and scenes as one of the reasons necessitating that greater attention be given to set decoration. Even the topographic titles of melodramas like Loaisel de Tréogate's *The Devil's Castle* (1792), Redon's *The Mysterious Castle* (1799), and Chaussier Armand's *Maria or the Forest of Limberg* (1800), to cite only three, indicate the new importance the setting of the dramatic action was assuming, replacing the classical notion according first place to 'character.' The Romantic dramas of Hugo, Dumas and Vigny would return, however, to the classical tradition of eponymous titles: so Corneille's *Le Cid* and *Horace*, Racine's *Phèdre* and *Esther*, Voltaire's *Mérope* and *Tancrède*, are parallelled in Hugo's *Hernani* and *Marion de Lorme,* Dumas's *Christine* and *Antony,* and Vigny's *Chatterton* and *La Maréchale d'Ancre,* and so on.

Pixérécourt, the principal writer of melodramas at the time, went much further than specifying mere settings. He has left us technical explanations of how some of the most spectacular of the special effects necessary to the action of his plays were to be achieved. For the 1819 production of *The Exile's Daughter,* for example, he describes how the set-designer and stage hands had brought off the chief attraction forming his play's climax, an onstage flood. They had needed to use all their resources of understage frames and supports equipped with rollers that passed through slots in the scenery, as well as strategically positioned strips of cloth simulating water, mounted on a chassis stretching all the way across the stage. They also needed trolleys to move scenery back and forth, and artificial mounds on the set, which was divided into well-defined planes. The final manoeuvre involved raising the 'water,' with every element on the set, right down to the smallest nuts and bolts, playing its part in achieving the effect (*MSF,* 25). Thanks to such special effects, audiences at *The Exile's Daughter* could expect, helped no doubt by their lively imaginations and ability to identify themselves with fictional characters, to 'see' the heroine 'floating offstage on a plank' (*FS,* 45).

An earlier melodrama, *The Colossus of Rhodes* by Augustin Hapdé, had, in 1809, as its apocalyptic climax, a storm accompanied by an earthquake which swallowed up the city of Rhodes 'in the midst of fire from below,' along with a volcano spewing lava which spread over the stage. The stage directions at that point in the drama contain some details helpful to the stage manager and set designer: 'The Colossus totters, sinking down to its waist, everything else disintegrates and falls into the sea. At that very moment, a mountain rises from the tidal wave ... with a volcano smoking at its summit.' After citing this stage direction, French drama theorist Jean-Jacques Roubine adds: 'Demand for such technical wizardry was so strong that no [popular] theatre could afford to ignore it' (*TF,* 604).

Such sets demanded the skills of architects, specially trained set-designers and expert stage staff. The most famous of contemporary set-designers, one who was to work on Hugo's *Hernani* and *Le Roi s'amuse* was Pierre Ciceri, whom Dumas would later call the 'father of modern set-design.' He had begun his career in 1809, painting landscape sets at the Academy of Music; named by Napoleon chief set decorator for the musical theatres of Paris in 1810, he was awarded the title of the Emperor's painter in 1812, and in 1814 Louis XVIII made him the King's painter. With Daguerre he developed the first experimental stage lighting using gas at the Opéra in 1822 for *Aladin ou la Lampe merveilleuse.* He also organized Charles X's Coronation ceremony in 1825 in Reims cathedral. But his real work was in the theatre.

As part of his job as official painter for the Academy of Music, Ciceri had also to provide sets for some of the minor Parisian theatres like the Panorama-Dramatique, which combined living actors, stage machinery and circular scenic views. With Ciceri as designer, the technique of painting sets moved closer to landscape painting, and his contributions thus fostered Paris' new interest in historical accuracy and exotic settings. The Romantic desire for 'local colour,' be it temporal or geographic, a desire that Hugo would champion in the Preface to *Cromwell*, found its ideal exponent in Ciceri. No longer might the same set serve to represent different epochs and places. Audiences demanded to see 'Mary Queen of Scots' bedroom,' 'the street' in which Henri IV was assassinated, the 'old marketplace' where Joan of Arc was burnt to death, the site of a king's execution, or the den of a group of conspirators. Ciceri and his colleagues would help Romantic dramatists to satisfy this demand.

In its less extreme form such set-design did not remain the exclusive province of the 'minor' theatres in Paris. The Comédie-Française, under its Commissioner, Baron Taylor, chose Ciceri to design Dumas' drama, *Henri III et sa cour*, which had a sensational success there in 1829. This was the year before *Hernani*, for which Ciceri also created the architectural set of Act 4. By the time the Romantic dramas of Hugo, Dumas, and Vigny began to appear, contemporary set designers were ready for them:

> People wanted to see everything in the theatre, and all their dreams were now satisfiable. Did authors want ships to transport the action onto distant seas? Stage managers constructed them, using ropes to move them. Did they want to see different historical periods, with their monuments, costumes, parades, and battles brought back to life down to the smallest detail? enter the world of legends? fly up to Milton's Paradise? or sink down into Dante's Inferno? The providers of 'special effects' (*trucs*) at the Opéra came to their aid ... Did their characters wander through streets or fields, cross rivers, walk by the side of moonlit lakes, lose themselves in forests, face the wild elements? A powerful band of set-decorators, exploiters of an industry in which Daguerre and Ciceri had owned the privilege of innovation, was ready to satisfy their desires. (*MSF*, 161–2)

To modern readers of Allévy and Carlson, their accounts of the 'industrial' proportions that the construction of sets, the provision of period costumes, and the designing of ever more spectacular special effects suggest nothing more clearly than the work accomplished in the Hollywood film studios in the first half of this century: 'Dream Factories' merely existed in Europe a little earlier.

One other phenomenon which affected the success or failure of the Romantic drama because it represented a direct manipulation of a play's reception has already been mentioned: the claque. *Claquer* in eighteenth-century French, meant to clap over-enthusiastically, a task undertaken by the officially sanctioned members of a group of spectators, also known as the 'Knights of the Chandelier' (from the principal light fixture of most Parisian theatres) and as the 'Romans' (because the first to guarantee applause for his own performances was said to be Nero). The claque's most recent historian, F.W.J. Hemmings, expresses some of the bewilderment that such an institution routinely causes those unfamiliar with the history of French theatre:

> The claque in the nineteenth century was an institution peculiar to France and even there, confined to Paris. Visitors from abroad found it eccentric, annoying, and quite inexplicable: if an audience was allowed, anywhere else in the world, to be sole judge of a play and applaud it or not as they thought fit, why was it that in this city a small body of men, in all the best theatres, were charged with the function of ensuring as best they could that every play and every actor in it should be cheered to the rafters? And why, in spite of complaints and objections from nearly everyone with an interest in the theatre, and in the teeth of every effort to rid the stage of this parasitic growth, did the claque persist and prosper from one end of the century to the other?[13]

The practice of buying applause mounted in the years 1800–30 to the point that actors, theatre managers, and playwrights seeking to save a first-night flop believed support from a theatre's official claque indispensable to their success. They therefore paid for applause in various ways: theatre managers appointed an official claque 'Chief' and through him supplied the money and free tickets necessary to pay his hirelings. The claque performed its commercial service at state and minor theatres alike, and at the Comédie-Française in the 1820s it was not unknown for the claque to outnumber paying members of the audience. Some actors, Joanny at the Comédie for instance, refused the professional blackmail exerted upon him, accepting that his performances would go unapplauded. A few playwrights, most notably Hugo during the run of *Hernani*, also declined to purchase the official claque's services.

The power exercised by a claque Chief should not be underestimated rather it should figure in any discussion of the contemporary reception of Romantic drama. Once again Hemmings offers the best information, this time on the responsibilities, status and prestige of Santon, leader of the claque at the Variétés:

> Santon ... knew the repertory there by heart, so much so that all the way

through a performance he would read the paper instead of following the play and yet would never fail to give the signal for a shout of laughter or a burst of applause at exactly the right moment. In the hierarchy of the administration, a *chef de claque* ranked, with the stage manager, immediately below the director; he sat in at dress rehearsals, taking notes that would serve him to give instructions to his subordinates when the play came to face the all-important opening performance, and afterwards he would have a private conference with the director, in which the play or musical comedy was analysed scene by scene in order to determine where it might need to be boosted a little, or where the *chef de claque* could safely rein in his men, confident that the scene would 'carry' without their help.[14]

Clearly, Hugo's refusal of such guaranteed, albeit tainted, support would cost him dear, if he were unable to replace it with his own, less professional, supporters. This passage also reminds us that in the nineteenth century, the house lights remained on during a performance, a fact which explains not only Santon's ability to read the newspaper during the play, but also contemporary spectators' confidence that they, and their jewels, were as much on show as the play itself. Not until Wagner doused the house lights at the Festival Theatre in Bayreuth in 1876, a practice followed later by Parisian theatres, was the audience 'compelled' to turn their whole attention to events onstage.

Our study of the conditions, physical, artistic, and commercial, affecting the period immediately preceding the production and reception of the first Romantic dramas by Hugo, Dumas, and Vigny is now almost complete. However, such a study needs to be complemented by an examination of the literary presuppositions of a cultivated Parisian audience of the 1820s, that prepared it, to the extent that it was prepared, to patronize the new plays. What 'models' of Romantic drama had they seen, and what influences had made them readier to accept the work of the new dramatists?

AVATARS OF THE ROMANTIC DRAMA: FROM DIDEROT TO HUGO

The theory of the French Romantic drama no more sprang newly born from Hugo's 1827 Preface to *Cromwell* than did *Cromwell* come to be written merely to illustrate the ideas in his manifesto. Historians of the Romantic drama trace its origins in France back to eighteenth-century attempts to undermine the absolute separation advocated by Boileau between the worlds of tragedy (inhabited by gods, royalty, and nobles) and comedy involving common people. Writers of 'bourgeois drama' like Diderot, or of 'serious,' or 'tearful' comedy, like Nivelle de La Chaussée, presented either bourgeois family dissension, or nobles whose dramatic dilemmas end unhappily. In plays like La Chaussée's *Le Préjugé à la mode* (1735), or like Diderot's *Le Père de famille* (1758), sentimental pathos replaced the classical comedy's happy ending. Beaumarchais wrote of the moral improvement he believed drama's emotional power produced:

> The spectacle of an honest man's misfortune strikes one to the heart, creating sympathy for him, at first gently then completely, eventually forcing you to examine yourself. When I see virtue persecuted, the victim of malice, but still fine, still splendid, and preferable above everything else, even in the midst of misfortune, then Drama's effect is not ambiguous, it becomes my only interest; and then, if I myself am not enjoying good fortune, if base envy is striving to blacken my character, if I am thus attacked in my person, my honour, or my fortune, how pleasing I find this kind of spectacle! and what a fine moral I can draw from it! ... Thus I come out of the theatre better than when I went in, for the simple reason that I was moved there.[15]

Beaumarchais, who, in *Le Barbier de Séville* and *Le Mariage de Figaro*, wrote the two most successful 'serious' social comedies in the French eighteenth-century repertoire, was particularly well qualified to explain the didacticism that such a mixture of light and moralistic genres produced.

It was Diderot, however, who proposed both a theory of the new 'bourgeois drama' and illustrated it with two plays, *Le Fils naturel*, written in 1757, performed once only in 1771, and *Le Père de famille*, published in 1758, and performed in 1761 and 1769 at the Comédie-Française. His theoretical works on the new dramatic form include his 'Entretiens sur *Le Fils naturel*' (1757), 'Sur la poésie dramatique' (1758), and 'Garrick et les acteurs anglais' (1770). The latter essay is the first version of what was to become upon its publication in 1830 the *Paradoxe sur le comédien*, in which he proposed his famous theory of acting: the greater the artistic control exercised by the actor, the greater the illusion of naturalness and spontaneity produced.[16]

Basing his remarks about the bourgeois drama on the criterion of theatricality, rather than literary prestige ('A play is made less to be read than to be performed'),[17] Diderot pleaded for serious comedy and domestic bourgeois tragedy, with subjects involving the imitation of modern, not Graeco-Roman, life. Such subjects would thus be social, rather than psychological, mythic, or dynastic, and would involve disputes between artisans and merchants, financiers and magistrates, middle-class fathers and sons. Such social dramas would emphasize 'real-life,' static, rhetorical debates or 'tableaux,' rather than dynamically surprising *coups de théâtre*, or peripeteia. Actors should create by their art the illusion of deep emotion, with the aim of moving the spectator to meditate upon the moral truths debated onstage. Diderot wrote his dramas in prose so as better to create the illusion of everyday life. A typical subject might be the story of the disagreements about an inheritance within a middle-class family, with characters expressing virtuous moral sentiments, since the aim of drama should be to 'inspire in man the love of virtue and the horror of vice.'[18] Of Diderot's principles, Hugo would only fully exploit in his Romantic dramas the combination of comic and tragic elements, although in his critical prefaces he would agree with Diderot on the didactic value of theatre.

Where else then did Hugo take his ideas from for the Preface to *Cromwell*? The answer becomes clearer if we consider Ubersfeld's definition of the principal characteristics of Romantic drama, since her summary offers us a thread leading through the theoretical battles of the period 1800–27: 'The Romantic revolution has three faces. It is a revolution in its themes, which are essentially historical; it is revolutionary in its forms; lastly, it is revolutionary in its ideas, its philosophy' (in *TF*, 548). We have already seen evidence of the importance of historical subjects in the work of writers of dramas and melodramas under the Empire and after the Restoration. In their historical plays, such authors as Schiller, and the French Romantic dramatists who came after him, dramatized, in the main, incidents they took from the Middle Ages and Renaissance, rather than from classical times. All of Hugo's dramas written between 1820 and 1843, for instance, were set in these periods or in the seventeenth century. The principal influences here are foreign, with Shakespeare and Schiller sharing first place.

Schiller's *The Brigands* was translated and played in France to great acclaim in 1792. The French Revolutionary audience, who were witnessing violent historical events in their daily lives, particularly enjoyed the violent historicality of Schiller's play, with its exaltation of patriotism, love, and of liberty conquering despotism. Hugo's hero, Hernani, would also be a brigand, opposed to the young Charles V, Holy Roman Emperor and King of sixteenth-century Spain. Schiller's other historical dramas, *Don Carlos, Maria Stuart, William Tell,* and his trilogy, *Wallenstein,* were translated into French and received enthusistic acclaim for their action, for their freedom from the restraints hampering French neo-classical tragedies, but most of all for their celebration of historical tragedy. One influential French critic, Benjamin Constant, added to his translation of Schiller's *Wallenstein* a preface in which he contrasted contemporary German and French dramatic practice, confessing that he still preferred French restraint to German violence: 'If [German] conventions were to be allowed, one would fear that the only things seen in our theatres would be scaffolds, fighting, feasting, ghosts, and set changes.'[19] Thus Schlegel's criticism in 1809 that French taste preferred its own literary conventions to attempts at reconstructing other periods and locales continued to be accurate.[20]

The Romantics were also to revolutionize various formal conventions of French drama. By refusing to observe Boileau's 'rules,' principally the unities, and by mixing, in Hugo's formulation, 'sublime' and 'grotesque' characters, language, and effects, Romantic drama once more showed its debt to German authors and critics. Lessing, for instance, had criticized French dictates on the unities in his *Hamburgische Dramaturgie*, translated into French in 1785:

> The French, who had no taste for true unity of action, and who had been spoiled by the barbarous plots of Spanish plays before experiencing Greek simplicity, considered the unities of time and place not as consequences of the unity of action, but as conditions indispensable in themselves ... Instead of a single place, they introduced an indeterminate space, which may be taken now for this place, now for that. All that was needed, they believed, was that such places should not be too far apart, and that none demanded a particular stage set, so the same one might serve just as well for one as the other. For the unity of time they substituted unity of duration; and they permitted to count as a single day any period of time, in which the sun neither rose nor set, in which no one went to bed, not more than once at least, whatever the quantity and variety of events that might take place (*DR*, 32).

The accuracy of Lessing's remarks will strike anyone who has seen or read neo-classical tragedies of the eighteenth and early nineteenth centuries. Romantic dramatists, convinced by Lessing's logic, as well as by that of Stendhal, who, in *Racine et Shakespeare*, made a similar criticism of French 'regularity,' abandoned the constraints on both time and place, restricting their attention to observing the unity of action.

German dramatic theory and practice found its most persuasive French advocate in Mme de Staël, whose 1810 work, *De l'Allemagne*, toned down the anti-French strictures of Lessing and Schlegel, producing a rhetoric more pleasing to the new generation of Romantic dramatists. She insisted that, rather than relying on the unities to create theatrical illusion, foreign dramatists believed that 'This illusion consists in the drawing of character, in truthful language, and in the exact observation of the customs of the time and country one desires to describe ... A tragedy can only seem true to us by the emotion it arouses in us. Now, if the nature of the circumstances dramatized, changes of place, and the imaginary prolongation of time increase our emotion, the illusion itself becomes all the more vivid.'[21] The production of the 'local colour' possessed by historical events when dramatized in their authentic time period and topographical setting became a principal distinguishing mark of the French Romantic drama. Once again, the cinema offers the most striking analogy in our own century. Modern film directors who abandon studio sets in favour of authentic locations, shooting the action of their screenplays on the very spot where it is represented as having happened, effectively satisfy the desire felt by Romantic dramatists for chronotopical precision.

When Stendhal proposed his definition of 'Romantic tragedy' in *Racine et Shakespeare* (1825), he too insisted on its formal characteristics: 'A Romantic tragedy is written in prose, the events the spectator sees onstage last several months and take place in several different places' (*RS* 105). His famous antithetical definitions of romanticism and classicism, when applied to Hugo's dramas, support the latter's desire to renew neo-classical tragedy by appealing to ideas important to the contemporary public, rather than to conventional wisdom and to models whose currency had come under challenge: 'Romanticism, [Stendhal wrote], is the art of presenting to nations literary works which, in the current state of their customs and beliefs, are capable of giving them the greatest possible pleasure. Classicism, on the other hand, presents them with the literature that gave the greatest possible pleasure to their great-grandfathers' (*RS*, 62). The new forms would make possible works appealing to the new ideas about the individual and society, about history and politics, current in the Romantic era.

François Guizot's philosophical view of the new symbolic hero, one that Romantic drama should feature, exemplifies the third of its revolutionary innovations. Guizot's 'Life of Shakespeare' served as preface to the 1821 edition of Le Tourneur's translation of his plays. At least some of the new hero's characteristics feature in the dramas of all the French Romantic dramatists. He will be an outlaw (Hernani), alone against all (Ruy Blas), out of sympathy with society's moral dictates (Antony), financial compromises (Chatterton), or political dishonesty (Lorenzaccio). He may even be the Romantic colossus himself, Napoleon (as in Dumas' 1831 *Napoléon Bonaparte*, for example). To Ubersfeld the Romantic hero has much in common also with some of the great mythic heroes and anti-heroes. She sees Lucrèce Borgia as Hugo's female version of Don Juan, and in the two warring brothers of *Les Burgraves* a version of the Cain and Abel fable, in which envy turns to fratricidal hatred.

Guizot also believed that Romantic authors should address their dramas to a contemporary audience who, matured by the historical events they had lived through, no longer wanted to watch intimate dramas involving the fate of a single individual: 'Nature and the destiny of Man have revealed to us all their simplest and most vivid features in all their breadth and dynamism. We need tableaux in which such a spectacle finds renewal, in which Man is shown in his entirety, provoking all our sympathy.'[22] Such a hero should be larger-than-life, able to personify the great social and political conflicts of his time.

In his essay on Shakespeare Guizot also proposed a theory of universal reception: he believed that the work of a national dramatist should appeal to all classes of society. Although the theatre is a feast for the people, a national theatre should not be reduced to popular melodrama alone, for if theatre appeals only to the masses, it excludes, he believed, those of superior intelligence and cultural sophistication. Dramas which appeal only to the upper classes, on the other hand, are condemned to the kind of degeneration he found in contemporary neo-classical tragedy. In the Romantic manifestos that the Prefaces to his dramas became, Hugo reformulated some of Guizot's ideas on the popular audience and on the Romantic hero.

One final source of theoretical and practical models affected Hugo in the 1820s when he was beginning his career as the principal theorist and practitioner of the Romantic drama: the theories and plays produced by the writers of melodrama. Etymologically, the name comes from a combination of the Greek *melos* and *drama,* of alternating music and action, which is precisely what it meant to Rousseau, who first used the term in his *Pygmalion* of 1774. By 1800, as we have seen, however, the term designated the exciting popular dramatic productions of writers like Pixérécourt, Ducange, and Caigniez, featured on the 'boulevard du Crime.' Commentators of the time and since have remarked on the genre's moralistic character or function and on its use of sensational spectacular effects. From both of these characteristics Romantic dramatists, though using some of the effects, structures, and emotional appeals of melodrama would distance themselves.

Charles Nodier and Pixérécourt himself have left explanations of the reasons for, and the functioning of, melodrama's ideological mechanisms in the first third of the nineteenth century. Nodier wrote, for instance, of the historical links between melodrama and the French Revolution:

> Given the circumstances surrounding its appearance, melodrama was a necessity. The entire [French] people had just played out in the streets and public squares the greatest drama in history. Everyone had been an actor in the bloody play, everyone had been either a soldier, a Revolutionary, or an outlaw. Such solemn spectators, still reeking of gunpowder and blood, needed to feel emotions like those of which the return to public order had deprived them. They wanted [to see] conspiracies, dungeons, battlefields, powder and blood, the unmerited misfortunes of the Great and Glorious, the insidious plotting of traitors, the perilous acts of devotion performed by honorable men. They had to be reminded of ... the great moral lesson in which all philosophical doctrines and religions may be summarized: even on earth, virtue never goes unrewarded, crime is never unpunished. And

make no mistake about it! Melodrama was no small thing! It *was Revolutionary morality*.[23]

Nodier's naive optimism concerning the values taught by melodrama reflects that of Pixérécourt himself who, in his own *Réflexions sur le mélodrame* which prefaced the 1832 edition of his *Oeuvres choisies*, contended astutely, and with a condescension born presumably of experience, that 'Melodrama will always offer a means of instructing the people, because the genre is, at least, within the people's grasp,' (*DR*, 89).

That Romantic dramatists like Hugo, Dumas, and Vigny did not take the same naively optimistic view of contemporary society as Nodier may be seen from the contrast Pixérécourt found between their works and his own: 'In the past we chose only what was good; but in modern dramas, you find only monstrous crimes that revolt morality and one's sense of shame. Always, everywhere, adultery, rape, incest, patricide, prostitution, the most shameful, filthiest vices, each one more disgusting than the other ... In the last ten years, a very large number of Romantic plays have been produced, that is to say evil, dangerous, immoral plays, plays deprived of interest and truth ... It was not I who founded the Romantic genre' (*SG*, 73). Pixérécourt's impassioned disclaimer is worth remembering when one reads, as one so often does, that Romantic drama is merely a 'literary' form of melodrama.

Modern scholars are more careful when assessing the Romantic drama. It is no longer enough to dismiss generic differences between Romantic drama and melodrama in order, as Ubersfeld frequently reminds us, 'to devalue Romantic drama.' Analysis of Hugo's Romantic dramas, for instance, reveals that they contain none of the sensational special effects of boulevard melodrama: there are no earthquakes, no tidal waves, no smoking volcanos. Although the Romantic dramatists would keep coincidences, recognition scenes, poisons and counter-poisons, spies, symbolic objects and so on, they did so in company with dramatic authors like Aeschylus or Shakespeare, Pirandello or Ibsen, Brecht or Pinter. Most often commented upon by scholars assessing Romantic drama's debt to melodrama is the striking contrast in social attitudes between the protagonists of the respective genres. Romantic anti-heroes who refuse the constraints of a bourgeois society, frequently preferring exclusion or death to conformity with its social norms, are at the opposite extreme to the conventionally minded heroes of melodrama, interested only in defeating the villain so as to restore bourgeois normality. Another Romantic character, the man of the people, either in a primary or secondary role, Ruy Blas or Gilbert in *Marie Tudor*, for instance, is the opposite of the melodrama's simpleton, whose naiveté supposedly represents that of the members of the underclass. The Romantic drama's unhappy ending is another of the generic marks distinguishing it from melodrama, whose conclusion presents a contented reintegration of (usually) the family group into society's bosom. Although both Romantic drama and melodrama aimed at popular audiences, melodrama appealed to popular sentimental optimism, whereas the Romantic drama encouraged in its spectators a more cynical or fatalistic reaction.

These remarks should not be seen as an attempt to argue the Romantic drama's greater aesthetic value by denigrating an 'inferior' genre, namely melodrama. In questions of generic evaluation, genres represent separate entities, which such invidious comparisons serve only to confuse. James L. Smith states this idea quite clearly in speaking of the folly of comparing tragedy with melodrama to the greater glory of the former: 'Critics who stress the fatalism of *Romeo and Juliet* usually conclude the play a tragedy which fails; they would judge it very differently as a melodrama of defeat. This is not to say that Shakespeare missed the marathon and won the egg-and-spoon race. Melodrama is not inferior to tragedy; it works by different means to different ends, and comparisons are only valid when they lie within a genre.'[24]

As we have already seen to some extent, and as the next chapter will reveal more clearly, Hugo's early dramas, written between 1812 and 1826, owe most to contemporary literary forms, Pixérécourt's melodramas and Walter Scott's historical novels among them. By the late 1820s, however, in *Cromwell*, *Marion de Lorme*, and *Hernani*, he enters his own dramatic world.

3. Hugo's Aesthetic Revolt (1), 1820–1827: *Inez de Castro, Amy Robsart, Cromwell,* and Its Preface

Passion combined with action, which is to say present life and past history, creates the drama.[1]

Victor Hugo was eighteen in February 1820, and already ambitious to succeed in a literary career so that he could marry Adèle Foucher. The 1820s were to be for him, in general, a period of intense literary activity leading, among his other activities as poet and novelist, to the first formulation of his theory of the Romantic drama in the Preface to *Cromwell* (1827) and to the writing of his first such dramas, *Cromwell, Marion de Lorme,* and *Hernani.* Along the way, he wrote dramatic criticism, an activity that introduced him to the realities of the theatre scene in Paris; and he also completed the prose melodrama, *Inez de Castro,* as well as *Amy Robsart,* part drama, part melodrama, also in prose, based on Walter Scott's novel *Kenilworth.* One play, on Pierre Corneille, he began but abandoned, incorporating some of the material in his later drama, *Marion de Lorme.* The 1820s were also the period of his happy married life with Adèle, the time when his children were born: Léopold, who died at two months in 1823, Léopoldine, born in 1824, Charles in 1826, François-Victor in 1828, and Adèle in 1830.

That it was a period in which he was still seeking his way in literary matters is clearly evidenced in the contrasts and contradictions between his dramatic works, both theoretical and practical, written at the beginning of the decade and the texts he wrote between 1825 and 1827. In the twenty-five or so theatre reviews he wrote for the *Conservateur Littéraire,* the review he founded in 1819 with his two brothers Abel and Eugène, he reserves his serious attention, for instance, for the neo-classical tragedies and comedies of the day playing at the Comédie-Française or the Odéon. Although charged with reporting on the theatrical premières taking place in the French capital between December 1819 and March 1821, he scorned, with a few exceptions, the melodramas playing on the 'boulevard du Crime.' His scorn was to some extent conditioned by the review's policy: in 1819, his collaborator on *Le Conservateur Littéraire*, Abel, had published a *Traité du mélodrame* in which, along with his collaborators, Armand Malibourne and J.-J. Ader, he had lampooned the genre. And yet, despite Hugo's scorn as a drama critic, it was to melodrama that he would turn for the structure and ruling conventions of his first play in this period, *Inez de Castro*. Nor was his passion for the theatre restricted to the plays he was reviewing: we know, for instance, thanks to a letter to Adèle, that, among other plays, he saw a French adaptation of *Hamlet* on 28 December 1819.

INEZ DE CASTRO

'In this period' may be a misleading phrase when referring to the composition of *Inez*. Once again, the editors of the chronological edition of Hugo's works are not certain of the dating of one of the early plays, placing *Inez* as early as 1819 and as late as 1822 (*OC*, 1, iv), the year it received unanimous approval from the reading committee of the Panorama Dramatique, one of the boulevard theatres devoted to the production of melodrama. Despite this enthusiastic reception, *Inez* was never performed, being banned by the censor, presumably, according to Éliette Vasseur, because the character of Alphonse, a weak king manipulated by his wife, was a reminder of Louis XVIII, another weak king accused of being too easily influenced by his favourites of both sexes. This was by no means the last time that one of Hugo's plays would be banned for the 'political allusions' which the government censor read into it.

There seems little doubt that *Inez* was a melodrama, rather than the first of Hugo's Romantic dramas: its enthusiastic acceptance by one of the principal contemporary centres of Parisian melodrama may be said to confirm this. Formally, it corresponds to Rousseau's etymologically inspired definition of the genre, being a mixture of *melos* and *drama*, as its title and generic description make clear: *Inez de Castro. A Melodrama in three Acts and two Interludes* (*OC*, 1, 433). The accompanying stage directions establish the musical and Terpsichorean character of the interludes. The 'First Interlude' is introduced thus, for example: '*The stage represents the Moorish camp, on the sea coast, from which the masts of the Moorish galleys can be seen. The tents are decked out with pennants and streamers. Soldiers are scattered about among battle trophies and piles of arms. A choir of young Moorish girls and Arab horsemen advances singing to the music of harps, drums, guitars and bugles*' (*OC*, 1, 444).

Music and action do not always alternate, however, as in Rousseau's definition. Music, for instance, accompanies the climactic event forming the play's ending: the appearance of the ghost of Inez, returned to comfort her distraught husband and children. And it is music also which distinguishes Hugo's melodrama from its most obvious source, Houdar de La Motte's sentimental or 'pathetic' tragedy *Inès de Castro,* which had enjoyed great success in Paris in 1723.

The subject had already been treated by Lope de Vega in 1630 *Amar sin saber a quién* (*Loving without Knowing Whom*) and by Luis Velez de Guevara in 1604, *Reinar despues de morir* (*Reigning after Death*).[2] It was probably the Iberian setting of the myth that drew the young Hugo to the subject. He follows the existing Spanish and French versions fairly closely, unlike Montherlant, for instance, whose 1942 version, *La Reine morte,* introduced major changes. In the modern version, Inez is pregnant, rather than already a mother, so the central figure, Ferrante, King of Portugal, must decide whether to put to death both his son's wife and his own innocent grandson. In the earlier myth, no such dilemma exists: although King Alphonse, softened by the tears of his grandchildren has forgiven Inez her crime of *lèse-majesté* in marrying his son, Don Pedro, she is poisoned by the Queen of Spain. Where Houdar emphasized intimate family details for pathetic purposes, Hugo develops the subject's melodramatic potential. The multiple settings, for example, include a dungeon in which Inez appears in chains and a funeral vault into which Inez's coffin is carried in order that the crown of Spain may be placed symbolically upon it. Here it is that her ghost appears above the tomb, bathed in heavenly light and 'surrounded by angels.' The supernatural element, the use of disguises (Don Pedro returns to Lisbon *incognito* to save his wife and children), the heartless villain (the Queen) and her treacherous helper, the Alcade d'Alpunar, all belong in the world of the writer of Pixérécourt-style melodramas. The ending even manages to encourage Don Pedro in his civic duty, for the message the ghost of Inez returns to pass on to her husband is this: 'A crime was going to separate us forever. If you wish us to be united for eternity, live for our children, live for your people. Life is short and many men still living need you on earth. I have been allowed, dear husband, to come from the resting place of the blessed to tell you this from the Lord: Live and suffer; a people's happiness sometimes demands a King's unhappiness (*OC,* 1, 464). The ending illustrates Ubersfeld's thesis that the melodrama's happy ending has an edifying purpose. In his Romantic dramas, all of which end unhappily, Hugo was to break the melodrama's conventions, in the process, as Arnaud Laster remarks, 'subverting the genre and constituting a definitive anti-melodrama' (*PF,* 378).

AMY ROBSART

The history of the composition of Hugo's next play, *Amy Robsart*, is complicated. Hugo began *Amy* in 1822, in collaboration with Alexandre Soumet, a
successful author of neo-classical tragedies who two years later would be
elected to the French Academy. Hugo agreed to write the first three acts,
and Soumet was to add acts four and five. In fact, Hugo completed his part
on schedule, but not apparently to Soumet's satisfaction. Unable to accept
Hugo's mingling of tragic and grotesque elements in the action, the conservative Soumet withdrew from the project, and Hugo put the manuscript
aside until after the critical success that greeted his Preface to *Cromwell* in
1827. He then quickly completed the play, but was unwilling perhaps to
have as his first performed play an adaptation of another author's work, in
this case Walter Scott's novel *Kenilworth*.[3] He therefore allowed the play to
go on under the signature of his brother-in-law, Paul Foucher. After the
one disastrous performance on 13 February 1828, however, Hugo immediately identified himself as the play's author and even claimed as his the
lines that had drawn the greatest number of catcalls and whistles. In any
event, his first venture on the Parisian stage was a total flop, and he withdrew the play after a single performance. Let us try to see why.

One criticism made in the press concerned the play's lack of novelty.
Although Scott's 1821 novel had only recently been translated into French,
Parisian theatre-goers had already been able to see three other dramatic
versions of it, including Soumet's *Emilia*, in September 1827. The character
of Flibbertigibbet, the grotesque actor who shows disinterested courage
and generosity in helping Amy, the wife of the Earl of Leicester and victim
of the royal favourite's ambition to marry Queen Elizabeth, aroused great
opposition from a Parisian public more used to laughing at such lowlife
figures. The public seems to have been unwilling to pay this character,
who combines the wit and word play of the medieval clown with the high-
minded values of a Romantic hero, the respect which his high-born adver-
saries in *Amy* sacrifice to ambition. Another reason for the poor reception
was the play's length, excessive by the standards of the day. It is easy to see
why, after sitting through about four hours of a play that in no way catered
to their critical preconceptions, the audience at the Odéon took exception
to the ending. They reacted most strongly against Hugo's sensationally
horrific treatment of his source. The authors of all three other dramatic
versions of *Kenilworth* that appeared in Paris at the time, had weakened
Scott's tragic ending, judging rightly that Amy's murder would offend a
contemporary audience. According to Henry Bonnier (*OC*, 2, 913, n4) the
first-night audience found Hugo's new ending just too horrible. Amy falls
into the abyss, lured by the sound of Leicester's hunting horn. Flames

destroy the ruined castle, and the murderers, Richard Varney and his sorcerer henchman Alasco, go to their deaths accompanied by the jeers of their triumphant adversary, the grotesque Flibbertigibbet. All this was too much for the audience.

We should not blame the play's staging for the flop. It is true that, according to Mme Hugo's account, rehearsals had not gone well because, as a result of the death of her mother, Hugo was distracted and unable to supervise them. The costumes were designed by Delacroix however, and, from the drawings that remain, they incorporated the grandeur and the schematic function that Hugo had prescribed:

> ELISABETH, *Queen of England. Splendid court dress, small royal crown.*
>
> LEICESTER. *Rich costume of white satin embroidered in gold; velvet cloak, scarlet or black, with the Decoration of the Garter, the collars of the orders of Saint Andrew, of the Golden Fleece, and of the Garter. Formal, narrow-brimmed hat with white plume; diamond gloves.*
>
> AMY ROBSART. *White dress, over which, in act three, she wears a dress of purple velvet, richly embroidered.*
>
> VARNEY. *In black, costume tightly fitting from head to foot; short cloak, small sword. Cap with fine coxcomb.*   (*OC*, 2, 798)

Amy's white dress suggests her innocence, just as Varney's black costume signals his role as the melodramatic villain and the heroine's would-be seducer. As for the actors, Lockroy (Leicester) and Mlle Anaïs (Amy), later to play Blanche in *Le Roi s'amuse*, Ubersfeld declares them 'honourable without being outstanding' (*VHTL*, 1, 1384), and Laster adds that they were 'the best possible for productions at the Odéon' (*PF*, 286). Once again, Hugo put the manuscript away, not intending it for publication. In fact, the manuscript was found after his death, in a secret drawer in his bedroom at Hauteville House, Guernsey, and published posthumously.

Despite the play's failure in 1828, Hugo's supporters have credited *Amy* with the importance attached both to its being Hugo's first staged play and to its significance in the history of the Romantic assault on the theatre. Théophile Gautier, for instance, spoke of it in 1838, as having been 'one of the first steps the new School took on the stage' (*HADF*, 1, 195), and Ubersfeld goes so far as to say that 'there is not a play of Hugo which does not owe to *Amy* some detail or some essential element' (*VHTL*, 1, 1384). Indeed, the most obvious resemblance between *Amy* and Hugo's later dramas is with the story of *Marie Tudor*, also set in Tudor England, also involving a Queen's relationship with her non-regal lover and his mistress. But the motif of the hunting horn will return in *Hernani*, and Sir Hugh Robsart's enumeration of Amy's glorious ancestors prefigures the portrait scenes in *Hernani* and *Les Burgraves*. And, just as Amy herself is the first in a line of Hugolian heroines who will sacrifice themselves for love (Doña Sol, Blanche, Tisbe), so Flibbertigibbet prefigures the same kind of generous-spirited and ingenious helpers in the plays Hugo included in his *Théâtre en liberté*, figures such as Airolo in *Mangeront-ils?* (*Will They Eat Something?*), and Glapieu in *Mille Francs de récompense* (*A Thousand Francs Reward*).

From the melodrama, *Amy* inherited its setting: a gothic castle in ruins, with secret passages and oubliettes, in which prisoners may be conveniently 'forgotten.' It retained the melodramatic villain in his black clothes, a 'vile seducer,' who in his monologues exults in his own evil-doing, in the process explaining his machinations to any uncomprehending spectators. The same careful provision of explanations for slow-witted spectators also accounts for the frequency of asides, addressed to the audience. In fact, in some scenes (Act 2, scene 5 is a good example), two parallel and directly contrasted discourses occur. In the dialogue, characters flatter and lie to each another and then, in their asides, reveal to the audience the truth about their feelings, designs, etc., thus developing the dramatic irony that allows the public, however bereft of subtlety, to believe itself superior in intelligence to the characters. *Amy* also has as a character the astrologer of melodrama: Demetrius Alasco, also called Dr Dooboobius, whose predictions may either determine the course of the action, or, as in the parodic form used by Hugo in *Amy*, merely serve to expose his role as charlatan. Opposed to the evil genius is, as we have seen, the other grotesque catalyst, Flibbertigibbet, who places his skill as 'fixer' or escape artist at the service of the villain's victim, Amy.

Amy contains not only elements of melodrama but, completed during the writing of the Preface to *Cromwell*, exhibits as well some features Hugo later used in his Romantic dramas. His insistence on the 'historical' character of the action is one such. Although the action derives from the historical novel of Scott, and although the allusions to Shakespeare's works in a drama whose action Scott situates in 1560 are anachronistic, the play *is* set in Tudor England, rather than in ancient Greece or classical Rome. Characterizations, such as that of Amy herself, display the intense Romantic passion we shall meet again in all of Hugo's dramas. And the ending of *Amy*, with the death of both heroine and villains in the final conflagration upon which no moralizing survivor bases any edifying maxims, clearly distinguishes Hugo's play from the Pixérécourt-style melodramas of the day. Also in keeping with Hugo's theories of the Romantic drama, as we shall see in his Preface to *Cromwell*, is the mingling within the same character, Flibbertigibbet, of noble sentiments with low birth, grotesque accoutrements, and behaviour. Hugo's refusal to respect the separation of genres contributed directly to the contemporary bourgeois audience's rejection of the play. They found the contradiction between Flibbertigibbet's low birth and high sentiments unbelievable because such a contrast clashed with their Worldview, one first expressed in Aristotle's *Poetics*, and espoused until the eighteenth century by European society, for whom the words, 'noble' and 'low,' when applied to characters in a play, identified social rank with moral behaviour.

In January–February 1825, Hugo wrote a fragment of a verse drama on Pierre Corneille, for him one of two great French seventeenth-century dramatists, along with Molière. In the first act, which is all that has survived, the Duke of Villaflor, the Spanish Ambassador to Paris and a descendant of the medieval Spanish hero El Cid, prefers to seek out the humble lodging of the bourgeois author of *Le Cid* rather than to present his credentials to Cardinal Richelieu, as diplomatic protocol would dictate. He informs his conventionally minded servant, Gomez, that 'greatness' should not be confused with political power or noble birth, and that a poem (the *Iliad*, for instance), is worth more than any pile of noble escutcheons as a proof of intrinsic merit. He finds, of course, that Corneille, whose genius 'all Europe envies France for possessing' (*OC*, 2, 949), is unknown to his own neighbours, despite the fact that his works are being attacked by the most influential French dramatic critics of the day. Hugo's vision of Corneille as the base-born Romantic hero, surrounded by inferiors to whose political and social power he falls victim, will find its most successful dramatic form in the figure of the lackey Ruy Blas, who loves a queen. Hugo abandoned the drama before Corneille's entry onstage, and it is difficult to see how he could have developed the conflict between the dramatist and his antithesis, Richelieu, astute manipulator of kings but a mediocre poet. Suffice it to say that, as *Cromwell* loomed on the horizon, he abandoned Corneille for Milton.

But before beginning work on *Cromwell*, the twenty-four-year-old Hugo scribbled down on a piece of paper, in late 1826 or early 1827, the following astonishing program of his planned future dramatic compositions:

> Dramas that I have to write:
> *La Mariposa.* Episode of [Don] Pantaleone. (Hist. of Cromwell.)
> *The Man in the Iron Mask.* (Mazarin. The child in the tiger's lair.)
> *Gennaro.* True love opposed to false.
> *Louis XI.* His death. (The great scene with Olivier le Daim.)
> *Sabina Muchental.* The same man loved by two women, a courtesan and a religious bigot.
> *The Childhood of Pierre-le-Cruel.* A girl sacrifices her honour to save her father.
> *The Death of the Duke d'Enghien.* Justification of Bonaparte.
> *Louis XVI.*

Charles I.

Philippe II. Don Carlos. The son struggling with his father, each attempting to poison the other.

The Death of [*Emperor*] *Charles V.*

Nero, a Roman tragedy. Depiction of the complicated Rome of the Caesars.

When that is all finished, I shall see.   (*OC,* 2, 973)

Elements from this list led to completed works or were featured in some form in later works. For instance, the name Gennaro became that of the hero of *Lucrèce Borgia;* Charles the First is constantly evoked in *Cromwell,* a play that modern scholars see as an allegorical version of the historical period that includes the French Revolution, the regicide of Louis XVI, and Napoleon's murder of the Duke d'Enghien, rightful successor to the Bourbon throne; the summary of *Sabina Muchental* recalls *Angelo,* a play dominated by the two antithetical female roles of Tisbe and Catarina; *Les Jumeaux,* an unfinished play, treats the theme of the 'Man in the Iron Mask,' that of a twin brother of Louis XIV sacrificed for dynastic and political reasons to protect the king's right to the throne.

CROMWELL (1827)

During the years 1825–7, when he was first meditating upon and then writing *Cromwell,* Hugo's political ideas were changing. In April 1825 he had been made a Chevalier of the Légion d'honneur and on May 29 had attended as an invited guest the Coronation of Charles X in Reims, a ceremony on which he published a celebratory ode in June. The royalism that he had learned from his mother still kept him apart from his father whom he identified with the Napoleonic party in France. But as he gradually overcame the influence of his childhood, his attitude to Napoleon metamorphosed into what some modern scholars have called his 'obsession'[4] with the former Emperor, whom he came to see as the architect of France's nineteenth-century glory, and whose victories confirmed, he believed, the triumphs of the Revolution. His desire to study the historical subject offered by the achievements of a great military leader, one who came to power thanks in part to an act of regicide, and who was then tempted to assume the throne, explains why he turned to seventeenth-century England for his subject. It would have been impossible in 1827 to persuade the censor to accept a play on the death of Louis XVI and on the quarrels between Bonapartists and Royalists concerning the Imperial 'usurper.' But his developing belief that exemplary historical figures should have a didactic role in the Romantic drama influenced him to dramatize the story of Cromwell, the regicide and Puritan King (almost) of England. The Protector's story was in the air at the time, as was the subject of seventeenth-century political conspiracies. Balzac was also writing a drama about Cromwell, and in July 1826 Hugo reviewed Alfred de Vigny's historical novel, *Cinq-Mars*, about a conspiracy to oust Cardinal Richelieu, the seventeenth-century minister of Louis XIII. On 6 August Hugo began writing Act 1 of *Cromwell*, completing the play in September 1827.

In the writing the play became the quintessential Romantic rejection of the French neo-classical theatre. Rather than obeying the dictates of propriety and verisimilitude, rather than fitting into the narrow material constraints of contemporary play production at the Comédie-Française, *Cromwell* broke all the practical 'rules' necessary for its successful production in a 'serious' Parisian theatre. Its gigantic dimensions ensured that it would be read, rather than staged.[5] It consists of 6,413 lines (about four times the length of a classical French tragedy). It has more than seventy speaking roles and an enormous number of supernumerary characters necessary for the crowd scenes, court ceremonials, and shows of military power called for in the plot. The action also requires five different sets, one of which, for Act 5, involves a representation of the Palace of Westminster for Cromwell's coronation. Such material considerations ensured that no theatre manager of the day, not even Baron Taylor, could afford to stage the play. As has been said, the play embodies Hugo's idea concerning the dramatic nature of Walter Scott's historical novels: by means of language they represent a whole society, all classes, all professions, and all political parties and religious factions at a moment of crisis.[6]

This is precisely what readers of *Cromwell* find as they open the text. The speaking roles include: Cromwell, Lord Protector of England; his wife, Elisabeth Bourchier; his son Richard; and four daughters, Mistress Fletwood and Ladies Falconbridge, Cleypole, and Francis. Twelve members of the Privy Council, including Carlisle, Lord Broghill, Stoupe, Thurloe, and John Milton, also play roles of diverse importance in the unfolding action. Eleven Royalist conspirators, outwitted by their intended victim, include Ormond, Drogheda, Davenant (poet laureate), and Sir William Murray. Fourteen Puritan plotters, among them, Lieutenant-Generals Lambert and Ludlow, Major-General Overton, Colonels Joyce and Pride, Barebone, a currier, as well as the evangelically named Praise-God Pimpleton and Death-to-Sin Palmer, and the fanatic Carr, bound in an unlikely alliance with their Royalist counterparts, also try to assassinate Cromwell. The poet Waller, Roundhead soldiers, Sergeant Maynard, Colonels Jephson and Grace, Lady Guggligoy (Lady Francis' companion), Manasseh-Ben-Israel, theological scholar and Jewish rabbi, and Dr Lockyer, Cromwell's chaplain, complete the Protector's household of retainers and spies. The courtiers and ambassadors necessary to display Cromwell's international power

and reputation in scenes involving diplomatic confrontation and manoeuv-
ring include: Don Luis de Cardenas, the Spanish Ambassador and his
suite; the French Ambassador, the Duc de Créquis, and Mancini, Mazarin's
nephew, and their suite; Filippi, Christine of Sweden's envoy, and suite;
Hannibal Sesthead, the King of Denmark's cousin, and his two pages;
three Waldensian envoys seeking Cromwell's protection from religious
persecution by the Duke of Savoy; and six envoys from the Netherlands. All
four of Cromwell's jesters, Trick, Giraff, Gramadock, and Elespuru appear,
serving as parodical chorus to the political events onstage. Tom, Enoch,
Nahum, and a group of workmen prepare in Act 5 the throne on which
Cromwell will sit to be offered the crown. The Coronation ceremony also
calls for the active presence and verbal participation of the Parliamentary
orator, as well as that of members, clerks, and ushers of Parliament itself.
The Lord Mayor of London, escorted by his aldermen, clerks, and ushers,
will offer Cromwell the ceremonial sword. The High Sheriff, his sergeants-
at-arms and archers, the Leader of the Ranters and his colleagues, and the
Town Crier complete the official party. But this is far from being all, since
the crowd will speak individually and in unison at different moments in
the action. Hugo's list of *dramatis personae* concludes with the following:
'Municipal ushers. – Halberdiers. – Archers. – Cavaliers, Roundheads,
Colonels, Lords, and Courtiers. – Pages. – Musketeers, Retainers, Gentlemen of the Protector's personal retinue. – City Bailiffs. – Burghers – Soldiers. – Townspeople' (*OC*, 3, 93). Such a cast would only be possible,
even nowadays, in the kind of cinematic, Cecil B. De Mille–style historical
epic, which used to be advertised as 'coming soon with a cast of thousands.'

Equally gargantuan in the number of its episodes and complications is
the plot. It is not unfair to say that, at four times the length of a neo-classical tragedy, *Cromwell* contains at least enough plot lines for four such plays.
Again, it is to novelistic construction that Hugo turned in order to organize the gigantic fresco of the English post-revolutionary society he wished
to represent. As was to become his practice in later dramas, he assigned
descriptive titles to the five acts of *Cromwell*, in so doing identifying them as
the five 'chapters,' or episodes, in the story of the Protector's successful
defusing of two conspiracies on his life by both sets of his enemies, the Cavalier supporters of the Restoration of Charles II, and his own evangelical
and military supporters, the Roundheads.

Act 1, subtitled 'Les Conjurés' ('The Conspirators') takes place in the
setting of the Three Cranes Tavern, described in the stage directions as 'an
old medieval house,' and presents all the principal Cavalier conspirators
as well as Cromwell's dissipated son Richard. Act 2, 'Les Espions' ('The
Spies'), set in the Banqueting House at Whitehall, with downstage, according to the opening topographical indication, 'The window through which

Charles I walked to the scaffold' (*OC*, 3, 141), shows Cromwell, onstage for the first time, as he bullies and manipulates the foreign diplomats, legates, and envoys who, by their timid acquiescence, bear eloquent testimony to the power and glory he enjoys throughout Europe and the world. Act 3, 'Les Fous' ('The Fools') dramatizes, in Cromwell's throne-room at White-hall, the striking antithesis of Cromwell's international prestige, as his fools reduce his reputation, character, and ambitions to shreds by their ridicule and derisive remarks. Cromwell spends Act 4, subtitled 'La Sentinelle,' disguised as the eponymous 'Sentry' stationed at the postern gate of the Park at Whitehall through which the royalist conspirators pass to kidnap the man they believe to be the sleeping Protector. The action takes place at night with trees onstage necessary to provide hiding places and vantage points for hidden witnesses to the various verbal exchanges. Act 5, 'Les Ouvriers' ('The Workmen') begins at 3 a.m. with the constructing of the throne in the splendidly decorated Great Hall at Westminster. The set contains benches and boxes for the spectators of, and participants in, Cromwell's coronation ceremony. The onstage amphitheatre then becomes the stage on which Cromwell awakens from his dreams of kingship and, in a long speech to the assembled microcosm of English society, first explains why he will not accept the crown and then displays his clemency by pardoning all those who have conspired against his life. The most interesting dramatic innovation, in terms of French theatre, is the presence onstage of a fairly numerous popular element who act as chorus, preparing by their comments Cromwell's eventual appearance before Parliament and acting as dramatic exemplars of the current state of English opinion on the Protector, his ambitions, and final clemency.

Cromwell also details the protector's Hamlet-like hesitations and meditations upon the political advantages and disadvantages incumbent upon acceptance of the crown which Parliament, thanks to his own machinations, offers him. Add to this secondary source of dramatic interest another subplot in which Cromwell, convinced of his son's treachery and parricidal intentions, is tempted to kill Richard onstage, appearing behind him with an upraised dagger, only to control his passion just in time. The conflict between father and son is later resolved by Richard's declaration of affection to his father, but further complicated by the son's refusal to act as Cromwell's successor after the latter's death.

In addition to such potentially tragic events, running through the play is an element of grotesque comedy, entirely in keeping with the dramatic theory Hugo outlined in the Preface. The principal grotesques are, of course, Cromwell's four jesters, whose clownish antics, songs, and ironic comments on the actions and motivations of all the characters around them are expressed in the most direct terms. Their crudeness represents an absolute contradiction of the neo-classical doctrine that the 'noble style' of 'serious' drama should exclude any but the most 'elevated' and conventional periphrases sanctified by centuries of dramatic usage. Not only does the language of the different speakers correspond to their social class and intellectual attainments, but the verse in which they express themselves deliberately sets out to shock contemporary taste. The play's first line is a case in point, the sacred alexandrine being made the vehicle for the most prosaic of utterances, that of expressing the date of the play's action: 'Demain, vingt-cinq juin mil six cent cinquante-sept' ('Tomorrow, the twenty-fifth of June sixteen hundred and fifty-seven').

This defiance of stylistic convention continues in Hugo's parodical use of a poet as a principal comic character. Wilmot, the Count of Rochester, a historical personage, appears both as Cavalier conspirator and as the burlesque suitor of Lady Frances, Cromwell's youngest daughter. In his efforts to win her, he, like Oronte, Molière's amorous marquis in *Le Misanthrope*, produces a love poem which he fondly imagines will end all resistance to his advances. Hugo's treatment of the deluded poet is both more severe and more farcical than is Molière's. Discovered by Cromwell on his knees before the affronted Frances, Lord Rochester, to save his life, must declare that his passion is addressed not to the Lord Protector's favourite daughter, but rather to the lady's aging duenna, the onomastically disadvantaged Dame Guggligoy. Delighted to be of help, Cromwell arranges the immediate marriage between the outwitted Rochester and the lady, who can scarcely believe her ears, but who, once married, pursues her new husband, insistently demanding his amorous attentions. At the end of the play the farcical pursuit continues, to Rochester's ultimate comic discomfiture.

Another central comic device in *Cromwell* is the intrusion into the atmosphere of political conspiracy and dynastic temptation of a type of commentary, provided by the Protector's four clowns, which has its origins in the medieval convention allowing the depiction of the 'world upside down.' In such a world, exemplified in Shakespeare's scenes between Lear and his fool, and in the 'feast of fools' in Hugo's novel *Notre-Dame de Paris*, the convention allows the fool to see more clearly than the wise man. The fool also possesses the licence necessary to tell the Emperor when he is naked and to comment in satirical terms on the actions of the highest court personages. In Hugo's verse play, the clowns express themselves in a series of comic songs at the beginning of Act 3, which is to say after two acts in which the conspirators (Act 1) and Cromwell (Act 2) have presented their own views on the current state of England under the Protector's rule. The fools' chorus deconstructs the declarations by both Cavaliers and Roundheads of their disinterested search for justice, revealing their real ambitions for power, as well as turning to ridicule the official pieties of Cromwell and his trusted associates. The intervention of the fools illustrates admirably Bakhtin's theory of popular carnival which, he believed, offered by its derisive laughter a reversal of the world as organized by rulers of any kind.[7]

By their refusal to take anything seriously, Trick, Giraff, Gramadoch, and Elespuru appeal to readers sceptical about the political motivations of all participants in the conspiracies. Such readers also suspect that those in power, in this case Cromwell, desire to retain their position at any cost. The fools' songs, whether they express doubt concerning a wife's virtue, as in Gramadoch's echo-ballad (*OC*, 3, 217–18), or identify the Cavalier and Roundhead 'Brutuses' as 'Plutos' (ibid. 218–19), and 'Our Jupiter' as 'a Scapin' (ibid., 219) or Molièresque comic valet, as in Trick's song, or express Elespuru's desire, to 'see Old Nick ... strangle Old Noll' (ibid., 220–1), or convey Giraff's equally disabused description of the situation: 'Yes. Cromwell is becoming King. Satan wants to be God' (ibid., 221) they do not simply vilify the Protector, as the conspirators' speeches attempt to do. Rather, the songs exhibit the deliberate projection of a grotesque, or belittling light on the characters and dramatic world of *Cromwell.*

But the fools' role as agents expressing derision of those in power is not restricted to the meta-theatrical one of ironic commentary on the drama 'staged' before them. In Act 5, ensconced in a public gallery from which to view Cromwell's climactic temptation, as the whole of the parliamentary establishment gathered together at the Palace of Westminster humbly begs him to accept the crown, the clowns almost succeed, by direct intervention in the dramatic action, in preventing the ceremony from taking place. Challenged by the Champion of England to pick up the gauntlet thrown down and so oppose Cromwell's right to the the throne, the assembled multitude maintains a cowed silence – until, that is, Gramadoch, to forestall the conspirators crowding around Cromwell's throne to assassinate him, and to ensure the continuation of the dynastic flummery, challenges the Champion of England, symbol of her might, to a duel. The exchange between the two contrasting figures, antithetical personifications of what Hugo will call in the Preface the 'Sublime' and the 'Grotesque,' clearly demonstrates Hugo's new 'liberal' disrespect for the bastions of the royalist establishment:

CHAMPION: What are you then?
GRAMADOCH: A seller of grimaces
            Like you. Both our masks are liars.
            My grin makes them laugh and yours frightens them.
            That's all.

CHAMPION: You look like a clown to me.
GRAMADOCH: And so do you. ...
CHAMPION: Wretched buffoon!
           Leave now, or I'll have you flogged.
GRAMADOCH: Such pride, such disdain!
           [You are] Just as much a puppet as I, your grimace is not as
           happy.
           I repeat, friend, Cromwell pays both of us
           To make a little noise in this bizarre concert,
           In which your voice is the chime and mine the cow-bell.
CHAMPION: Rogue!
GRAMADOCH: Without stooping from custom, we can, I think,
           Do battle for and against Cromwell
           I carry his train, you his megaphone.
CHAMPION (*angry*): What weapon do you choose?
GRAMADOCH: I?
           (*Drawing his Harlequin's bat.*)   This wooden sword.
                                   (*He waves it about with a martial air.*)
           This is just the weapon to use against a straw soldier.   (5, 10)

This exchange exemplifies the contempt for the conventional powers-that-be that would constantly bring Hugo into conflict with French theatrical censorship, the official arm of the political establishment.

Despite the high seriousness of its subject which accords with Hugo's developing theory that the Romantic drama should teach lessons about contemporary events, two misunderstandings provide evidence of the grotesquely comic nature of the plot of *Cromwell*. The *quiproquo*, a device quite conventional in comedy, would have seemed totally out of place in the type of 'serious' drama of which tragedy supplied the paradigm in France until the nineteenth century. The first such dramatic error occurs when Rochester mistakes his love poem for Frances for the letter Lord Ormond receives from Charles II. When Cromwell intercepts the letter, thanks to the incompetence of the lovesick poet, he learns of Ormond's presence in London and is able to set the trap for the conspirators in Act 5. The second such burlesque plot device also concerns the unmasking of the conspirators and again involves betrayal of their plot by one of their own colleagues. Barebone, a currier, has caused to be constructed at his own expense, but counting upon a princely recompense from Cromwell, the throne the Protector will occupy for his 'coronation' at Westminster. As a member of the Puritan plot, Barebone learns from his colleagues of their plan to assassinate Cromwell as he presides over the ceremony. Fearing for his investment, the slow-witted and miserly Barebone reveals the plot to its intended victim. So financial gain (a motivation that to Boileau identified French classical comedy as a low form, in which only non-tragic actions could be presented), becomes for Hugo another means of demonstrating the mingling of genres, which he will declare in the Preface to *Cromwell* to be the central characteristic of the Romantic drama.

Evidence of the more serious, even tragic, elements present in *Cromwell* is, however, not far to seek. Already mentioned is the potentially tragic slaying by Cromwell of his son. Among the play's serious concerns must also be numbered the Protector's certainty that, despite his having the right to choose his successor, Richard's refusal to succeed his father would lead to a restoration of the Stuarts. And, throughout the play, Cromwell reveals in his speeches and actions his complex nature, one in which faults and virtues battle for dominance. By his pedantic quibbling with his Puritan entourage, or with Rochester over different interpretations of Biblical incidents and parallels, he displays the petty pride of the scholar in his own subject of specialization (2, 15). On the other hand, Act 4 displays dramatically his practical grasp of the problems involved in ruling a country riven by political and religious dissent. Disguised as a sentry at Whitehall, Cromwell personally intervenes to trick the royalist conspirators into making incriminating declarations of intent. He also persuades them to kidnap the sleeping Rochester, whom they believe to be Cromwell himself, an act which leads to their entrapment and incarceration. Having shown, albeit parodically, such a grasp of the practical wielding of power both in military matters and in the ruling of England, Cromwell amply demonstrates his authority as the first ruler of Europe by his rhetorical treatment of the ambassadors sent by their sovereigns to solicit his favours. Thus Act 2, scene 2, shows the ambassadors of France and Spain attending on his pleasure, while he delights in spurning their offers and in breaking their pride and pretentions, manipulating them into becoming agents of his own foreign policies. As represented, English power under Cromwell, thanks to his capacities as ruler and international statesman, achieved an apogee that would not long survive the Protector's death. And yet, Cromwell himself loses the ability to act decisively whenever he meditates upon the crown.

In Act 2, scene 15, for instance, unaware of the doubly ironic asides of Rochester (also present onstage) who has not recognized him as the Lord Protector, Cromwell meditates upon kingship:

> What do you want, Cromwell? Say? a throne! What for?
> Are you called Stuart? Plantagenet? Bourbon?
> Do you belong among those mortals who, thanks to their ancestors,
> Have looked upon the earth from childhood as its masters?

What sceptre, fortunate soldier, does not break under your pressure?
What crown is great enough for your brow?
You, Chance's son, King! for future races
Your reign would count as only one of your adventures!
Your house, a dynasty! ...
A King of Parliament!
With the bodies of your victims as steps beneath your feet!
Is it thus that one mounts to a legitimate throne?
What! Are you not wearied from so much marching,
Cromwell? Has the sceptre some hidden charm?
See: the entire universe lies in your power;
You hold it in your hand, and what a small thing it is.
The chariot of your fortune, upon which you base your right,
Rolls on, and with royal blood has splashed kings!
What! Powerful in peace, triumphant in war,
All is nothing without a throne! Vulgar ambition!

As the scene continues, Cromwell's will sways now one way, now the other, and for once the asides of the watcher, whom the speaker does not see, add by their unconscious humour a piquancy rather than merely a lack of verisimilitude to the scene. It is impossible, of course, not to think of Shakespeare's heroes as one reads such a soliloquy: Hamlet's hesitations, Richard II's regrets and recriminations, and Henry V's disillusionment with the trappings of kingship come easily to mind. But so too, do the plottings of Richard III.

Perhaps the most serious subject in Cromwell, however, is not so much historical as philosophic. Concerned less with the aspiration to rule, than with the condition of superiority giving one a legitimate right to the first place in society, Hugo places in direct conflict, at least twice in *Cromwell*, the Protector and his personal secretary, John Milton, representative for Hugo of the poetic genius, at once Magus and Seer. In one sense, Milton's interventions dramatize the workings of Cromwell's Puritanical conscience, even more than do the extremist pronouncements of the fanatic Carr, who lives in a world of absolute values and who, equally ready to die or face internment for life, dismisses Cromwell's offer of clemency with the following paradox: 'In my cell, perhaps / I am the only Englishman of whom you are not the master; / Yes, the only free man! (5, 14). But Carr's persuasiveness is impaired by his earlier betrayal of the plot by his Puritan comrades. This lofty declaration of high principles is therefore open to question.

No more idealized than Carr, Milton, who does not appear until Act 3, scene 2, immediately following the derisive songs by the fools, begins by displaying his pettiness in an exchange with Cromwell about the respect due to his (Milton's) social status : 'You might treat me with more civility! / I am the son of a notary, an alderman in his city' (*OC*, 3, 228). In the same scene, both Cromwell and Rochester criticize Milton's poetry, declaring it inferior both to Donne's and to the courtly verses of French baroque poets like the now long-forgotten Racan. Milton's reply marks him as the epitome of the Romantic stereotype, the poet misunderstood and despised by society for his refusal, which society unworthily condemns as his inability, to accept conventional bourgeois values and attitudes:

> I am silently contemplating a strange plan.
> I live in my thoughts, and Milton finds consolation there.
> Yes, in my turn, I wish, like some bold emulator
> Of the supreme creator, to create by my words
> A world, between hell, earth, and the heavens.   (3, 2)

Cromwell will complete Milton's humiliation in their final conversation when, after pardoning the conspirators, he naively asks for Milton's approval. Piqued by his secretary's refusal to flatter him or to accept the position of poet laureate, which he has just offered him, Cromwell dismisses Milton's 'poet's reasons,' adding: 'And you want to reign, and constantly rebuke / Rulers of nations, you, who spend your time / Twisting words into frivolous metres!' (3, 13). In Hugo's world, a great poet's relations with the politically powerful can only lead to misunderstanding and mutual contempt.

As well as his role as representative of the misunderstood Romantic genius, Milton also plays a dramatic part in warning Cromwell about the plot by the conspirators to kill him, as well as in dissuading him from accepting the crown. Blind like Tiresias, Milton can predict the threat to Cromwell's life, and like the soothsayer in Shakespeare's *Julius Caesar*, even warn him to 'Beware ... Think of the Ides of March' (5, 12; *OC*, 3, 404). But it is Milton's great speech attempting to dissuade Cromwell from accepting the crown which best displays the character's oratorical skills. Reminding him that so far, as Secretary of the Privy Council, he has remained mute, Milton warns Cromwell against the treachery of his ministers who are urging him to be king. The speech is constructed upon a central organizing antithesis which contrasts Cromwell's youthful republican desire for liberty with his present dynastically-inspired desire to enslave his fellow Englishmen by imposing upon them his regal authority:

> They lure you astray with a fatal diadem,
> Brother, and I have come to plead for you, against yourself.

> So you want to be king, Cromwell? And in your heart
> You say: 'It is for me that the people was victorious.'   (3, 4)

Warning him against such pride, Milton, in a nostalgic *anamnesis*, recalls the days of Cromwell's true, republican greatness:

> Powerful in thought and powerful in battle,
> You were so great, that in you I believed I had found my dream,
> My Hero! I loved you above all in Israel,
> And no one placed you higher in heaven!
> And for a title, a word as empty as it is high sounding,
> The apostle, the hero, the saint is dishonoured!
> In his deepest designs, that was what he always sought,
> The purple robe, an empty rag! The sceptre, a vain bauble!   (3, 4)

'Think,' Milton says, in the highly charged deliberative rhetoric of a member of Cromwell's Privy Council, of the historical precedent you have set:

> Think of Charles the First
> Do you dare, after plucking up the crown from his blood,
> With his scaffold to remake a throne?
> What! You want to be King, Cromwell! Is that what you contemplate?
> Do you not fear that one day, swathed in crape,
> This same Whitehall, where your greatness is now on display,
> Will open once again the fatal window? ...
> Think of Charles Stuart! Remember! Remember!
> When the King had to die, when the axe stood ready,
> There came a hooded executioner who cut off his head.
> The King, in the view of all his people, perished helpless,
> Without even knowing who was ending his days.
> By the same road you are going to the same disaster.   (3, 4)

He concludes this *ominatio*, or prophecy of evil, by urging Cromwell to return to his former republican glory. And as Cromwell's musings show after Milton's departure, the Seer succeeded in persuading his listener, at least to take care:

> He is right, basically. Yes, but he badgers me too much.
> Charles the First? . . . No, you misread my fate
> Kings like Oliver don't die like that,
> Milton. They are stabbed to death, not condemned by courts.
> I will consider it, though, this sinister alternative!   (3, 4)

If the fools introduce derision into the serious topic of Cromwell's royal ambitions, Milton's intervention transfers the Protector's desire to reign as King of England into the realm of the sublime, where philosophical values transform personal and political reasoning.

It would be absurd to judge *Cromwell* by the criteria appropriate to the evaluation of historiography. The seeker of historical accuracy, of the authority which the exhaustive consultation of archives and primary sources confers on the historian's interpretations of past events and personages, will inevitably be disappointed. No more than Shakespeare in his time, or Peter Shaffer in ours, did Hugo create the principal figures and events of his plays by choosing to reproduce only extracts from authentic documents. His belief in the allegorical and didactic functions of Romantic drama, as shown in the parallels between his representation of Cromwell and the historical Napoleon, in itself militates against historicity. And his philosophical theory that the history of humanity is one of continual progress, outlined first in the Preface to *Cromwell*, reappears in his critical writings throughout his career. It explains his choice of 'legendary' central figures (Cromwell, Holy Roman Emperor Charles V, Francis I, Lucrezia Borgia, 'Bloody Mary,' 'The Man in the Iron Mask', and Torquemada, for example), that is, historical characters whom the popular audience knew from current mythology and *doxa*. From such monstrous stereotypes, he believed the French people could learn lessons about the costs of progress, lessons valuable in the nineteenth century.

In the Preface, he clearly separates the genres of historical drama and historiography thus: 'The ode sings of eternity, the epic solemnizes history, the drama depicts life.' And in a note to this passage, attempting to meet the objection concerning the relationship between scholarly historiography and historical drama, he adds:

> But it will be said that the drama also depicts the history of nations. Yes, but in terms of everyday *life*, not of *history*. The drama leaves to the historian the precise series of general facts, the chronological order of dates, mass movements, battles, conquests, the splitting up of empires, everything external in history. The drama takes the internal events. What history forgets or disdains, details of costume, customs, faces, the underpinnings of events, life, in a word, belongs in the drama; and drama can be immense in aspect and in overall picture when these small things are taken into a great hand, *prensa manu magna*. But one must be careful not to look, even in the *historical* drama for pure history. The drama writes down legends, not archives. It is a chronicle, not a chronology. (*OC*, 3, 57)

It would be equally naive, however, to imagine that such a disclaimer has convinced all of Hugo's critics, many of whom have reproached him with the historical inaccuracies present in the plots and characters of his dramas. Nevertheless, his paradoxical defence of the 'legendary historicity' of the Romantic drama possesses a logic, albeit a Romantic one, from which the law of the excluded middle finds itself excluded.

The size and attendant costs of *Cromwell* prevented any possibility of its being performed in the Paris of 1827, despite the enthusiastic reception that Hugo's two readings of extracts from the play received from his fellow Romantics. By 1827, thanks to his gifts and energy, the young Hugo headed the new 'school,' or '*cénacle*' of French writers striving to transform the literary tastes of the contemporary public. The group, which included for a time Vigny, Sainte-Beuve, Émile Deschamps, Alexandre Soumet, Baron Taylor, Balzac, Musset, Dumas, Mérimée, Nerval, and Delacroix, met regularly at Hugo's house in the rue Notre-Dame-des-Champs. The Romantic 'school' combined liberals and conservatives, and Hugo's own nascent liberalism in this period flourished partly under the influence of Sainte-Beuve, the young critic most favorable to Romantic literary endeavour. It was Sainte-Beuve also who advised Hugo to tone down the grotesque elements and reduce the scale of *Cromwell*, advice which Hugo ignored, of course, reducing in the process the play's performability. Partly to satisfy the *cénacle*'s demands for some expression of the new literary credo, partly because he was reluctant to see his play vanish without trace, without, that is, its having changed anything on the French literary scene, Hugo added to *Cromwell*, in September-October 1827, a seventy-page Preface which was to become the manifesto not only for enthusiasts of the Romantic drama but for the French Romantic movement generally. Its relationship to his own Romantic dramas we shall study in later chapters.

THE PREFACE TO CROMWELL (1827)

Well-informed contemporary readers of the Preface, familiar with the works of Schlegel, Constant, Mme de Staël, Stendhal, Guizot, and other literary theorists and historians that we examined in Chapter 2, would not have been particularly impressed by the 'novelty' of Hugo's ideas. With the exception of the central importance Hugo was prepared to assign to the 'grotesque' as one of the two defining elements of Romantic literature generally, and of the Romantic drama specifically, many of his ideas were already in the air, as we have seen. What was new in the Preface, however, was the vigour of the Romantic *Weltanschauung* Hugo proposed, as well as the organizational power of his imagination and argumentation. That the Preface emanated from the most promising young poet, novelist, dramatist and literary personality of the day, one whose name was becoming increasingly well known with the appearance of each of his works, gave the Preface a certain rhetorical authority also. But what ensured its success was that it expressed in unequivocal terms ideas which the literary public was ready to hear. Almost forty years after the French Revolution, a revolution in French literature had become increasingly necessary, as the old genres gently expired under the weight of second-rate imitations. Hugo's Preface proclaimed the necessity of abandoning the old in favour of something new.

He begins by proposing a metaphorical view of human history which posits the three ages of man: childhood (the 'primitive' age), development (the 'ancient' period dominated by Greece), and maturity (the 'modern' age, since the rise of Christianity). That he took such ideas from Herder (via Mme de Staël) and Chateaubriand, for instance, is immaterial. They enabled him to propose as the dominant and appropriate genre for each of the three periods respectively, lyric poetry, the epic, and the drama, the last of which being, in Hegelian terms, the synthesis of the two preceding genres. Hugo argues that the drama came into being because Christianity imposed a view of the total man, soul and body, and in so doing, destroyed once and for all the separation between 'noble' and 'popular' dramatic forms, between tragedy and comedy. Thus the Romantic drama will combine Longinus's 'sublime' poetry with a medievally-inspired representation of life that Hugo calls 'grotesque,' at once comic and horrible.

It is worth remembering that the function 'Longinus' assigned to discursive sublimity (which he contrasts with profundity), is rhetorical: the sublime is capable of overcoming resistance to persuasion: 'Sublimity consists in a certain excellence and distinction in expression, and ... it is from this source alone that the greatest poets and historians have acquired their pre-eminence and won for themselves an eternity of fame. For the effect of elevated language is not to persuade the hearers, but to entrance them; and at all times, and in every way, what transports us with wonder is more telling than what merely persuades or gratifies us. The extent to which we can be persuaded is usually under our own control, but these sublime passages exert an irresistible force and mastery, and get the upper hand with every hearer.'[8] Hugo planned to combine the hyper-persuasive power of 'Longinus''s concept of the sublime, which French neo-classical critics mistakenly equated with the '*style noble*,' with the power to shock possessed by the 'grotesque.' It behoves us therefore to try to understand this latter concept.

The following definition of 'grotesque,' by insisting upon its etymological derivation, reveals something of its medieval and Renaissance origins: 'The word *grotesque* comes from the Italian *grottesco*, from *grotta*, a grotto. At the time of the excavations in Rome in the fifteenth and sixteenth centuries, a number of rediscovered ancient underground chambers were called *grottoes* and the name *grotesque* was given to their decorative ornamentation. Literally, grotesques are fantastical figures representing real or imaginary characters or animals, accompanied by various types of ornamentation. Later, *grotesque* was used to describe anything that distorts nature, anything that includes extravagantly ridiculous traits. Notice that Victor Hugo never clearly defines the word 'grotesque,' and that by it he means anything ridiculous, comical, distorted, physically and morally ugly, strange or monstrous.[9] In the absence of a definition by Hugo, modern scholars have attempted to describe the properties forming the category of the grotesque. Claude Duchet, for instance, lists the terms in the Preface included in the concept as well as the linguistic techniques Hugo used in forging it:

> Its semantic field is constituted step by step as much through contamination and refraction of successive meanings, as through opposition to the category of the sublime. As one progresses through the text, here is what may be classified under the heading 'grotesque': temporary, bestial, body, ugly, distorted, evil, shadow, laughable, stupid, comedy, incomplete, terrible, clown[ish], ridiculous, parody, grinning, bizarre, (witches') sabbath, Satan, hideous, burlesque, fantasy, gambol, crawl, free, frank, bold, formless, passions, vices, crimes, abyss, storms, trivial, low, populace, commoners ... A complete enumeration, including all the names, proper, mythological, historical, and literary used to illustrate the type would be too long; but we ought to include in the list the following semi-portrait of Cromwell, of his grotesque half: he is evil and petty, his family's plaything; he surrounds himself with fools and believes in astrology; he is a social climber and coarse soldier; stiff on matters of etiquette, a clumsy orator, an excessively timid hypocrite who enjoys buffoonery. (*OC*, 3, 32–3)

Clearly Hugo hoped that the combination of such all-embracing opposites as the sublime and the grotesque, would, if skilfully used, be capable of making an overwhelmingly powerful emotional appeal to audiences of the Romantic drama.

Hugo's arguments in favour of the incorporation of the grotesque into the 'serious' dramatic genre which the historical drama was to become are partly pragmatic, partly ethical. He asserts that ugliness, both physical and moral, being multiform, offers far more possibilities for exploitation in the drama than does beauty, uniform and therefore less interesting. And Christianity, he claims, had long before the Romantic dramatists seen the necessity of examining both high and low aspects of man: 'Christianity brings poetry to truth. In like manner, the modern muse will take a higher, broader view of things. She feels that everything in nature is not *beautiful* in human terms, that ugliness exists by the side of beauty, the mis-shapen beside the graceful, the grotesque on the reverse of the sublime, evil next to good, shadow as well as light ... She will begin to act like nature, mingling (but not confusing) in her creations light with shadow, the grotesque with the sublime, in other words, the body with the soul, the bestial with the spiritual' (*OC*, 3, 50). To 'high' tragedy, therefore, the Romantic drama will add comedy and horror, derision and anguish, thanks to its incorporation of 'low' or grotesque forms and devices. And Hugo, writing in 1827, having just seen the English actors perform in Paris, takes Shakespeare as the supreme example of the modern dramatist, since he combined tragedy and comedy to produce an impression of the 'totality' of life: 'We have arrived at the poetic summit of modern times. Shakespeare is the drama; and the drama, which combines in one breath grotesque with sublime, the terrible and the clownish, tragedy and comedy, drama expresses the appropriate character of poetry's third age, the literature of the present day' (ibid. 57). With the principle of combination outlined, Hugo can then go on to discuss ways and means of achieving the new dramatic genre, which for him represents 'complete poetry' (ibid. 58).

First, negatively or extensionally, Hugo defines the drama by what it is not. It is not, for instance, neo-classical tragedy, because it refuses the 'rules' of that genre. Hugo the polemicist excoriates the 'two' unities (time and place), keeping the unity of subject, the 'only true and well founded one' (*OC*, 3, 62). The new verisimilitude will make necessary the representation of action on a set built to display the authentic historical scene of the events dramatized. It will not allow the action to 'take place' in the wings with reports arriving onstage thanks to 'messengers.' The vague, multipurpose sets of neo-classical tragedy will no longer serve:

> What is more unlikely and absurd in fact than the vestibule, the antechamber, the banal scene where our tragedies are enacted, to which arrive (Who knows how?) conspirators to declaim against the tyrant, who in his turn comes to the same place to declaim against them ... Where has anyone ever seen such a vestibule or peristyle? What is more contrary, we won't say to truth, the Scholastics thought little enough of that, but to verisimilitude? The result is that anything that is too typical, too intimate, too specific to take place in an antechamber or at a crossroads, which is to say the whole drama, happens in the wings. We only see, as it were, the elbows of the action, its hands are elsewhere. Instead of scenes, we have narratives; descriptions, rather than tableaux. Grave-looking characters, situated, like the ancient chorus, somewhere between us and the dramatic action, come forward to tell us what is happening in the temple, palace, or public square, so that often we feel like shouting out to them: 'Really! Take us there then! That's where the action is, so it would be fine to see it!' (*OC*, 3, 62–3)

Hugo goes on to present the Romantic doctrine of 'local colour,' necessary because contemporary audiences insisted upon seeing the authentic place where the historical events dramatized had in fact taken place. In this regard he mentions Joan of Arc, burnt at the stake in the Old Marketplace in Rouen, thus indirectly criticizing Schiller's play on the subject in which Joan is killed in battle.

Just as the unity of place fell under his criticism of absurdity, the unity of time must yield to historical and dramatic necessity, he declares: 'The unity of time is no more solid than that of place. Action, when forced into the twenty-four hour frame, is as ridiculous as when limited to the vestibule. Every action has its own time-frame and its own location! Pouring the same dose of time on all events, applying the same measure to everything! A cobbler who tried to make one shoe fit all feet would be laughed to scorn!' (*OC*, 3, 64).

Hugo is now launched on the major theme of the Preface, namely that the Romantic genius should have complete artistic freedom to construct his own vision of the world. Such freedom would not come without great risks, he allows, but the true genius would know how to overcome them. In pleading for the 'liberty of art against the despotism of [all] systems, codes, and rules' (*OC*, 3, 77), Hugo is anticipating his well-known declaration, made during the rehearsals for *Hernani* just over two years later in January 1830, on what constituted the new 'Romanticism': 'Romanticism, so often badly defined, is simply, all things considered, and that is its real definition, *Liberalism* in literature ... Liberty in art, liberty in society, that is the dual goal towards which all consequent and logical minds must tend; that is the dual banner under which, with the exception of some few minds (which one day will see more clearly), the whole of today's youth, so strongly and patiently rallies.'[10] But, eager to show how the Romantic genius might avoid the pitfalls of poetic licence, Hugo outlines how to ensure that the drama would differ from the common run of dramatic productions by rejecting the bourgeois philistinism which, as spokesman for the Romantic *cénacle*, he was committed to opposing.

Unity of subject would concentrate the drama, preventing its construction from slipping into the episodic and the unfocused structure of melodrama. If the drama was to be a mirror held up to nature, as Stendhal, in *Le Rouge et le noir*, was to say of the novel,[11] Hugo's metaphorical mirror sets in the foreground and focuses, rather than merely reflecting, the objects it reproduces: 'The drama is a mirror in which nature is reflected. But if this mirror is an ordinary one, a plain, flat surface, it will reflect only a dull and flat image of objects, faithful, but colourless. It is well known what colour and light lose by being merely reflected. The drama must therefore be a concentrating mirror which, far from reducing rays of coloured light, picks out and intensifies those which turn a glow into a bright light, a light into a flame. Only then can the drama be acknowledged as art. The theatre offers a perspective. Everything that exists in the world, in history, in life, in man, everything can and must be reflected in it, but subject to the magic wand of art' (*OC*, 3, 70–1). By insisting upon the concentrating power of art, Hugo is here rejecting the notion of dramatic 'realism' of the 'slice of life' variety, in favour of the necessary 'illusionism' of the drama. He would continue to do so, for we find him writing between 1830 and 1833: 'The theatre is not the real world: it has cardboard trees, cloth palaces, skies made from rags, diamonds of glass, gold made from tinsel, paint on the peach, rouged cheeks, underground suns. It is the world of truth: there are human hearts on the stage, human hearts in the wings, human hearts in the audience' (*OC*, 4, 948–9).[12]

The most obvious way to separate the Romantic drama from contemporary 'reality,' apart from situating its action in the historical past, as he was to do in all but one of his dramas, was to compose in verse, specifically in alexandrines. Far from wishing to abandon the twelve-syllable alexandrine as an archaic throwback to French neo-classical tragedy, Hugo insisted in the Preface on the central function it was to serve in the Romantic drama, where it would replace the common prose vernacular. But the new alexandrine, as wielded by Hugo, would accept none of the artificial constraints, rhetorical or prosodic, imposed on seventeenth- and eighteenth-century verse dramatists. Rhymed alexandrines, treated with new suppleness, were to become the medium he used in eight out of the twelve plays he identified, in his prefaces or elsewhere, as 'dramas.'[13] In the Preface to *Cromwell*, he explains why:

> Poetry is the visual form of thought. That is why it is especially suited to the stage. If used correctly, it emphasizes things that, in its absence, would be dismissed as insignificant and vulgar ... If we had the right to say what, in our view, should be the drama's style, we would want a line at once free, frank, faithful, daring to say anything without prudery, to express everything without effort; passing from the natural manner of comedy to tragedy, from sublime to grotesque; by turns positive and poetic, altogether artistic and inspired, profound and quick, broad and true; able at the right moment deliberately to disregard or displace the caesura so as to disguise the alexandrine's monotony, more allied to enjambement that lengthens [the line] than to inversion that confuses [the spectator]; faithful to rhyme, at once its queen and its slave, the supreme grace of our poetry, generator of our metre; inexhaustible in the variety of its tricks, unmatched in elegance and workmanship; like Proteus, able to adopt a thousand forms without losing its shape and nature; avoiding tirades, at ease in dialogue, always

> hidden behind the character speaking; careful above all to remain in its its
> place, and when it happens to be *beautiful*, being so, as it were by chance,
> despite itself and without knowing it; lyrical, epic, dramatic, according to
> need, able to run through the whole dramatic gamut, from high to low,
> from the highest to the most vulgar of ideas, from the most comic to the
> most serious, from the most concrete to the most abstract, without ever
> exceeding the limits of a spoken scene; ... the old poetry was descriptive, the
> new will be alive. (*OC*, 3, 74–5)

The alexandrine, thus described, would need to be combined with the '*mot propre*,' the appropriate word or expression, in order to be able to 'say anything without prudery.' Only by systematically exploiting all levels and riches of the French language, he believed, rather than by allowing himself to be limited to a single form of discourse – the *style noble* with its precious euphemisms and pompous periphrases – could the modern poet produce a revolutionized, Romantic drama.

This, then, is the program Hugo set for the new drama in the Preface to *Cromwell*. The program was received with the greatest enthusiam by the young Romantics who were to support the plays of Hugo, Dumas, and Vigny in the next fifteen years in Paris. It was accorded an equally enthusiastic rejection by the partisans of neo-classicsm, a fact that was to produce the confrontation between the two parties at the first performances in February 1830 of the flagship of the Romantic drama, *Hernani*.

No one has seriously questioned the success, either at the time or since, of the Preface. Its influence makes it the most persuasive dramatic program that appeared in France in the nineteenth century, and even today its effects remain with us. Théophile Gautier, who was of Hugo's generation, described its power over their contemporaries thus: 'The Preface to *Cromwell* shone in our eyes like the Tables of the Law on Sinai and its arguments seemed to us irrefutable.'[14] Mme Hugo reports that in 1827: 'The Preface exploded like a declaration of war against received doctrine and provoked battles in the newspaper. Those hostile to it attacked everything in it, both its ideas and its style ... Its defenders were no less fiery in their attacks: young people declared themselves energetically in favour of the theatre's independence, and the Preface to *Cromwell* became their rallying sign.'[15] Modern critics have argued that, even after the the decline of the Romantic drama, the Preface continued to influence dramatic production in the twentieth century: 'The whole of the modern theatre, in which a play may obey the rules or not, without one even dreaming of worrying about the matter, proves that the Preface succeeded in its demand for liberty, in its protest against the rules ... Victor Hugo's theory of the grotesque has become the fundamental law of all our theatre, since, among literary plays, not a single drama, however dark, could be cited in which there is not some flash of gaiety, no really funny comedy in which there is not a little sadness.'[16] Fernand Baldensperger, writing in 1929, saw this period (1827–8) and especially *Cromwell* and its Preface as the turning point in the 'liberation of art forever' in France.[17]

By October 1827, Victor Hugo had produced a persuasive theory of the Romantic drama, then, but he had not yet managed to have one of his plays performed successfully in a Parisian theatre. It was to this task that he next bent his literary endeavours.

4. Aesthetic Revolt (2), 1828–1831: *Hernani* and *Marion de Lorme*

If we study the history of the French stage in the nineteenth century, we are forced to acknowledge that Hugo's output, the eight plays he signed and which were produced from 1830 to 1843, represent by far its most important event before Antoine's Naturalist renewal of the director's art.[1]

After the excitement aroused by the Preface to *Cromwell*, Hugo's first attempt at writing a successful play involved, as we have seen, his completing *Amy Robsart*, performed with such disastrous results in February 1828. Temporarily discouraged, he turned his efforts to fiction, beginning to take notes for his medieval novel, *Notre-Dame de Paris*, and composing his first fictional denunciation of capital punishment, *Le Dernier Jour d'un condamné à mort*, between October and December 1828.

Meanwhile, Alexandre Dumas' Romantic drama *Henri III et sa cour* had been enthusiastically accepted by the Comédie-Française in September, opening triumphantly there on 11 February 1829. The time seemed once more to be right; so Hugo spent the month of June 1829 writing *Un Duel sous Richelieu*, the drama whose title he was to change to *Marion de Lorme* at the request of Marie Dorval, who would to play the title role in 1831. At first, all the auguries were good. On 9 July 1829, Hugo read the play to the principal members of the Romantic *cénacle* assembled in his house. His audience included Balzac, Auguste Barbier, Armand and Louise Bertin, Louis Boulanger, Eugène Delacroix, Émile and Antony Deschamps, Achille and Eugène Devéria, Alexandre Dumas, Magnin, Mérimée, Alfred de Musset, Sainte-Beuve, Soumet, Taylor, Villemain. So impressed were the assembled experts, and so quickly did the word spread, that Hugo was soon receiving offers to stage his play. On 11 July, just two days later, Jouslin de La Salle, director of the Porte-Saint-Martin Theatre wrote asking his permission to do so. On 14 July, the Comédie-Française accepted the play. Their prompt decision, and Baron Taylor's enthusiasm for the play and for the new Romantic drama generally, promised a lavish production and an early triumph.

But it was not to be. On 1 August, Hugo learned from Charles Brifaut, the censor to whom *Un Duel sous Richelieu* (the first title of *Marion de Lorme*) had been submitted, that Martignac, the Minister of the Interior, had decided to ban the play, presumably because in that period of King Charles X's unpopularity, Hugo's critical portrait of Louis XIII would be read as a criticism of the current monarch. Hugo immediately took the necessary steps to appeal the decision, writing to Martignac, without result, and obtaining a private audience with Charles X himself at Saint-Cloud on 7 August. The king and his advisers then handled the situation with the kind of clumsiness that was to lead in the following year to the July Revolution. In an attempt to buy Hugo off, the king took out a subscription with Gosselin, Hugo's publisher at the time, agreeing to purchase fifteen copies of two books of poems by Hugo, the *Odes et ballades* and *Les Orientales* (but not, of course, *Le Dernier Jour d'un condamné à mort*, which harshly criticized the regime for its maintenance of capital punishment). On 13 August, La Bourdonnaye, the new Minister of the Interior, confirmed to Hugo that the ban was to stand, Charles X declining to intervene. He went on to offer Hugo a seat on the Council of State and a post in the Administration. Hugo, uninterested in entering politics, and profoundly out of sympathy with the regime, refused. And on the following day, informed by La Bourdonnaye that Charles X was increasing, 'as a proof of his satisfaction,' Hugo's annual pension from 2,000 to 6,000 francs, Hugo once more refused the bribe, saying: 'I had requested that my play might be performed; I ask for nothing else.'[2] In the weeks that followed, when the newspapers got wind of the affair and then publicized the principal events, giving to them the 'spin' that accorded with their particular political orientations, no sign of the lifting of the ban appeared.

Still without a play with which to launch his career as a Romantic dramatist, Hugo set furiously to work once more. Between 29 August and 24 September 1829, he wrote the five acts of *Hernani ou l'Honneur castillan*, cause of the 'battle' fought between the Romantics and their opponents during many of the play's first 39 performances in 1830. During *Hernani*'s run at the Comédie in 1830, the July Revolution deposed Charles X and brought Louis-Philippe to the throne and, as well, abolished for a time State censorship of the theatre. One result of the July Revolution was, therefore, that

Marion de Lorme could finally be performed, although not at the Comédie-Française, in August 1831.

One price that Hugo had to pay for the furious pace of his literary activities in this period involved his personal relations with his wife. After her fifth confinement in less than eight years of married life, Adèle ended conjugal relations with Hugo. And, at the time of the 'battle' of *Hernani*, when the house on the rue Notre-Dame-des-Champs was frequently invaded by Hugo's motley gang of supporters, eagerly planning their campaign against their classical enemies, the shy and retiring Adèle avoided the hubbub in favour of more intimate conversations with Hugo's great friend and one of his first supporters, the poet-novelist-critic Charles Augustin Sainte-Beuve. The friendship became a love affair, whether physical or not matters little. It increased the growing estrangement between Hugo and Adèle and ended the 'brotherly' relationship between Hugo and his friend. Informed by Sainte-Beuve of the situation, Hugo even suggested that Adèle be allowed to choose between them.[3] Inevitably, personal conflict would lead to literary disagreement. No longer was Sainte-Beuve to be the trusted lieutenant whom Hugo relied upon for favourable notices. That he was to have need of such notices, from any quarter, had already become evident during the preparation and rehearsals for *Hernani* between October 1829 and February 1830.

HERNANI (1830)

The reading committee of the Comédie-Française accepted the play without a dissenting vote on 5 October 1829. But if we are to believe Maurice Descotes (*DRGC*, 119) the vote was not a free one, Hugo having arrived for the reading backed by a group of his most enthusiastic supporters. In such conditions, the actors found it impossible to criticize passages which, as actors used to neo-classical tragedy and to the audience at the state-supported Comédie, they found strange, to say the least. They did not hide their discontent long. The rehearsals, which began the following day with a distribution of roles, then proceeding to more than a month of 'Italian' runs through the play with the actors seated around a table, and then to acted scenes involving movement, gesture, and dialogue, were difficult. The four principal roles went to the most distinguished and influential actors at the Comédie. Mlle Mars, at fifty, would play the adolescent Doña Sol. Joanny, an actor of great presence and professional standing, received the role of Don Ruy Gomez de Silva. These were not their first Romantic roles: they had already triumphed in *Henri III et sa cour*, and they starred as Desdemona and Othello in *Le More de Venise*, Vigny's adaptation of Shakespeare's tragedy successfully produced at the Comédie-Française in October 1829. Firmin, an actor with almost twenty years' experience in all types of roles at the Comédie, was to play the young bandit Hernani; and Michelot, with twenty-five years at the Comédie would play Don Carlos (Charles V).

Modern scholars no longer accept uncritically Dumas' account in his *Memoirs*[4] of the 'stormy' nature of the rehearsals of *Hernani*, although agreeing with him that the actors were subjected to great pressure from a clique of anti-Romantic journalists, critics, and government censors, many of whom were themselves minor playwrights. Such a group could hardly be called disinterested: the production of their own dramatic works at the Comédie-Française would clearly be made less likely by any sustained Romantic success. Both Dumas and Mme Hugo have recounted, for instance the conflict between Mlle Mars and Hugo, who, Dumas alleges, had finally to assert his authority over her by asking that she give up the role. If this in fact happened, it was a battle Hugo won. He lost the battle, however, over Mlle Mars' costume and hat. As the star of the house, Mlle Mars had the right to dictate in such matters and, despite Hugo's protests, played the sixteenth-century heroine in a dress fashionable in 1830, choosing to complement it with a wide-brimmed, coolie-style hat with an enormous panache which, in Maloeuvre's engraving looks like an ostrich plume.[5] Such was her power over mere playwrights at the Comédie that five years later, in 1835, she wore the same hat as Tisbe in Hugo's *Angelo*, again ignoring his complaints.

Mme Hugo also blames the weather for spoiling the rehearsals, saying that it led to a falling off of interest in the play among the actors. The winter of 1830 was exceptionally cold, with the Seine freezing over and playwright and actors attending rehearsals in gloves and mufflers. Among the men, only Joanny pleased Hugo by learning his role early and playing Gomez as the author envisioned him. Michelot, particularly, had little confidence in the pivotal role of Don Carlos, the would-be ravisher of Doña Sol in Act 1, who, after his election as Charles V in Act 4, must assume the character and concerns of Holy Roman Emperor. But such a lack of enthusiasm hardly proves that the actors hated the play and set out deliberately to sabotage it, as Dumas alleges. Ubersfeld gives a more credible assessment of what may have happened: 'As is well known actors, except on exceptional occasions, keenly support the work they are playing ... *Hernani* had its dangers for them; all the more so, it must be said, because they had to change their style and vocal habits. The alexandrine's monotonous rhythm and caesura was distorted, crushed, and swallowed up [in Hugo's play]; in the face of such violence they found it difficult to remain on the gentle slopes that were their usual lot. And the actors of the Comédie-Française knew better than anyone just on which lines they risked being hissed, just what would draw hoots of laughter (*RH*, 47). It is in this context – that of a difficult play which spurned the old, safe techniques of neo-classical tragedy in favour of new aesthetic tenets, and which deliberately set out to change the prejudices of the regular audience at the Comédie – that the actors asked for changes in the text.

Mlle Mars asked Hugo to alter, for instance, her line: 'You are my lion proud and generous' to 'You are, Sir, valiant and generous' (3, 4). All zoosemiotics aside, Mlle Mars probably judged the expression unacceptable according to the norms governing neo-classical, noble vocabulary. The word 'lion' also had, in the 1830s, the unfortunate associated meaning of social celebrity or dandy, clearly inappropriate to the Spanish setting and Renaissance period of the dramatic action. Hugo agreed with her, rewriting the line in accordance with her wishes, as the prompter's copy of the play shows. Similarly, Mlle Mars' reluctance to play the role of silent listener during most of Act 3, while Hernani, Gomez, and Don Carlos occupy centre stage is understandable. As the unrivalled star of the house, she was expected to hold forth, and her public would brook little usurpation of her right to speak. It is true, however, that Doña Sol dominates Act 5, a fact ensuring the eventual triumph of Mlle Mars.

Hugo assiduously attended the more than fifty rehearsals, as was to be his custom until the production of *Les Burgraves* in 1843. While *Hernani* was in rehearsal, he also had to make changes to the script to suit the male actors and Baron Taylor. Judged too long, the portrait scene in Act 3, for instance, was cut, losing in the process passages describing four of Gomez's ancestors. But the longest cuts came in Act 4: Don Carlos' soliloquy on the responsibilities of the Emperor was reduced from 174 to 107 lines, though Hugo restored the missing lines in the printed text, published on 9 March 1830. There was little that the author could do, however, if actors changed lines onstage, as happened, or if they persisted in extraneous stage business they believed necessary to placate the public. Firmin-Hernani, for example, thought that the line: 'Oui, de ta suite, ô roi, de ta suite, j'en suis' ('Yes, one of your followers, O King, I am one of your followers' 1, 4) because of its repetitions and word play might be hissed. He therefore indulged in the following extraordinary mime as he said it, presumably in an attempt to distract attention from the script, or to take distance from it: 'He said *de ta suite*, then stamped his feet, flung himself about, ran to right and left of the stage, came back to stage centre, seizing in the midst of all this action a moment to utter as if in secret the words *j'en suis*' (*DRGC*, 122). Nothing Hugo said was able to alter Firmin's interpretation of this line, so the line itself had to be changed.

Hugo was also at the mercy of the censor who, although allowing the play to be performed, insisted on the following 'necessary' cuts and/or edulcorations:

1. Remove the name of Jesus throughout.
2. Substitute less harsh and cutting remarks for the insolent and inappropriate expressions addressed to the King: 'You are a coward, a madman'.
3. The following line must be changed: 'Do you think then that *I* hold Kings to be sacred?'
4. Remove or change the line beginning: 'A bad King ...'. Odious allusions are to be feared in this passage.
5. Replace the two lines referring to courtiers in which the meaning is too bitter and the form too strong: 'A farm-yard where the King, subject to shameless entreaties. Scatters to all these starvelings the crumbs of his greatness. (*RH*, 38)

An exchange of letters over three months between Hugo and Baron Trouvé, the censor in question, produced a sort of compromise, just in time for the play to go on. In exchange for making most of the changes imposed, Hugo was allowed to retain the epithets 'cowardly, insane, and bad' referring to the Spanish King, Don Carlos (*RH*, 41).

By February 1830, however, Hugo had other concerns. Aware that the play would arouse violent hostility in the audience at the Comédie-Française, and not trusting the loyalty of the official claque, he refused Baron Taylor's offer to put it at his disposal. Instead, he appealed to his friends and, through them, to a more youthful audience of students and artists than the collection of middle-aged bourgeois citizens who formed the majority of the Comédie's regular public. In so doing, he created the conditions that led to the 'Battle of *Hernani*,' the most famous and influential theatrical event in France in the nineteenth century. Accounts vary, naturally, about what actually happened, running the gamut from Enid Starkie's epic version,[6] to more recent attempts to reveal the truth about the play's first performances by reproducing Hugo's notes on a prompter's copy (*VHT*, 165–85). Published for the first time by Jean Gaudon in 1985, Hugo's 148 annotations, taken during a March performance of *Hernani*, record the exact points at which the audience voiced its approval or disapproval of happenings onstage. We shall return to this source.

Hugo's supporters, the *chevelus* (longhairs) – the synecdoche contrasting them with their opponents, the supporters of neo-classical tragedy, the *genoux* (literally, knees; figuratively, hairless, baldies), or *perruques* (the wigs) – had to wait outside the theatre on the afternoon of 25 February 1830, Starkie tells us: '[A]ll who passed saw an extraordinary crowd dressed in every kind of fancy dress, some with Spanish cloaks, some in Robes-

pierre waistcoats, some in medieval tunics, one with a Henri III hat and
Gautier in his famous scarlet doublet. Many of the young men were
unwashed and they looked a regular pack of ragamuffins. The respectable
people stared with amazement and disapproval at this motley gathering
and soon a crowd collected to watch them while they retaliated by making
grimaces. Then the crowd began to attack them, seizing as weapons anything they could find – sticks, stones and garbage from the gutters – and
began to pelt them with it. Balzac received a cabbage stalk full in the
face.'[7] Once allowed into, and then locked inside, the unlighted theatre,
Hugo's claque ate the highly spiced evening meal that they had brought
with them, swilling it down with copious libations. The lavatories being
closed to them, they pissed in the corners, (*RH*, 60). The disgust of the
beau monde on their arrival before 7 p.m., when the play was scheduled to
begin, can be imagined. They immediately assumed that such barbarians
had no aesthetic sense and blamed Hugo for appealing to such a 'rabble' –
worse, for introducing such savages into the Comédie-Française, the
sacred temple of French theatre. The battle between the two parties began
early in the play.

Contemporary accounts of what then happened on that cold February
evening need to be read with care. Mme Hugo's version, as well as those of
Dumas and Gautier, principal participants in the struggle, while picturesque and emotionally satisfying, are too close to fiction to serve even as
approximate historiography. So too are the hostile press accounts which
appeared after the first performance of *Hernani*. More recently scholars
like Jean Gaudon, for instance, have relied on a less biased document
which affords a view, if not of the first night, then of one of the early performances. The record that Hugo left, written line by line in a prompter's
copy, of one particular audience's reactions to the play provides material
for an empirical study of its early reception. Unfortunately, Gaudon's
idealized view of Hugo, who [he maintains], recounts no fables, who
embroiders nothing, 'who shows no obsequiousness, who tells the truth,
the whole truth, nothing but the truth' (*VHT*, 165),[8] reduces the potential
value of his interpretation of Hugo's very useful 148 annotations, all of
which concern an audience's actual reaction to the play. We need to dis-
count Gaudon's Hugolatry in order to judge the value of the notes.

Hugo made the notes in a printed copy of *Hernani* which he could not
have had before 9 March at the earliest (he may have had a presentation
copy of the text, published on that day). In his notes, Hugo carefully lists
four different kinds of reactions that the March audience manifested at
specific points in the play. He distinguishes *bruit* (noise), from *rires* (laughter), *sifflets* (whistling), and *mouvements* (agitation). He also noted hyperbolic forms of the first two categories: *grand bruit* (loud noise), and

ricanement (derisive laughter), as well as lines that drew combinations of laughter and noise, laughter and whistling, noise and whistling and even on one occasion, noise, laughter and whistling. Finally, Hugo notes one twenty-line passage, in Act 4, scene 2, when the noise was so great that nothing could be heard of the action onstage. By far the largest category of reactions (96 out of 148) concerns laughter alone; on another 13 occasions laughter accompanied noise and whistling. What such behaviour patterns reveal, of course, remains to be seen.

Gaudon's analysis of the statistical spread of such interruptions to the performance indicates several interesting facts: 'The distribution of the 148 interruptions – on average, one every twelve lines in a play already reduced by 12 per cent – conforms to what was reported by those present at the very first performances. Act 1 was interrupted "only" 16 times, the second act 22 times, the third 39 times, the fourth 32 times, and the fifth 34. We might say that the opposition was forming in the first two acts, came together in Act 3 – with the portrait scene serving as catalyst – and then maintained, and even increased its volume, since Act 5 was interrupted every ten lines' (*VHT*, 167–8). As well as indicating the distribution, one might say the rhythm, of the audience's 'interruptions,' Gaudon's statistical approach to Hugo's notes enables him to run to ground a canard reported since the first accounts of the battle. Hugo's notes reveal no opposition whatsoever to the enjambement that, in defiance of the 'rules' of classical French prosody, 'stretches' the meaning of the play's first alexandrine into line two. (In this celebrated case, the separation between substantive and qualifying epithet *escalier / dérobé* [secret staircase], occurs irregularly at line's end.) More generally, and most convincingly, Gaudon is able to state unequivocally that 'Among all the interruptions Hugo noted, there is not a single one aimed at specific versifying effects' (*VHT*, 169). Then, adding as further proof of this statement the parodies that followed hard on the heels of the first performance of *Hernani*, texts in which 'metrical problems are of little interest to [Hugo's] opponents,' Gaudon makes the startling assertion that 'It therefore appears legitimate to say that this "cultivated" public is almost totally insensitive to rhythmical questions' (*VHT*, 169–70). Gaudon's point is extremely well taken, given that the history of scholarship on *Hernani* and on Hugo's theatre generally shows an inordinate amount of effort expended to prove the contrary of what the empirical proof provided by Hugo's notes clearly demonstrates.

But, if the contemporary audiences at the Comédie-Française were not attacking Hugo's innovations in the use of the alexandrine, what then were they attacking? Gaudon's further analysis of Hugo's notes will not help us much here, since he offers no semiotic analysis of behaviour, merely assuming that 'laughter,' 'noise,' 'agitation,' 'whistling,' and so on represent the audience's opposition to the play. In most instances, he is right, although one would like to know how the different behaviour patterns display different types of opposition. Is laughter, for instance, to be taken as expressing a less extreme degree of opposition than 'noise,' 'agitation,' or 'whistling?' Was some laughter appreciative? It might have been provoked, for example, by agreement with Hugo's disrespectful references to such markers of nobility as the chivalric 'Order of the Golden Fleece': 'It's a golden sheep that hangs around one's neck' (1, 4). More importantly, in Act 1, scene 2, and Act 2, scene 1, Don Carlos' remarks on his period of concealment in the cupboard, which caused laughter in the audience according to Hugo's notes, may have merely fulfilled their dramatic function, rather than expressing opposition to the play. Given Hugo's insistence that the Romantic drama should combine both sublime and grotesque elements, it would seem only logical that some of what Gaudon calls the 'trivial' category of utterances ought to provoke laughter. The fact that Hugo noted 96 cases of laughter would seem to confirm that, in some cases at least, such laughter, although probably exaggerated for exhibitionistic effect, derived from the incongruity intended by Hugo, whose noble or royal characters frequently use popular expressions when speaking of courtly, regal, or imperial subjects. So, when the King, Don Carlos, expresses in 'low' terms his exasperation at being forced to hide in a cupboard, itself a grotesquely comic event, his unregal language could be relied upon to provoke laughter, not necessarily of the derisive or belligerent variety. On the other hand, it is understandable that some of the public reacted negatively – having been taught to expect that their social superiors communicated onstage exclusively in the *style noble*. The public's reaction proves simply that Hugo was ahead of his time in his refusal to kowtow to the pretentious language affected by monarchic regimes in general and more specifically by the then current French monarchy and its supporters. That said, however, it must be allowed that the neo-classical aesthetic had controlled stage language more tightly than any particular regime.

Hugo's remarks concerning 'derisive laughter,' however, might reflect more clearly the audience's opposition to the play, in fact their refusal to take it seriously or to accord to it the respect due a serious work of art; but he noted only seven examples of such laughter, so the point loses some of its force, given the violent partisanship of the contending parties at the play's opening performances. Similarly difficult to categorize precisely are Hugo's notes concerning 'noise' in the auditorium. Clearly, a play gains most from being listened to in an appreciative silence, but as Ubersfeld reminds us, such an attitude belongs more to our time than to Hugo's: 'We can scarcely imagine, at the end of the twentieth century, [which is] rather polite and respectful towards artists, what in the 1830s might happen during a performance that was booed ... The best proof we have of [Hugo's] struggle is the diary kept by Joanny, the actor playing Don Ruy Gomez de Silva ... On March 5, Joanny analyses the [following] contradiction: 'The house is full and the whistling continues twice as obstinately. There is in all this an implied contradiction: if the play is so bad, why do they come? If they are so keen to come, why do they whistle?' (*RH*, 72, *OC*, 3, 1443–6). One possible answer to Joanny's query is that by 5 March, *Hernani* had ceased to be merely a play and had become what we in the twentieth century have learned to call a cultural event, a 'happening,' or Bakhtinian 'carnival,'[9] in which the public assumes that its own role is as important as that of the (other) actors or performers. What such interventions did interrupt, presumably, was the deliberations upon the play's merits in which the 'cultivated' leaders of 'good taste,' the 'true' patrons of the Comédie-Française usually indulged themselves.

At any rate, Hugo's notes on the audience's reactions to *Hernani* throw new light upon the famous 'battle' which, after continuing throughout the play's 39 performances in 1830, mysteriously fizzled out, and became conspicuous by its absence from subsequent productions. The main reason for this change in reception is not far to seek. As Hugo's ideas on royalty and his belief in artistic liberty came to be shared by a wider public, so the 'cultivated' public grew to accept his convictions favouring the absence of rules and the individual's right to appreciate artistic innovation as such rather than in social or political terms. In such a cultural climate, *Hernani* came to represent the norm rather than a transgression from it: the 'battle' had been won.

When *Hernani* was revived in 1867, after fifteen years during which the Imperial censorship had closed all Parisian theatres to Hugo's plays, the result was a triumph. The twenty-three-year-old Paul Verlaine and thirteen other young French poets who were seeing for the first time a production of one of Hugo's plays, signed a letter of homage to him, then in exile in Guernsey. In a text published in the newspaper, *L'International*, Verlaine waxed lyrical about the experience:

> *Hernani*'s success was enormous, unheard of, colossal, overwhelming! And peaceful, which won't do any harm ... Good sense has, over the last thirty years, dealt according to their desserts with the ludicrous prejudices of a few fans of Tragedy ... [W]e are the cubs of those great lions [our fathers of 1830]. What a fine thing this drama is, leaving aside all thought of school or tradition! It combines the Cornelian sublime, Shakespearean emotion, and something especially moving and sublime belonging only to Hugo! What is there in the Spanish theatre, however proud, to compare with the splendid portrait scene? And doesn't the fifth act raise the French lovers to the stat-

ure of *Romeo and Juliet?* Also, what unanimous cries of 'Vive Hugo' were repeated over and over, in the intervals and at the end! What a fury of enthusiasm! What delirious joy and true happiness shone in all eyes! (*PF*, 266)

Thus did the young Symbolist generation glorify the revolution in French theatre wrought by their Romantic forebears.

But in 1830, artistic innovation had not yet received so favourable a press. Hugo's new staging techniques in *Hernani* might be assumed to have provoked particular opposition in the play's first audiences. Once again Hugo was far ahead of all but a small minority of the dramatists of his time in believing that an author should personally direct the actors of his plays. We should remember that the position of director only achieved its modern prominence in France in Antoine's *Théâtre Libre* in the 1890s. Marvin Carlson emphasizes Hugo's contribution to the recognition of the importance of the director's function: 'Hugo and Dumas were particularly closely involved with their productions, suggesting not only stage groupings and movements, but even gestures and vocal inflections, and were thereby important contributors to the growing awareness of the expressive powers of stage composition' (*HR*, 7). Carlson's research into dramatic technique has enabled him to pinpoint Hugo's innovations in stage composition in *Hernani*. With regard to the positions adopted by actors during a scene, for instance, Carlson shows that, traditionally, actors at the Comédie played in an almost straight line, 'facing full or three-quarters front' (*HR*, 10). This practice continued during the Restoration, with the actors generally grouped downstage centre in a semi-circle around the prompter's box. By analyzing the original script and prompt book of *Hernani*, Carlson discovered that the 'blocking patterns throughout show how much more Hugo utilized the entire stage space than any director earlier in the century' (*HR*, 19). Carlson's account of the actors' movements shows that the lineup of actors disappeared in favour of a more relaxed, natural set of attitudes, probably influenced by what Hugo had learned from the visit to Paris of the English actors in 1827–8. Most striking in this regard is the adoption by Hernani in Act 1 of the position later called in France the *dos anglais* (the English back), much affected by the English actors and later imitated by French Romantic actors like Bocage. Rather than facing the audience, Hernani turned his back on them and, says Carlson, 'remained down left in this position, leaning against the cupboard' during the confrontation between Gomez and the interlopers he discovers in Doña Sol's bedroom. Act 2 saw other irregular movements onstage, with Doña Sol's struggles against Don Carlos being first interrupted by Hernani's dramatic entry, and later by sword play between the two men, all of which necessitated some innovative choreography.

Hugo also exploited to the full the lavish set constructed by Ciceri for Act 4, which takes place in Charlemagne's tomb in Aix-la-Chapelle. He was fully cognisant of the problems such a massive set presented to scene-changers and therefore to the dramatic illusion itself. For the 1867 revival, he advised the stage manager at the Comédie-Française on how best to exploit the staircase and reduce the time necessary for its deployment: 'One very important observation: the staircase in Act IV, which confers grandeur on the entry of the electors into the vault, must be usable. It must be set up, all ready, and be in place backstage before the beginning of Act I; otherwise the time taken to erect the set would be interminable, and a long interval between Acts III and IV would dampen all enthusiasm for the performance. I used to time the scene-setting, watch in hand. Long intervals frighten me' (*PF*, 265–6). In 1830 Hugo used the massive staircase occupying centre stage by ensuring that movement occurred on, or around it, throughout the act. Carlson calls this 'the most striking act in scenic terms,' because 'Hugo achieved patterns of considerable variety by keeping the conspirators on the lower level and by allowing other actors to appear on the stairs at any one of three levels. From a literary point of view the great monologue of Don Carlos dominates this act, but scenically the high point was the coronation procession down the great stairs, with lavish period costumes' (ibid.). Carlson illustrates the blocking for this scene (4, 4), by showing the relative positions of the actors on the staircase and at the ballustrades of Ciceri's set.

Lavishness in set design was accompanied in *Hernani* with splendid costumes, thanks to Baron Taylor's determination to produce a Romantic success. Marie-Antoinette Allévy describes as follows some of the principal costumes, which Hugo's enemies declared were ruining the Comédie by their extravagance: 'The principal roles changed their costumes in every act: dark cloaks, broad-brimmed hats, belted leather breast-plates, very local-colour "alpine" costumes, black velvet doublets with broad low-cut collars, costumes of silken velvet in the Castilian style with voluminous slashed sleeves and ample damask tunics. Louis Boulanger designed all this finery which was still so new to the actors of the Comédie-Française and into which they, as men of the Restoration, had some difficulty sinking their identities' (*MSF*, 94). Allévy is right to mention the problems the conventionally trained actors were having adapting to Hugo's wishes as director of *Hernani*. Mlle Mars, for instance, attempted a long drawn-out death scene in Act 5, in the style of the English actors, but without success, according to Carlson, and one newspaper described Firmin's feverish antics as 'epileptic.'

Despite the vigorous opposition to Hugo's language in the play, there was, however, nothing but praise for the *mise en scène*. The solemn procession of Charles V's electors down the great staircase in Act 4 was particularly admired. Hugo had suppressed the musical accompaniment usual in such scenes, a directorial decision that drew approving comment. He did use music effectively in Act 5, however, to suggest the celebrations accompanying Hernani's marriage to Doña Sol. Carlson summarizes as follows the influence that Hugo's staging of *Hernani* had upon French theatre in the nineteenth century, and specifically upon staging techniques at the Comédie-Française: 'The patterns established by *Hernani* and other Romantic dramas there were not abandoned; they in fact formed the base for staging the more realistic dramas offered during the 1840s and 1850s at the Comédie. But the Hugo productions, *Hernani* in particular, remained the most advanced examples of stage composition for another twenty years' (*HR*, 25). Now, having seen how *Hernani* was written, rehearsed, staged and, in part, received, we shall examine the play itself as Hugo's first successfully-performed Romantic drama.

The action of *Hernani* may best be approached by reference to its three subtitles, because they encapsulate the contrasting, yet interwoven propositions in the plot's logic. Hugo's definitive subtitle, 'Castilian honour' corresponds to the supra-human constraint that in *Notre-Dame de Paris*, the novel he wrote in the same year as *Hernani*, is called ΑΝΑΓΚΗ, (fatality). In the medieval novel, Claude Frollo's sexual desire for Esmeralda is fatal both to her and himself and to her protector, Quasimodo. In *Hernani*, Don Ruy Gomez's absolute subjection to the honour of his house causes his own death and those of Doña Sol and Hernani. Castilian honour explains why Gomez is ready to protect his hated rival for the hand of his niece, even at the risk of his own death or her abduction as hostage by Don Carlos, King of Spain. Castilian honour explains why in Act 5 Hernani, pardoned by Charles V, restored to all his lands and titles, and married to Doña Sol, drinks poison at his own marriage feast. Having himself abused Gomez's trust and hospitality in Act 3 and sworn an oath to give his own life in exchange for the right to avenge his father – by killing Don Carlos – Hernani cannot face the shame of breaking his oath, and so dies. Doña Sol, unable to understand or sympathize with such a male, or *macho*, principle, pleads with him to reject male honour in favour of female happiness and so ignore Gomez's sarcastic gibes – to no avail, however. Hernani, bent entirely on vengeance, is unable to overcome the fatal power of honour, symbolized in the plot by his death pact with Gomez: bloodlust is stronger than sexual passion or desire for conjugal bliss.

The second subtitle, found on the first page of the manuscript, 'Tres para una' ('Three [men] for one [woman]') clearly indicates the position of Doña Sol at the centre of a triangle of male rivalries. She remains the object of Gomez's and Hernani's desires throughout; but Don Carlos's election as Holy Roman Emperor in Act 4 dehumanizes him, raising him above such emotional attachments. Gomez and Hernani, as antithetical personifications of old age and youth, show their feelings by their contrasting elegies. Gomez complains of the pain an old man suffers out of jealousy of his younger rivals, both real and imagined (3, 1); and Hernani, in his love scenes with Doña Sol, expresses the equally sharp pain of youthful sexual longing and ultimate frustration (2, 4; 3, 4). Doña Sol so little hides her love for the bandit Hernani, spurning in the process the offer of Gomez to share his wealth and prestige, that one of the play's censors described her as, 'the daughter of a Spanish Grandee ... shameless, without dignity or modesty' (*RH*, 32). What his report neglects to say about Doña Sol's moral character is that she is so little 'shameless' that she proudly rejects the offer made by her would-be abductor, Don Carlos, of the Spanish throne in return for her sexual favours:

DOÑA SOL
There can be nothing between us, Don Carlos,
My aged father spilled too much of his blood for you.
I am his noble daughter, and jealous of his blood.
Too high for a concubine, and too low for a queen.

DON CARLOS
Princess!

DOÑA SOL
                King Carlos, to girls of no account
Take your passing fancy, or I could very well,
If you dare treat me after your notoriously vile fashion,
Show you that as well as a lady, I am a woman!

DON CARLOS
Very well! Share both my throne and my name.
Come now, you will be the Queen, the Empress ...

DOÑA SOL
                                              No.
It's a trick. And besides, Highness, frankly
Even if it were not you, if I must say so,
I prefer to live as a wanderer with my Hernani, my [real] king ...
Than to be an Empress [and live] with an Emperor!   (2, 2)

It is impossible not to see that what the 1830 censor obviously believed 'shameless' in Doña Sol's behaviour was her rejection of a king's offer of concubinage and her preference for sharing the life of an outlaw.

Hernani's third subtitle came from members of the French press who, as early as October 1829, were speaking of the play as the first part of a trilogy, calling it 'The Youth of Charles V.' It is true that in a note published in the newspaper *Le Constitutionnel*, on 25 February 1830 and distributed to the first-night audience, Hugo does refer to the whole life of Charles V so it might be inferred that he intended to treat it in a series of sequels. But, in fact, the note seems to focus on other concerns:

> It is perhaps germane to place before the public's eyes what Alaya's Spanish chronicle says ... touching upon the youth of Charles V, who figures in *Hernani*, as is well known: 'Don Carlos, as long as he remained merely Archduke of Austria and King of Spain, was a young prince keen on his pleasures, a great one for love affairs, serenades and violent attacks under the balconies of Saragossa, quite willing to steal beauties away from their gallants and wives from their husbands; he was sensual or cruel as he saw the need. But, from the day that he became Emperor, his character suffered a revolution (*se hizo una revolucion en el*), and the debauched Don Carlos became the skillful, wise, clement, haughty, glorious, bold and prudent monarch that Europe has admired as Charles V' (*Grandezas de España*, descanso 24). (*SG*, 159)

In quoting this note, W.D. Howarth, concludes that, in the absence of any trace of the text Hugo gives as supporting evidence for his claim concerning the 'revolution' in Carlos's character, the note represents an example of 'deliberate *mystification*' by the dramatist. Be that as it may, the note aims to establish the historical accuracy of the 'revolution' in the king's character, rather than to promise future sequels to *Hernani*. In fact, Don Carlos's sudden change from lover ready to kidnap and (presumably) to rape Doña Sol, and even to suggest a more 'modern' sexual arrangement – that of sharing her with Hernani (2, 2) – to the idealized Imperial Sage, ready to pardon all plotters and to 'award' Doña Sol to Hernani, reinstated lord of all his lands, and with new titles and honours, does take some swallowing. It does so particularly if, disregarding the red herring of historicity, we seek verisimilitude of a classical or rationalistic nature in *Hernani*. The reason is that Hugo's first successful drama rejects the neo-classical theory of character psychology. In so doing, it may be taken as the paradigm prefiguring all of his later ones. In order to understand why, we need to ask why audiences accept as 'likely' certain dramatized acts, emotional attitudes, or rhetoricized thought processes. We will approach the problem by considering some reactions to this question among Hugo's critics.

Hugo's opponents have traditionally argued that the 'psychology' of characters in the French neo-classical theatre represents those plays' most valuable, 'obvious' (and therefore unattackable) value. Such critics dismissed Hugo's characters as 'incoherent,' the kind of personages whose actions reveal no underlying plot logic. Jean Massin, in arguing against such dismissive accounts, proposes that the type of psychological activity revealed in Hugo's dramatic works, far from being 'Cartesian,' or rationalistic, derives from his understanding of what we now call 'depth psychology' (*la psychologie des profondeurs*).[10] Massin contends that the superficial incoherence in the characters of Hugo's heroes should be read as evidence of the kind of unconscious, inexplicable motivations we meet in dreams, and that psychologists identify with repressed memories, desires, or other psychic activities. The action of Hugo's dramas, he therefore concludes, is 'symbolic.' It follows then, according to this interpretation, that Hugo's characters personify values, impulses and conflicts in a secret world where appearances do not correspond to realities. Hugo's world is, however, open to scrutiny if one possesses the right key. For Massin, Ubersfeld, Seebacher and many of the other contributors to the chronological edition of Hugo's complete works, the key allowing one to decode their meaning is the psychoanalytical approach to his life. The plays, novels, poems, etc. that he wrote display to the *cognoscenti* his deepest and most carefully hidden inhibitions, or alternatively his unconscious desires and repulsions.

On the other hand, formalist critics, while not rejecting as totally unconvincing this psychoanalytical approach, treat the plays, novels, etc., as something other than disguised or unconscious autobiography on Hugo's part. Rather than proposing allegorical interpretations of the plays, formalists offer descriptions of their dramatic functioning. They explain verisimilitude, for example, in terms of generic, rather than 'real-life,' or rationalistic constraints. For such critics, Hugo's characters offer an audience satisfaction of a specifically literary kind, deriving from an audience's informed appreciation of the author's treatment of the relevant literary codes. Hernani, for them, is a Romantic hero, whose reactions must be understood not by reference to non-literary models. They would point out that, logically and even ontologically, any psychological activity in a play must originate as much in the actor and audience as in the character, a creature of ink and paper. They would further point out that the actor's desire to make believable or verisimilar thought processes or emotional outbursts as well as an audience's desire to find them believable derives as much from their own thought processes and emotions as from the printed page. The playwright's skill should therefore be judged on his rhetorical ability to convince certain actors and audiences to sympathize with his characters to the point of overlooking any actions which, rationally, they would find incredible.

Related to the formalist approach is the view that Romantic experiments resulted in a non-mimetic, or 'anti-illusionist' type of drama. Using this criterion, Frederick Burwick clearly distinguishes Hugo's dramas from neoclassical theatre, first by explaining the theory behind it: 'On the one hand, there is the theatre as the mirror of life that imitates reality and exploits the illusion of the proscenium arch as invisible fourth wall to the stage setting. On the other hand, there is the theatre of myth and ritual, of allegory and masque, which makes no attempt at verisimilitude.[11] The example Burwick uses to illustrate anti-mimetic theory is that of Hugo's characters who, he argues, should not be judged by their 'truth-to-life,' but rather by their ability to personify Romantic irony. This self-reflexive type of reference to the action as a dramatic performance, is both illusion-shattering and illusion-creating: 'In the drama, the characters are caught up in their own illusory perceptions, and they "escape" only to remind the audience that they are acting ... [T]his act of "falling out of the role" (aus der Rolle fallen) reinforces rather than disrupts the spontaneity of stage illusion. If a character falls out of one role, after all, he inevitably falls into another.'[12]

Hugo's characters 'fall out of the role' in two ways: either thanks to dramatized changes of identity brought about by disguises, masks or anagnorisis, or by assuming in Hugo's plays the roles of actors performing meta-theatrically. Hernani, Ruy Blas, as well as all the protagonists of Les Burgraves belong in the first category; the lovers in Marion de Lorme and Count John in Les Jumeaux, who perform roles in the play-within-a-play that Hugo incorporates into these two dramas, represent the second. In both cases, the character who has stepped out of his or her role is still playing a role assigned by Hugo. Equally clearly, the complex, contradictory natures of many Hugolian characters, made up of opposing sublime and grotesque characteristics, remove them from naive allegory. Burwick's distinction and the criterion upon which it is based, should reduce the temptation to treat Hugo's characters as mimetic representations of 'real people.'

If we adopt the formalist approach, it is not difficult to see the dramatic action of Hernani as being organized by two major devices which, although frequently in conflict, achieve final resolution at the play's end. The two devices in question, dramatic irony, and the type of peripeteia the Greeks called anagnorisis, or recognition, characterize all of Hugo's dramas that are fables of identity, as we shall see. In Hernani, for instance, the identity of the hero remains hidden until the end of Act 4, where the dénouement of the love plot involving the rivalry among Carlos, Gomez and Hernani occurs. It has been often said that *Hernani* is a play with two endings. Like *Cromwell*, although to a lesser extent, *Hernani* has 'too much' action, a fact that leads Howarth to conclude that it is plot-dominated at the expense of character development. This argument is a form of the 'character-more-important-than-plot' position of some modern critics. It is sufficient to quote Aristotle's contrary belief in the superior importance of plot over character for the relativity of both such value judgments to become clear.[13]

In fact, Act 5 of *Hernani* presents the triumph of Doña Sol, a character who until that point has remained largely unexploited, representing merely the 'object of value' sought by the three rival male characters. (It is significant in this regard that of the four principal characters, Doña Sol is the only one not referred to directly in the titles that Hugo appended to the five acts: 'The King; The Bandit; The Old Man; The Tomb; The Wedding Feast'). Until Act 5, she accomplishes no decisive act, being simply the pawn in the men's quarrels. In the final confrontation, thanks to a peripeteia representing the symbolic recognition of her worth as woman and lover, she it is who seizes the poison from Hernani: by drinking it first, she both sets him the example to follow and reminds him of the superiority of female generosity over the macho oath for vengeance that is causing both their deaths, and that of Gomez:

HERNANI
                For pity's sake, give me back
The poison! For love, for our immortal souls! ...

DOÑA SOL *sombrely*
You want it? (*She drinks*)
                Take it now! ...
Don't complain about me, I've saved you your half ...
You would not have left me mine!
You have not the heart of a Christian wife.
You do not know how to love as a Silva loves.
But I have drunk first and am at peace. Now,
You drink, if you wish!   (5, 6)

To have ended *Hernani* happily, at Act 4, scene 5, would have truncated it. The play would have lost not only the *anagnorisis* of Doña Sol, not only the final 'love duet' between the just-married couple, but would also have implied consummation of the marriage. But the logic of Romantic drama is quite different from that of the melodrama.[14] As Romantic lovers, Hernani and Doña Sol 'must' accomplish the *Liebestod*, the 'love-death,' ensuring their entry, still young and beautiful into myth: any thought of them, or of Romeo and Juliet, or of any other Romantic couple 'living happily ever after' breaks the reading contract implicit in the generic designation, the 'Romantic drama,' by introducing a convention appropriate to comedy or melodrama. A melodrama entitled *Hernani* might well end with the ex-bandit and his bride celebrating their good fortune and praising the solid, bourgeois virtues that writers like Pixérécourt supported, and indeed, hoped to foster in their audiences.

Complementing the device of dramatic reversal is that of dramatic irony, a source both of suspense and of that feeling of superiority an audience enjoys when it sees more clearly than the characters whose fates it vicariously shares. Suspenseful when it allows the audience to foresee pitfalls into which the uninformed characters risk falling, the device causes us, in Act 4 of *Hernani*, for instance, to fear for the bandit's life, since we have seen his intended victim enter Charlemagne's tomb, from which hidden vantage point Don Carlos can surprise the plotters' plans to assassinate him. In Act 3, scene 6, a double dramatic irony creates the suspense attendant upon the audience's knowing that Hernani is hidden behind one of the de Silva portraits and also that the veiled Doña Sol has not been recognized by Don Carlos. The King's demands force Gomez to waver in his duty to save his guest and, in approaching the portrait in question, he arouses the audience's fears for the bandit's life. Later, after Gomez has overcome the temptation to betray his guest's hiding place, Doña Sol reveals her identity for a more pragmatic reason, when Don Carlos, reduced to threats, orders Gomez's arrest. Doña Sol's intervention is decisive, as the accompanying stage direction indicates: 'Doña Sol, *tearing off her veil, and throwing herself between the King, the Duke and the guards, exclaims,* "King Don Carlos, you are a bad king! ... / Highness, you have not the heart of a Spaniard"' (*OC*, 3, 987). By her action, she forces Don Carlos both to pardon Gomez and to take her with him as hostage to Aix-la-Chapelle. Without her intervention, the love plot and the election of the Emperor would have no link and there would be no reason for Hernani and Gomez to leave Spain. In this instance, dramatic irony serves as an agent producing structural verisimilitude.[15]

But perhaps the two most striking uses of the device occur in Act 5. The first forces the audience to guess at the identity of the figure in the black mask circulating among the wedding guests:

> DON GARCI
> Have you noticed, Gentlemen, among the flowers,
> The women, the costumes of all colours,
> That spectre who, standing by a ballustrade,
> Stains the ball with his black domino? ...

DON GARCI *(running to the black domino)*
Fair mask! ...
(The domino turns around and stops. Garci recoils.)
On my soul,
Messires, I saw a flame gleam in his eyes!

DON SANCHO
If he's the devil, I will give him someone to speak to
(He goes up to the black domino, who has not moved.)
Evil one!
Do you come to us from hell?

THE MASK
I do not come from there I go there!
(He begins to circulate again, disappearing on the stairs. Everyone stares after him with a kind of terror in their eyes.)
(5, 1)

Audiences who have remembered the fatal pact between Hernani and Gomez in Act 3 should quickly suspect whose identity the black mask conceals, who it is that personifies death at the wedding feast. It is interesting, but dramatically unnecessary, to compare Gomez, as does Burton R. Pollin, to Poe's 'Masque of the Red Death,'[16] or to the Commander, come to drag Don Juan down to hell (*OC*, 3, 910–11). The device works by creating the dread that the sound of Hernani's horn will trigger.

At this juncture occurs the second example of dramatic irony in Act 5, where the device increases the poignancy of the lovers' tragic predicament coming, as it does, in the midst of their wedding celebrations. The audience, well aware of the horn's meaning, can only listen as Doña Sol, the happy bride, recognizes the sound as Hernani's horn, but not what it signifies. Her incomprehension of Hernani's reaction is likely to claim an audience's pity:

HERNANI *(aside)*: Ah! The tiger is below howling, and wants his prey.
DOÑA SOL: Don Juan, this harmony fills my heart with joy.
HERNANI *(rising in terrible anger)*:
Call me Hernani! Call me Hernani!
I have not finished with that fatal name!
DOÑA SOL: What's wrong?
HERNANI: The old man!
DOÑA SOL: God! What a deathly look!
What is wrong?

HERNANI: The old man, laughing in the shadows!
              Do you not see him?
DOÑA SOL: Where is your mind wandering to?
              What old man?
HERNANI: The old man!
DOÑA SOL (*falling to her knees*):   On my knees
              I implore you, Oh! Say, what secret rends your heart.'
              What is the matter?
HERNANI: I have sworn!
DOÑA SOL: Sworn?
(*She follows all his movements anxiously. He suddenly stops, hand on brow.*)
HERNANI, *aside*:   What was I going to say?
              Try to spare her.
                      (*Aloud.*) I, nothing. What have I been talking about?
DOÑA SOL: You said ...
HERNANI: No. No. My mind was disturbed ...
              I'm in a little pain, do you see. Don't be frightened.   (5, 3)

The device tightens the screw governing the audience's suspense, at once
delaying the fatal moment and increasing their fears for the lovers. It also
prepares Doña Sol's powerful reaction to the threat to Hernani's life once
she learns the truth. But powerful as her reaction is – she first threatens
Gomez with a dagger, then implores his mercy for her husband, before
finally taking the poison herself – it does not satisfy Jean Massin, who
writes: 'I think that any of today's readers, whether they admit it to themselves or not, feel on first reading the play some disappointment when
Doña Sol throws down the dagger and falls in supplication at the feet of
the Commander [Gomez]; the only permissible conclusion would be a
brave thrust of the dagger, that would – finally – send the old man 'to get
himself measured by the gravedigger' (*OC*, 3, 916).

It is testimony to the power of the last act of *Hernani* that it can affect a
critic of Massin's stature strongly enough to make him want Hugo's
Romantic drama to achieve something of the bloodiness of *grand guignol*,
or to prefer that it end with the inconclusiveness more frequently encoun-
tered in modern drama, absurdist or otherwise. The fact of the matter, as
proved by the whole corpus of Hugo's dramas, and what distinguishes
them from the 'comedies' in the *Théâtre en liberté*, is that they must end
unhappily for the protagonists in order to create the desired thought-
provoking catharsis. *Hernani* is an early drama and the didactic element
remains as yet undeveloped. We shall follow – as it occurred – the growing
importance Hugo attached to the didactic function of the Romantic
drama.

Initial press reaction to the play was hostile except, as we have seen, to the *mise en scène*.[17] Only the *Globe* and to a lesser extent the *Journal des Débats* were more generally favourable. In the absence of a friendly review from Sainte-Beuve, Hugo the new liberal was subjected to the attacks of the conservative press and even to those of some radicals. Ubersfeld has shown how Armand Carrel's hostility in the *National* derived partly from his political differences with Hugo, partly from Hugo's financial success (*RH*, 85–97). Having sold the rights to the publisher Mame for 5,000 francs, Hugo drew some consolation on the work's appearance on March 9. *Hernani* also succeeded financially at the Comédie, far exceeding the receipts for any neo-classical play that year. The receipts in February–March 1830, after the record set by the première of more than 5,000 francs, never fell below 2,350 francs. By 5 June, however, with receipts of 1,505 francs, *Hernani* clearly was approaching the end of its run,[18] which continued at irregular intervals into November.

More ambiguous than receipts as a sign of popular interest in the play were the numerous parodies that it provoked. Lyonnet lists the following titles:

> *Oh! que nenni! ou le Mirliton final* (*Oh! Not I! Or the Final Cream-Horn*).
>
> *Harnali ou la Contrainte par cor* (*Harnali or Constraint by Horn*).
>
> *Réflexions d'un infirmier de l'Hospice de la Pitié sur le drame d'Hernani* (*Reflections by a Male Nurse at the Hospice de la Pitié on Hernani's Drama*).
>
> *N-i-ni ou les Dangers des Castilles, amphigouri romantique en 5 actes* (*N-either-Nor or the Dangers of Bickering, Romantic Rigmarole in 5 Acts*).
>
> *Fanfan le troubadour à la représentation d'Hernani, potpourri en 5 actes* (*Fanfan the Troubadour at a Performance of Hernani, a Medley in Five Acts*).
>
> (*PVH* 35)

Harnali, by Auguste de Lausanne, generally regarded as the most amusing of the bunch, was produced at the Vaudeville Theatre in March 1830, and again in 1838 during a revival of *Hernani* at the Comédie-Française in which Firmin again played the title role with Marie Dorval as Doña Sol. The meta-theatrical verse parody presents as principal figures: Arnali, an ex-casher of cheques in exchange for tickets and Quasifol (Almostcrazy), the niece of Dégommé Comilva (Fired As-he-goes), an old shareholder in the theatre. The play burlesques the roles, incidents, and language of the original. It includes a portrait scene, an oboe warning the lovers by playing 'My father the cuckold,' and a final death scene in which Quasifol, now called Estragon, and Harnali sit on cushions waiting for the end.[19]

To redress the balance a little, from the grotesque towards the sublime, as it were, it should be noted that up to 31 December 1978, *Hernani* had proved itself to be Hugo's most popular play at the Comédie-Française with 979 performances, just 22 ahead of *Ruy Blas*, the second most popular of his plays at the state-funded theatre. (*Ruy Blas*, however, only entered the Comédie's repertoire in 1879, almost fifty years after *Hernani*.) Evidence of *Hernani*'s influence on French authors includes a poem, 'Un Soir à Hernani,' which records a visit made by Edmond Rostand, the author of *Cyrano de Bergerac*, to the Spanish village that had supplied Hugo with his hero's name. In the poem, printed in 1902, Rostand writes:

> I still remember the [play's] final verses:
> I murmured: 'Must such a day end?'
> I came out of Hugo as out of a dream.
> And I went back down the street and when I
> Passed under an old wrought-iron balcony,
> A man said, in a proud, surly voice:
> 'Señor, it's there, in that old street,
> That Urbieta was born, the bravo to whom
> Francis the First surrendered his sword!' Then I,
> I said: 'It is there that was born, in that ancient street
> The drama to which The Cid might surrender his.[20]

MARION DE LORME (1831)

With the fall of Charles X and the abolition of censorship consequent upon the July Revolution of 1830, Hugo was approached by Baron Taylor, Commissioner of the Comédie-Française, by François Harel, director of the Odéon, and by Crosnier, manager of the Porte-Saint-Martin Theatre, all of whom wished to stage *Marion de Lorme*. But, despite their interest, the play's première did not take place until 11 August 1831. In the Preface to his play, Hugo states that his hesitation to see the play produced stemmed from his refusal to allow a play of his to be seen as containing critical allusions to current events. He was willing, he wrote, to applaud the people's Revolution, but not to curse Charles X (*OC*, 729): he therefore did not want the negative portrait of Louis XIII in Act 4 of *Marion* to be read as contemporary satire. In fact, his reasons were somewhat more complicated. In the first place, he expected *Hernani* to run at the Comédie into 1831 and was ready to offer *Marion* partly as an inducement to the subsidized house in order to ensure this. But *Hernani* came off in November 1830, despite his manoeuvering. Also, the Comédie, because of its subsidy – which the Government could suspend at any time – could not guarantee the play from cuts, despite the apparent abolition of theatre censorship; so Hugo and

Crosnier signed a contract, according to which Hugo promised to sell to the Porte-Saint-Martin Theatre the exclusive rights to two full-length plays a year, of his own composition (this provision excluded works in collaboration). In return, Crosnier guaranteed his plays against censorial interference. As the director of a non-subsidized popular theatre, he was not subject to the same governmental pressure as the Comédie. Crosnier also gave Hugo full casting rights over his plays, a privilege Hugo was very happy to have obtained, and which he used to the full in preparing *Marion* for the stage.

The year 1831 saw the triumph of Dumas' Romantic drama, *Antony*, at the Porte-Saint-Martin Theatre. Hugo then engaged both of its stars, Marie Dorval and Bocage, to play Marion and Didier, the tragic couple of his own drama. His relationship with Mme Dorval during rehearsals was both less stressful and more dramatically productive than that between himself and Mlle Mars during the rehearsals of *Hernani*. It was Dorval, for instance, who persuaded him to change the ending of *Marion*, a feat beyond the persuasive power of Mérimée after Hugo's first reading of the play to the *cénacle* in 1829. Mme Hugo's account of both events is generally accepted as accurate: '"Monsieur Hugo," she [Dorval] said with her graceful smile, "Your Didier is nasty. I do everything for him, and he goes off to die without even a kind word to say to me. Tell him that he is wrong not to forgive me." This advice, already given by Mérimée on the evening of the first reading, made [Hugo] think. On the way back [from rehearsals], he went for a walk in the Champs-Élysées and decided at the last moment to change Didier's inflexibility' (*VHR*, 491). Almost all commentators have praised the new ending for increasing the poignancy of the final meeting between Marion and her puritanical lover. Marie Dorval also persuaded Hugo to change the play's title from the sociologically-sounding, *A Duel in Richelieu's Reign*, to *Marion de Lorme*, an alteration which served to emphasize her own role, of course.

Like Marie Dorval, Bocage had become a star thanks to *Antony*, and would appear in the dramas of Hugo, Vigny, and particularly Dumas until 1843. He would have preferred to play the pusillanimous Louis XIII, a role Hugo offered, despite Crosnier's protests, to Gobert, an actor who had recently starred with great success as Napoleon at the Porte-Saint-Martin Theatre. Hugo found it more striking to cast the actor who had played the powerful Emperor as a King notorious for his weakness. As L'Angely, the King's fool, a pivotal role, he chose Provost, giving to Auguste that of the Marquis de Nangis, an old man who, like Gomez in *Hernani* and M. de Saint-Vallier in *Le Roi s'amuse*, pleads his case vainly before a youthful king. Although the actors at the Porte-Saint-Martin were in general younger, more agile, and more passionate, 'in the English style,' than the troupe at the Comédie, they were less skilled in verse-speaking, a defect for which they, particularly Marie Dorval, would be reproached by the critics.

Hugo attended the rehearsals diligently, directing the actors in their parts and in some instances modifying the text in accordance with their demands or particular needs. Because of Marie Dorval's inexperience at speaking French alexandrines, Hugo was forced to make his lines easier to say. In order to make them suppler, less stilted, more human, he broke up the monotony of the twelve-syllable line with caesura at the hemistich by means of exclamations, expletives, and emotive repetitions, all of which introduce secondary or tertiary caesuras into the verse. In the following speech, for example, commented upon favourably by most Hugo critics since Descotes, the italics indicate expressions which were added during rehearsals and have the effect of interrupting the alexandrines' prose-like rhythm with short emotional outbursts:

> Ah, Sire! May the King sympathize with our grief.
> *Do you know what it's like?* Two young fools,
> Pushed down into the abyss for a duel!
> Death, *Great God,* death on a foul gibbet!
> You will have pity on them! *I, a mere woman,*
> *Don't know* how to speak to a king. *Weeping is wrong maybe;*
> But *your cardinal is a monster! ...*
> *At their age, both of them! Killing them for a duel!*
> *Their mothers, just think ... Ah! It's horrible! Oh God!*   (4, 7)

Descotes comments also on the dramatic possibilities such highly charged lines afforded to an actress of the calibre of Marie Dorval: 'The text allows for the most *English* scenic effects: supplication on bended knee, beseeching hands, a voice hoarse with grief. In this scene, which was made for her, Dorval was to win all the acclaim she could hope for' (*DRGC*, 218).

Another text that affords us a glimpse of Victor Hugo's direction of the actors in his dramas concerns the 1873 revival of *Marion* at the Comédie-Française with Mounet-Sully, Sarah Bernhardt's frequent partner in Romantic roles, playing Didier. Hugo intervened by letter from Guernsey to explain how the great scene of *anagnorisis* (5, 6), in which Didier reveals that, despite Marion's efforts to conceal her past, he knows that she is Marion de Lorme the notorious courtesan, rather than the simple Marie she had claimed to be. Here is the moment, one of the emotional climaxes of the play:

> MARION
> Speak to me, speak, call me by my name: Marie! ...

DIDIER
Marie, or Marion?

MARION (*terrified, falling to the ground*)
          Didier, be merciful!

DIDIER (*in a terrible voice*)
Madame, it is not easy to get in here!
State prisons are guarded day and night
With iron gates and walls twenty feet thick.
In order for the prison to throw its gates open to you,
To whom did you prostitute yourself?   (5, 6)

Having just, with the utmost repugnance, given herself to the odious M. Laffemas, 'Richelieu's hangman,' in order to save Didier from the gallows, Marion is crushed by Didier's cruelty, which is likely to arouse a sensitive audience's indignation. Mounet-Sully proposed, therefore, to soften the blow, but Hugo would have none of it, as Laster tells us (Hugo's remarks are in quotation marks):

> Make of *Marie or Marion?* 'a thunderclap' which must be 'terrifying' because 'the whole drama explodes in these two words' and the cry must burst from Didier's bosom 'like a jet of lava.' The audience 'must tremble at this cry which blasts Marion to the ground' ...
>
> Mounet-Sully wanted to say *Marie* tenderly, and *Marion* gravely and severely, without emphasis and without rising to his feet. Hugo insisted: 'the explosion, *Marie or Marion?* demands that Didier be on his feet. He draws himself to a terrible height on the words, and Marion is broken, falling at his feet. [If he is] seated, the effect is lost.' Hugo specified further the need for a pause after this 'first flash of lightning' to prepare 'a second flash' with the eight subsequent lines climaxing with *To whom did you prostitute yourself?* 'Do not run them together!' He also recommended for Didier's forgiveness of Marion 'two cries: *Come! Ah, come to my arms!* (Passionate embrace). *I'm going to die. I love you.* (A second broken-hearted explosion.)' And finally, he wanted *Come, poor woman!* spoken 'aloud,' and *Oh! Let me die,* 'more intimately,' with neither embraces nor goodbyes after the clock strikes nine. (*PF*, 267)

Hugo's remarks on acting show that he believed violence and hyperbole, rather than subtlety and understatement, should characterize the expression of passion in the Romantic drama.

Passion also marks the two principal themes dramatized in *Marion de*

Lorme. Written just six months after Hugo's great denunciation of capital punishment, *Le Dernier Jour d'un condamné à mort, Marion* also treats of legal murder, with Didier and Saverny decapitated for duelling by the arbitrary power of Richelieu, despite Marion's having obtained a pardon for her lover from Louis XIII. The play's second theme, which was to become one of the Romantic clichés of which modern audiences have grown weary, presents the prostitute's rehabilitation brought about by pure love. Ubersfeld dresses the idea in terms more usual nowadays when she speaks of the play being 'an interrogation on the relationship between woman and love, the existence of the self, and personal integrity,' adding that: 'The tragic conflict is between the demands of the [woman's] self and man's irrepressible jealousy' (*VHTL*, 1, 1396). At the service of these two themes, Hugo wrote a drama set in the Loire Valley in 1638, and in which dramatic irony once more delays *anagnorisis* almost until the final peripeteia.

Act 1, 'The Rendez-Vous,' begins in Marion's bedroom in Blois, introducing the lovers and setting the scene for the play's final dramatic climax by witholding from Didier, an archetypical Romantic hero – a foundling, profoundly at odds with contemporary society – the information that Marion, to whom he declares his desire for a chaste love, is the notorious Parisian courtesan, twenty of whose lovers are listed in the course of the action. Saverny, saved from brigands by Didier in Act 1, will by tragic irony cause his rescuer's arrest for duelling in Act 2. This Act also presents the kind of historically-inspired view of life in Blois in the reign of Louis XIII, reminiscent of the vision of the Lord Protector's England presented in *Cromwell.* Nobles, townspeople, town crier, the King's jester, L'Angely, and the lovers pass through the town square discussing current events like Corneille's disfavour in Paris and Richelieu's new edict banning duelling. In Act 3, 'The Comedy,' the arrival of a troupe of strolling players preparing to enact Corneille's tragi-comedy, *Le Cid,* introduces the grotesque into the Château de Nangis whose owner, clad in mourning, walks the corridors plunged in grief for the death of his nephew Saverny, who, unknown to him, is also present in disguise there. Marion and Didier, after the latter's escape from custody during the interval, are assigned by Le Gracieux, the chief of the players, the roles of Chimène and the swashbuckling braggart respectively. In the play-within-a-play rehearsed onstage, Marion must declaim an extract from one of Chimène's speeches in Corneille's *Le Cid* before Laffemas, who seeks to recapture Didier, and she seizes the opportunity to warn her lover against his enemy:

> Since, to prevent you racing to your death,
> Your life and honour are but feeble attractions,
> If ever I loved you, dear Rodrigo, in repayment
> Defend yourself now and take me away from Don Sancho.

Fight to free me from a position
In which I am joined to the one I hate.
Shall I go on? Go, think about defending yourself,
To overcome my duty, and command my silence;
And, if you still feel in your heart some love for me,
Be victorious in the battle which has Chimène as prize!   (3, 10)

But Didier has learned from Saverny the truth about Marion's past life and, no longer wishing to live, reveals his identity to Laffemas who, rejecting Saverny's generous effort to save Didier by revealing his own identity, arrests them both for duelling, the penalty for which is death on the scaffold.

In Act 4, 'The King,' set in the royal palace of Chambord, satire replaces irony as the dominant mode. Hugo contrasts the pleadings of Nangis and Marion for the lives of Saverny and Didier with the tergiversations of Louis XIII, a bored, weak king, jealous and fearful of Richelieu's power but lacking the energy to oppose it. After Act 3's *Hamlet*-inspired scenes involving the players, Act 4 presents the *King Lear*-like dialogue between the grotesque King and his fool on the meaning of life, death, and the burdens of kingship. L'Angely, the wily fool, outwits Louis, obtaining a pardon for the duellists, a decision the fearful King immediately regrets but is too weak to revoke. Act 5, 'The Cardinal,' set in the prison yard at Beaugency, opens with workmen demolishing part of the wall through which Richelieu's palanquin will pass, allowing the Cardinal to witness the execution of Didier and Saverny. Dramatic reversals succeed one another rapidly, piling hope on disappointment and sustaining suspense until the tragic *dénouement*. First, Marion arrives with the King's pardon for Didier then Laffemas counters with the Cardinal's rescinding order; Laffemas proposes Didier's freedom in exchange for Marion's sexual compliance; she refuses, then agrees; the jailor offers to save only Saverny, who refuses, preferring to die with Didier; next, Marion arrives with the means for Didier's escape; he refuses her offer, because of her past; finally, after kissing Saverny and refusing to kiss Marion, Didier's last act is to reverse himself, thus effecting a reconciliation at the foot of gallows:

DIDIER (*He rushes to Marion, panting and bursting into tears.*)
No! No, my heart is breaking! It's horrible!
No, I have loved her too much! It's impossible
To leave her like this! No! It's too hard
To be stone-faced when your heart is broken!
Come! Oh, come to my arms!
                    (*He clasps her convulsively in his arms.*)
                    I am going to die. I love you!
And to tell you so here is my supreme happiness!   (5, 7)

Even now, Marion hopes still to arouse the Cardinal's pity, as the stage direction makes clear:

MARION (*dragging herself on her knees to the [Cardinal's] litter, her arms raised in supplication.*)
In the name of your Christ, in the name of your race,
Mercy! mercy for them, My lord!

A VOICE (*from the litter*)
                    No mercy!
Marion falls to the ground. The litter passes, and the procession with the two condemned men sets off behind it. The crowd rushes noisily to follow them.

MARION (*alone. She half rises, dragging herself on her hands and looks around her.*)
What did he say? Where are they? Didier! Didier! Nothing more.
No one here! ... The people! ... Was it a dream?
Or am I mad?
(*The people come back in disorder. The litter reappears downstage, returning from where it had disappeared. Marion rises and gives a terrible cry.*)
                    He's coming back!

THE GUARDS (*moving the people aside*)
                    Make way! Make way!

MARION (*on her feet, her hair dishevelled, points out the litter to the people*)
See, all of you! The man in red going by!
                    (*She falls to the ground.*) [Final curtain.]   (5, 7)

The dying moments of *Marion de Lorme* demonstrate clearly how Hugo uses rhetorical *pathos*, the appeal to an audience's emotions, to persuade them to accept his political and social beliefs. They illustrate his agreement both with rhetorical theorists as least since Quintilian, and with neo-classical moralists like La Rochefoucauld who advised his readers that 'the passions are the only orators that always achieve persuasion. They are Nature's art whose rules are infallible; the simple man who has passion persuades better than the most eloquent speaker who has none.'[21] Both Hugo's choice of Marie Dorval, the most impassioned and pathetic actress of her time, and his decision to end his play by provoking this pitiful catharsis show him exploiting the final moments to make the strongest possible appeal to his audience's sense of justice.

His stage directions concerning the actions of his characters also prove conclusively that he wrote his plays to be performed, rather than simply to be read. They involve no considerations of literary style or versification. Their function is entirely practical and pragmatic. They exist principally to help actors prepare their roles, and to make his plays more dramatically affecting for an audience viewing them in performance. While it is a critical commonplace to comment, favourably or otherwise, on Hugo's words in the plays, critics have given much less attention to the stage directions by which he both shaped the actors' stage behaviour and, in so doing, influenced an audience's reactions. *Marion de Lorme* is particularly rich in significant stage business, as analysis reveals.

In Act 2, scene 1, for instance, the following stage direction indicates the means by which Hugo creates the bustle of the town square in seventeenth-century Blois: '*A crowd of people enters from the streets and houses, covering the square. In the middle, the town crier, on horseback, with four liveried municipal retainers, one of whom sounds the trumpet, whilst another beats the drum ... Brichanteau [speaks] to a juggler in the crowd who has a monkey on his shoulder*' (*OC*, 3, 759). Without such stage directions, which serve the same purpose as description in a novel, a director would be left to create his own stage dressing. By including it, Hugo is able to suggest some, at least, of the onstage elements he believed necessary to create the illusion of the scene's appropriate historical setting.

More typical of a different dramatic function served by Hugo's stage directions – that of economically conveying and concealing information, simultaneously or otherwise, to audience and characters – is the following which shows how to organize a character's entrance so that the action alone will inform the audience of a character's mental and emotional state: '*Downstage passes the Marquis de Nangis, an old man. White hair, pale face, arms crossed on his breast. Dressed in the style of Henri IV. Deep mourning. The star and ribbon of the [Order of the] Holy Spirit. He walks slowly. Nine guards, dressed in mourning, halberd on the right shoulder and musket on the left, follow him in three ranks at a certain distance, stopping when he stops, walking when he walks*' (3, 2). The paragraph enriches considerably the atmosphere Hugo wished to achieve in the 'sublime' scenes of Act 3: their grandeur and grief contrast with scenes in which the players enact their comic roles and grotesque tricks. The contrast accords, of course, with Hugo's dramatic tenet as set down in the 'Preface' to *Cromwell.*

In order to create dramatic irony, a stage direction may also apprize the audience of facts of which one or other of the characters remains unaware. In Act 3, scene 6, for instance, the didascalia makes clear that Saverny recognizes Marion, whom he had known in Paris, but that he does not see Didier for whom he is searching: '*Marion rises quickly from beside Didier. At the same time as Le Gracieux, Saverny enters, stopping upstage to observe Marion attentively, but without seeing Didier, who has remained seated on the bench, and who is hidden by a bush*' (*OC,* 783–4). In this instance, the stage direction indicates how both dramatic irony and suspense are to be created. The audience, who observe Saverny watching Marion, have also seen Didier, who remains hidden to Saverny. The audience also probably fears that Saverny, a former lover of Marion, may well betray the truth about her past life to Didier, once he finds him.

One piece of stage business that Hugo considered but abandoned, as too melodramatic perhaps, figures among the play's variants. In this passage, an alternative version of the final climactic recognition scene (5, 6), Didier is onstage but lost in his own thoughts when Laffemas, having forced Marion to have sex with him, insists on a final kiss. Because of his power as Richelieu's hangman, she acquiesces and the following stage direction outlines the result: '*Laffemas seizes her in his arms and kisses her. At the sound of the kiss Didier wakes from his reverie, turns around, picks up the dark lantern, and shines it on the faces of Marion and Laffemas, and all three remain for several moments motionless, as if petrified. Finally, Didier bursts into horrible laughter*' (*OC,* 877). After his experience with *Amy Robsart* and the easily offended Parisian public, Hugo may well have judged the incident, with all its tragic irony, too likely to create indignation in an audience sympathetic to Marion. In any case, the example does reveal the emotional power possessed by Hugo's stage directions which, without the added resource of dialogue, permit skillful manipulation of the action and of an audience's emotional reactions.

Marion was a qualified success in 1831. It certainly did not enjoy the triumph at the Porte-Saint-Martin Theatre that had greeted Dumas' *Antony.* Despite Hugo's care in casting and rewriting his play to suit his star performers, there was some hissing during the run, which soon discouraged them, unused as they had become to such rough treatment, Mme Hugo tells us (*VHR,* 493). The press was lukewarm, no longer expressing the violent hostility with which they had greeted *Hernani.* They criticized Hugo's lack of historicity, the performers' clumsy verse-speaking, and the Romantic 'excesses' such as the mixture of sublime and grotesque elements in the play. In her study of the contemporary reception accorded to *Marion,* Ubersfeld puts adverse critical reaction down chiefly to uncertainty as to Hugo's political opinions: 'Another cause of uncertainty: they didn't know how to take Hugo; despite appearances, the author's political choices are difficult to read in the play. Hugo's depiction of the couple, Louis XIII-Richelieu is not very different from Vigny's incontestably legitimist view in *Cinq-Mars.* But at the same time, the whole fable binds the image of monarchy to that of oppression, violent death, and decapitation; *volens nolens,* the King brings death, and the work, which rests on monarchical presuppositions, finishes up by appearing to be a Liberal attack against the monarchy' (*RB*, 64). If Ubersfeld is right, Hugo refused to allow himself to be influenced by the public's lukewarm reaction to his fable about a weak king. In his next play, he was to dramatize the crimes of a celebrated French king whom he represents as a dissipated tyrant.

5. The Worst ... and the Best of Times, 1832: *Le Roi s'amuse* and *Lucrèce Borgia*

Censorship is my literary enemy, censorship is my political enemy. Censorship is without legal principle, dishonest and disloyal. I indict censorship ... These censors, most of them dramatists, all self-interested defenders of the literary and political *ancien régime*, are my opponents and of necessity my natural enemies.[1]

Between 3 June and 20 July 1832, Victor Hugo did an extraordinary thing: he wrote two plays back to back, without waiting to see the first one produced.[2] His extraordinary activity was not provoked, as in 1829, by censorship problems. Unlike *Marion de Lorme*, banned by Charles X's ministers in that year, *Le Roi s'amuse*, written in June 1832, was not even in rehearsal when Hugo, in July, wrote *Un Souper à Ferrare* (*A Supper in Ferrara*), the drama that he would later retitle *Lucrèce Borgia*. Nor were theatre conditions in Paris so encouraging that he needed to over-produce in order to satisfy the public's passion for drama. In fact, the spring of 1832 was a particularly bad season for Parisian theatre managers. The city was suffering through an epidemic of cholera, with many theatres closed despite the subsidies that Louis-Philippe's government was offering them to stay open. On 28 April, Victor Hugo's own son, Charles, was stricken by the disease and his father suspended everything to take care of him. And in June, when Hugo was writing *Le Roi s'amuse*, a Republican insurrection in Paris sought to oust Louis-Philippe, making the streets dangerous and again closing some theatres. In such unpromising conditions, why then did Hugo write two plays virtually at the same time?

The answer to this question involves many elements in Hugo's developing thinking about the Romantic drama. In his theoretical texts written in 1832–4, principally in the Prefaces to *Lucrèce Borgia* and to *Littérature et philosophie mêlées* (*A Mixture of Literature and Philosophy*), we see see him meditating upon such topics as the conditions of theatrical production in Paris, the need to heal the split between contemporary audiences at the Comédie and at the boulevard theatres, the drama's power to act as a civilizing agent in nineteenth-century French society, and the striking symmetry between the dramas he was writing at this time. In his correspondence, he also announces his ambition to produce his own plays, or at least to ensure for them the best possible conditions for rehearsal and performance. All of these considerations played a part in triggering the process of dramatic composition in June–July 1832.

Among critics who have pondered Hugo's dramatic production in 1832, Ubersfeld has produced the most persuasive hypothesis, the one, that is, that covers most of the data. She begins by admitting that the evidence for her interpretation of Hugo's motivation in this regard is only inferential, because 'We have no evidence about what Hugo thought about the semi-success of *Marion de Lorme*' (*RB*, 77). But there is little doubt that such half-measures were unlikely to satisfy him. Thus, by June 1832, Hugo had had no unqualified success in the theatre: all of his dramas had met with resistance or with outright condemnation. In contrast, Dumas, Hugo's friendly rival as Romantic dramatist, had enjoyed three triumphs by that date. In 1829, *Henri III et sa cour* had somewhat taken the wind out of *Hernani*'s sails by becoming the first drama by a young Romantic dramatist to succeed at the Comédie-Française. Then in 1831, *Antony* enjoyed great financial success, conquering the popular audience at the Porte-Saint-Martin Theatre. And most recently, in May 1832, *La Tour de Nesles*, Dumas' drama about the medieval queen Marguerite de Bourgogne, who first enjoyed and then consigned her lovers to the Seine, especially as acted by Mlle George, became, despite the cholera and trouble in the streets, what Maurice Descotes calls 'the Romantic drama's greatest triumph,' with daily receipts of 4,000 francs (*DRGC*, 239). It is possible that Hugo wished to surpass his rival, but he could have done so with one triumph. Why then write two plays?

The answer, according to Anne Ubersfeld, is that in 1832 Hugo conceived the hegemonic ambition of dominating the whole theatrical scene in Paris by writing dramas which would be equally successful at the Comédie and at the Porte-Saint-Martin. As we have just seen, Dumas had already managed this feat. But the difference in Hugo's project arose, she asserts, from his desire to triumph at both houses *at the same time*. In order to do so, he would need to write a prose drama that would appeal to the popular public at the Porte-Saint-Martin and a verse drama that would please the delicate ears of the élite at the Comédie-Française. In fact, Hugo did write a verse drama, *Le Roi s'amuse*, which was performed, once, at the Comédie, and a drama in prose that triumphed at the Porte-Saint-Martin. But Ubersfeld, obliged at this point to explain the absolutely opposite receptions accorded to the two dramas – *Le Roi* suspended and then banned outright after a single performance, and *Lucrèce* producing some of Hugo's best notices and highest receipts – puts forward a most ingenious thesis, which she bases on evidence from Hugo's critical writings in 1832–4:

> He then conceives an original project. By a kind of cross-over strategy, he will write for the Comédie-Française a grotesque drama whose hero will be a court jester, a drama that will respect neither the unities nor the proprieties, but which will be written in verse and in the sustained style [of tragedy]. For the Porte-Saint-Martin, on the other hand, he will create a kind of 'tragedy of the Atreides,' with a direct, diagrammatic plot line, but he will write that one in prose. The characters, spatial elements, and language will be treated with nobility and dignity: [it will be] a drama with classical concentration; but the violent situations and images will allow modern dramatic actors to show off their strengths free from constraint. He aspired therefore to take possession of the whole of the French theatre with a double breaking of the theatrical codes, at the Porte-Saint-Martin, raising prose melodrama to the heights of tragedy by the power of his writing, [and], by contrast, displaying before the eyes of the distinguished audience at the Comédie-Française Triboulet, the low-born, monstrous clown, the king's hunchbacked fool, and wrecking the tragedy by grotesquely extravagant vocabulary and spatial settings. (in *TF*, 572–3)

Ubersfeld's thesis is ingenious and possesses the advantage of accounting for most (but not all, as we shall see) of the elements in the puzzle concerning Hugo's motivation for writing two plays at virtually the same time.

His desire to control the performance and reception of his plays had already surfaced in early 1831 when, with Baron Taylor absent again from Paris and with receipts more disastrous than ever, the Comédie, so it was reported in the Parisian press, appeared to be coming under the joint management of Victor Hugo and Alexandre Dumas, the most successful of the new dramatists. In a letter to Victor Pavie, a friend who had expressed dismay at the thought of Hugo's (more particularly of Mme Hugo's) descending into the daily strife that enlivened the Comédie's green-room, Hugo both reassured his friend that such was not his intention and revealed his utopian theatrical ambition: 'I have never dreamed of *directing* a theatre, but rather of *possessing* one. I don't want to direct a troupe of actors, but to own a company, be master of an atelier in which art could be worked upon life-size, having everything – both manager and actors – at once under my control but at a distance. I want to be able to shape and reshape the clay to my liking, to melt down the wax over and over, and for that to be possible, both clay and wax must belong to me (*OC*, 4, 1021). The letter continues, expressing more of the pipe dream of the rich amateur that Hugo could not afford to be. As we shall see, when Hugo and Dumas did later manage the Théâtre de la Renaissance, he was far from being the absentee playwright he goes on to envisage in this letter.

Another element in Hugo's decision to write two plays, also covered by Ubersfeld's hypothesis of a cross-over strategy on his part, derives from his belief in the need to fuse the two audiences, popular and distinguished, that frequented Parisian theatres in the 1830s. That he was unhappy with the split between state-subsidized and boulevard theatres is clear from his desire, often expressed in the Prefaces to his dramas and in his other theoretical texts, to create a new public, the 'people.' In the Preface to *Marion de Lorme*, Hugo emphasized the artist's pragmatic duty to study the theatre public, finding encouragement in the 'new' public that the 1830 Revolution had created: 'For the artist who studies the public – and it is necessary to study it unceasingly – it is most encouraging to see developing in the masses an increasingly serious and deep understanding of what best suits this century, both in literature and in politics' (*OC*, 4, 466). But Hugo's notion of the 'people' is not an exclusively populist one – equating 'people' with 'the masses,' nor is it a Liberal one – limiting the 'people' to the 'bourgeoisie.' Liberal critics of the day reproached him because in his dramas he chose royal and aristocratic characters and subjects drawn from the past. Why not deal with modern subjects in bourgeois settings?, they asked. Hugo's reply was optimistic. The modern public, thanks to its direct participation in two Revolutions, was becoming more clear-sighted, more appreciative of 'high' art, verse drama, for instance, and so no longer needed prose dramas on everyday modern subjects. At the same time, the public that frequented the Comédie-Française possessed a discernment born of many years of exposure to the greatest dramatic works, both French and foreign. The Romantic dramatist who jettisoned such experience in search of easy popularity would do so to his cost and to that of French theatre: 'Popularity is doubtless the magnificent complement of the conditions surrounding accomplished art but, in this as in everything else, whoever has only popularity has nothing. And then, we must distinguish between different kinds of popularity. There is a wretched kind of popularity which has devolved merely into the banal, the trivial, the common ... Such popularity is merely vulgar. Art disdains it ... There is another popularity formed by the successive voices of a small elite in each generation; over centuries, they too form a crowd. It must be said that they are the real people to whom genius appeals' (*OC*, 5, 42). Modern plays must therefore appeal, he believed, to both the popular and the distinguished audiences by sharpening the appreciative powers of the former and giving to the latter a better understanding of the passions of suffering humanity.

Quite obviously, Hugo had already embarked, in this 1834 text, upon the campaign that he was to pursue throughout the rest of his dramas and their Prefaces, as well as in his novels, in favour of didacticism in art, a concept he repeated most memorably perhaps in an 1863–4 article entitled the 'Utility of Beauty.' Hugo's theory of didactic drama finds its clearest expression in the Preface to *Littérature et philosophie mêlées*:

> The theatre, we repeat, teaches and civilizes ... Attract the crowd to the drama like a bird to a mirror; fill the multitude with passion about the poet's glorious fantasies, and make the people forget the government of the day; make women weep over a woman, mothers over a mother, men over a man; at the right moment, show the beauty of morality under physical deformity; penetrate surfaces to essentials; give to the great respect for the poor and to the poor ways of measuring the great; teach that there is often a little evil in the best and almost always a little good in the worst; ... without their being aware, thanks to the pleasure you are giving them, take advantage of the masses' attention [to the drama] to teach them the seven or eight great social, moral, or philosophical truths, without which they would not understand their own times. That for the poet is, in our opinion, real usefulness, true influence, and forms a true collaboration in the work of civilizing [one's fellows]. (*OC*, 5, 40)

As well as expressing the general belief in the social value of art, this passage points to the thematic symmetry – 'make women weep over a woman, mothers over a mother, men over a man' – observable in the two dramas Hugo wrote in 1832.

He discussed this symmetry in the Preface he appended to *Lucrèce Borgia* on that drama's publication in February 1833. It is this same symmetry which clashes most fundamentally with Ubersfeld's thesis that seeks to explain Hugo's simultaneous composition of the two plays by his hegemonic desire to dominate the French stage. According to Hugo, *Le Roi s'amuse* and *Lucrèce Borgia* occupy the two balanced sides of a rhetorical diptych in which are represented two monsters, one male saved by paternal affection, and one female saved by maternal love:

> He [the author] believes he must say that these two plays, so different in substance, in form and in fortune, are tightly mated in his mind. The idea

that produced *Le Roi s'amuse* and that which produced *Lucrèce Borgia* were born at the same moment, in the same place in his heart. What is, in fact, the private thought hidden under three or four concentric layers inside *Le Roi s'amuse?* It is this. Take the most hideous, the most repulsive, the most complete *physical* deformity; situate it where it will stand out most clearly, at the meanest, the lowest, the most despised level of society; illuminate this miserable creature using a sinister, contrasting light; and then toss him a soul, putting into it the purest sentiment given to man, paternal love. What will happen? This sublime sentiment, if nurtured under the right conditions, will transform this degraded creature before your very eyes; this mean-spirited being will become great. In the final analysis, that is *Le Roi s'amuse.* And *Lucrèce Borgia,* what about that? Take the most hideous, repulsive, complete *moral* deformity; place that where it will stand out most clearly, in the heart of a woman who enjoys every advantage of beauty and royal grandeur, making it [her moral deformity] stand out all the more; and now, mix into this moral deformity a pure sentiment, the purest that woman can feel, maternal love; inside your monster, place a mother; and the monster will become interesting, and the monster will bring tears, and this creature of terror will arouse pity, and this deformed soul will before your very eyes become almost beautiful. So, paternity sanctifying physical deformity, there you have *Le Roi s'amuse;* maternity purifying moral depravity, that is *Lucrèce Borgia.* (*OC,* 4, 654)

There exists no clearer formulation of Hugo's desire, expressed earlier in the Preface to *Cromwell,* to present in the Romantic drama characters combining sublime emotions and attitudes with immoral, even criminal tendencies and acts. What the rhetoric of this passage most clearly confirms also, for anyone interested in Hugo, is the astonishing attraction he felt for the figure of antithesis, and for dichotomous thinking in general. There is no doubt that the symmetries between the two dramas he completed during that fruitful seven-week period in 1832 do exist, as analysis will show. But whether he wrote them as Ubersfeld suggests, 'To lay siege to all that counts in the French theatre?' (*RB,* 88) of his day, remains moot.

LE ROI S'AMUSE (1832)

To understand the paradox surrounding this play and its reception both on its disastrous creation in 1832 as well as on its mainly disappointing revivals since then, we need to examine both the play itself and the political and literary pressures influencing its different audiences. Critics of Hugo have been unable to explain, for instance, the reasons why Hugo's drama has never enjoyed the success that Verdi's opera *Rigoletto,* based on

Le Roi s'amuse, continues to have. I suspect that it is more than the change of genre, from Romantic drama to grand opera, and of medium, Hugo's verse drama being replaced by Francesco Maria Piave's libretto and Verdi's music, that accounts for the contrasting fates of two works having in common the same subject and dramatic argument, the same principal characters (albeit with different names) and peripeteia. We will begin by looking at the circumstances surrounding the first production at the Comédie-Française on 22 November 1832.

It was Baron Taylor who persuaded Hugo to give his drama to the Comédie rather than to François Harel at the Porte-Saint-Martin theatre. Hugo attended the first reading in early September, already proposing, as was his right, a provisional cast: Bocage, Dumas' favourite actor, to play the King, Mlle Mars to play Blanche, with Ligier as the King's jester – Triboulet, and with Joanny as the aged M. de Saint-Vallier, and so on. He also requested (or stipulated) that three new sets should be built for the three different scenes of the action and that Ciceri should be engaged to build them. He was even, at Bocage's request, able to impose him on the production at the Comédie, only to be told by Bocage himself later that, in fact, the role of the King was too small. Hugo then gave the role to Perrier, whom the Parisian press would criticize for his lack of royal elegance and distinction. Mlle Mars also refused the role offered to her, and so Blanche was played by Mlle Anaïs. As Mme Hugo was to write, *Le Roi s'amuse* was created by the Comédie's 'second team' of actors (*VHR*, 505).

Disturbing as these changes were, more serious ones reduced the effectiveness of both the set and the costumes. Since the actors refused to pay the expenses involved, no new sets were in fact built as Lyonnet recounts sarcastically:

> Act I. 'A feast at the Louvre at night. Splendid reception rooms,' says the manuscript. A set was cobbled together out of a piece of the gothic chamber that had served in Vigny's *Othello*; a fragment of Alexandre Dumas' *Henri III*; a bit of Joseph Chénier's *Charles IX*.
> Act II. 'The most deserted recess in the Bussy cul-de-sac.' A set from *Dominique the Possessed* will do!
> Act III. 'The King's antechamber in the Louvre.' Don't we still have Desdemona's bedroom?
> Act IV. 'A deserted part of the Seine's bank below Saint-Germain.' Here, we won't trouble ourselves much about that! The 'deserted bank of the Seine' becomes a public square with a tumble-down house. On the left, a wooden frame for a parapet; and, since there has to be a backdrop in any case, we'll ask Ciceri to paint a quick daub of old Paris with a few steeples.
> Act V. Same set as Act IV.   (*PVH*, 63)

The same desire to cut down on expenses resulted in costumes 'borrowed' from earlier productions by Dumas, Vigny, and Hugo. In all, the total production expenses for staging *Le Roi s'amuse*, a drama which is supposed to display orgies at the Louvre in the brilliant Renaissance court of François I, amounted to only 7,200 francs, a fraction of the sum expended on *Hernani*, and an infinitesimal part of the expenses involved in any production of *Rigoletto*, in the nineteenth or twentieth century.

A 'second team' of actors, worn-out sets, and tired costumes. And how did the rehearsals go? Not well, for several reasons. Hugo was less than regular in his attendance, with the result that he was not available to help with historical explanations, role interpretations, and line readings. His lack of coaching proved crucial for actors who, like Ligier in particular, had to play difficult roles to an unappreciative audience. (Ligier was more accustomed to playing less controversial roles in Casimir Delavigne's plays.) Descotes, who believes Triboulet to be one of the heaviest roles in the French dramatic repertoire, explains its special demands as follows: 'The difficulty comes first from its exceptional length; then from its monotonousness. For five acts, Triboulet expresses hardly anything other than a single sentiment, paternal love. In addition, Triboulet spares himself nothing. The great scene when he hurls insults at the courtiers (3, 3) demands that he commit all his extraordinary resources: screams, sobs, laughter, supplication on his knees, even physical struggles. He has no shortage of monologues, and he dominates the whole of the last act. Actors like Beauvallet and Silvain, who have played Triboulet, have been terrified by the role. Only a single actor would probably have had the strength to bring it off: Frédérick [Lemaître]' (*DRGC*, 242). But Baron Taylor, pressured by the troupe at the Comédie, would not allow Hugo to cast his favourite actor in the role in 1832, and sadly, by the time of the play's first revival, Frédérick was already dead. Without great actors and without Hugo's active participation in the production, with mediocre sets and costumes, *Le Roi s'amuse* prepared to meet its first-night audience.

That night the whole of literary, artistic, journalistic and political Paris seems to have been inside the Comédie-Française, along with 150 of Hugo's supporters armed with free tickets. Vacher, the leader of the official claque, was there too, but he had sold off to outsiders the tickets with which he was supposed to pack the house with more supporters. All accounts of the première of *Le Roi s'amuse* insist upon two constrasting elements in the audience. Hugo's young supporters were there again, arriving early and misbehaving in the theatre but, as Mme Hugo points out, they were fewer in number than at the première of *Hernani* in 1830, and were dominated by the brilliance of the assembled public. Both Jehan Valter and Anne Ubersfeld have studied contemporary accounts and offer lists of the great names present in the theatre (*RB*, 121). They include, among writers both Romantic and neo-classical, Eugène Sue, Nerval, Musset, Nodier, Sainte-Beuve, Vigny, Balzac, Marceline Desbordes-Valmore, Béranger, Stendhal, Victor Cousin, Scribe; members of the French Academy, Soumet, Casimir Delavigne, Népomucène Lemercier; painters, Gérard and Boulanger; musicians, Liszt, Berlioz, Rossini; all of the Parisian newspaper critics, naturally; actors, Marie Dorval, Mlle Mars, Bocage, Lockroy; the comte d'Argout and his head of Cabinet, Mérimée; other dukes and duchesses, etc. In short, the whole of the *gratin* of the fashionable Saint-Germain quarter of Paris was there in force. And what did Hugo choose to serve up to the *crème de la crème* of Parisian high society?

Act 1 opens with the King taking his pleasure at an orgy (*Lucrèce Borgia* will close with an orgy, as we shall see). At the Louvre, François I, bored with Diane de Poitiers his ex-mistress, announces that he's been following his next conquest through the streets. Then, under the eyes of their husbands, he dallies with the wives of two of the courtiers, all the while complacently rejoicing to his crippled and deformed jester over his satisfaction with life and its pleasures:

> Oh, how happy I am! ...
> These women; it's charming!
> I am content! ...
> The joyful day my happy mother conceived me! ...
> To be able to do anything one wishes, to possess everything!
> Triboulet! What a pleasure to be in the world, and how good life is!
> What fortune! (1, 3)

Triboulet fulfills his duties as the King's semi-official pander, displaying his viciousness when he tries to persuade the King to put to death a courtier jealous of the King's advances to his wife. The jester's hatred of courtiers brings down on his head the curse of M. de Saint-Vallier, father of Diane de Poitiers seduced by the King, whom the old man insults. The courtiers, enraged at the jester and believing wrongly that he has a mistress, conspire to deliver her to the King's bed in order to avenge themselves on Triboulet, and thus to make François I, a victim of his lust, the dupe of their plot. There seems little so far that would upset the sophisticated audience at the Comédie in 1832.

Act 2 takes place in the cul-de-sac outside the house where Triboulet keeps his 'mistress' immured. Triboulet, the loving father, reveals that his daughter Blanche, means everything to him, deformed and scorned by the world as he is, and condemned to amuse a King he despises. Was it the suggestion of incestuous love between father and daughter that caused an uproar? Certainly Triboulet's expression of love to his daughter is ambiguous, to say the least:

> Darling child! My city, my country, my family,
> My wife, my mother, and my sister, and my daughter,
> My happiness, my riches, and my cult, and my law,
> My world is you, always you, nothing but you!   (2, 3)

Some press reports would describe Triboulet's love for his daughter as excessive (only the right-wing *Figaro* would add, however, that he should think himself lucky to be able to procure his daughter for the King [*RB*, 134]), but contemporary accounts say nothing of a disturbance in the house at this point. The disturbance came later in the act when the courtiers, with Triboulet's help, kidnap Blanche and bear her off to the Louvre. The reason for the audience's discontent must have been caused by the scene's dramatic shortcomings rather than by moral outrage. Unable to believe that Triboulet's acts should so blatantly contradict his words, they found his conduct incomprehensible. Their incomprehension was caused by a blindfold – supposed to muffle the jester's eyes and ears – that apparently slipped at the first performance. This, plus the inadequately darkened set, and the omission by Samson, playing Clément Marot, of two lines of explanation, resulted in bemusement for the audience, who saw an apparently willing Triboulet helping the courtiers to kidnap Blanche and so avenge themselves upon himself.

Act 3 presents the King's seduction of Blanche. Triboulet's frustration at being physically prevented by a body of jeering courtiers from rescuing his daughter from the King's bed finds expression in the curses and insults the furious and despairing jester heaps upon his tormentors. The act ends with his oath of vengeance against the King.

Act 4 begins with Blanche's confession that she still loves the King and still believes him faithful to her. Triboulet is able to prove to her that she is mistaken, thanks to a set which was the most complicated spatial construction in Hugo's theatre to date, as his stage direction makes clear:

> *The deserted strand next to Paris's old Tournelle Gate. On the right, a hovel wretchedly furnished, with crude pots and wooden stools; above in the garret a straw mattress can be seen through the window. The front of the hovel is turned toward the audience and is so wide open that the whole interior is on view. There's a table, a fireplace, and upstage a steep staircase leading to the garret. The wall to the left of the actors has a door that opens inwards. The wall is badly constructed, full of holes and cracks, so that it is easy to see through, to what is happening inside. There is a barred peephole in the door, which is covered on the outside by a canopy with an inn sign on top. The rest of*

the stage represents the river bank. On the left, there's an old ruined parapet, below which flows the Seine, and in which is fastened the support for the bell to call the ferry. Upstage, beyond the river, is old [i.e., sixteenth-century] Paris. (OC, 4, 591)

The hovel is clearly a voyeur's ideal and, with the arrival of the King, who is intent upon having sex with Maguelonne, the sister of Saltabadil, a hired assassin and the hovel's other permanent occupant, the audience can watch both the King's attempt at seduction and the assassin's preparations to kill him. The audience can also watch Triboulet outside the hovel as he tries to persuade Blanche to allow him to take vengeance on the King, as he pays the assassin, and examines the best way of disposing of the body in the Seine. Later, the audience sees Blanche outside, debating whether to sacrifice herself to save her unfaithful lover, and then glimpses her death on Saltabadil's knife just inside the hovel's door. But the set, complicated as it is, must be properly lit and constructed. If, as was also the case in the kidnapping scene in Act 2, darkness is not perceived by the public to be a sufficient reason preventing the appropriate character(s) from seeing what is going on – thus creating the dramatic irony necessary to the scene's suspense – the public may well find the action unconvincing. Similarly, if the set's entrances and exits do not function correctly, actions which should, in ordinary circumstances, require little suspension of disbelief become ridiculous and incomprehensible.

The final act of the première of *Le Roi s'amuse* encountered disasters on both counts, disasters made even worse by the inappropriate set cobbled together to save money. The act presents Triboulet's triumph over the dead seducer of Blanche. In fact, it is Blanche's body that is in the sack prepared for the King's corpse, and it is essential that the jester not recognize the real victim. The audience in 1832 clearly was not satisfied that the illusion was sufficiently convincing, for all accounts confirm that continuous hissing and whistling made it impossible to hear anything said in Act 5. (At one point, Ligier, as Triboulet, repeated four times to Blanche 'Do you hear me?,' to ever louder roars of derision from the audience.) The climactic dramatic reversal in Act 5 occurs when Triboulet, having exulted in a long monologue over the body of his 'dead' master, is preparing to throw the body into the Seine. He suddenly hears the King leaving the hovel singing the song about woman's fickleness that Verdi was to turn into La donna è mobile. At this point, Hugo's stage direction is precise and efficient, indicating clearly the contrasting action going on at different parts of the stage: '*He takes the sack by one end and drags it to the water's edge. Just as he gets it onto the parapet, someone cautiously opens the door of the house. Maguelonne comes out, looks anxiously around her, gestures like someone who can't see anything, goes back in, and reappears a moment later with the King, to whom, using signs, she explains that there is no one there and that he can get away. She goes back in, closing the door, and the King crosses the river bank in the direction indicated by Maguelonne. It's the very moment when Triboulet is getting ready to slide the sack into the Seine* (*OC*, 4, 613). Apparently, on the night, the door through which the King was to make his exit was blocked, so that he had to exit upstage, without passing close enough to Triboulet to make convincing his recognition by the frantic jester. Mme Hugo, who was there, says that it sounded as if some reveller totally unconnected with the action onstage were reeling home much the worse for drink. She continues: '*The tumult became inexpressible Triboulet stands next to his daughter's corpse, amid lightning flashes; there is a hurricane onstage just as there is in the jester's heart; the rising tide of laughter, of booing and whistles covers his paternal sobbing; the onstage storm is only a soft murmur compared to the storm in the auditorium* (*VHR*, 508).

We should remember that the public at the Comédie that night included, as well as Hugo's enemies, 150 of his friends, and the most distinguished writers and critics of the day. No conspiracy theory will explain this audience's rejection of Hugo's latest drama. But sloppy preparation, poor execution and the impracticable staging demands made by the plot's melodramatic action, and most importantly, the emphasis Hugo places in the play on its grotesque and squalid elements, may well do so. Such appears to have been Hugo's opinion, at any rate, because, after the catastrophic evening at the theatre, he went home to make cuts, almost entirely in the grotesque details of Triboulet's characterization and language (*RB*, 130). But he burned the midnight oil in vain: the play was not to have another chance to prove its merits for fifty years. The next morning Jouslin de La Salle, stage manager at the Comédie, informed Hugo that the Ministry was suspending the play *sine die* for offences against public morality. The following day, 24 November 1832, the Minister banned the play outright. Hugo's immediate response was to take his case to the bar of public opinion. In order to do so, since he could not sue the Minister, he was obliged to sue the Comédie-Française for breaking the contract he had signed with Baron Taylor guaranteeing the play's run. The result of the trial, at the commercial court which judged such cases, was a foregone conclusion: the court declared its incompetence to try political disputes involving government censorship, and Hugo was ordered to pay the legal costs. But before the court handed down its verdict on 2 January 1833, Hugo had published *Le Roi s'amuse* with a Preface in which he had already presented his response to the government's treatment of the play.

In the Preface, Hugo quite rightly points out that since the July Revolution of 1830 had abolished censorship, the government had acted illegally in banning his play. He quotes from the Charter of Rights, amended in 1830, which re-established freedom of the press, and which asserted that 'Censorship can never be re-imposed' (*OC*, 4, 524). He then goes on to refute the three offences alleged against the play: it was immoral, it contained a political attack on Louis-Philippe, and it was unacceptable at the state-funded Comédie-Française because of its scandalously inferior liter-ary qualities. Hugo proves quite easily that the play's morality or immoral-ity depends entirely upon the view of the critic speaking: his own moral reading is, in fact, no more nor less convincing than his opponents' asser-tion of the play's immorality. Unfortunately, however, his proof does noth-ing to explain the play's failure on the night: the distinguished audience was hardly expecting to witness a morality play.

As to the criticism that the play, about a sixteenth-century king, could be read as a criticism of Louis-Philippe – who, incidentally, only three days before the première of Hugo's play, had survived an assassination attempt – he simply denies it. Despite his adoption of this rather cavalier attitude to his political critics, it is not difficult to agree with Hugo that the Minister's reading of the line used by the government to ban the play as directly defamatory to royalty, represents an interpretation that finds little support in the text. The line occurs in Act 3, when Triboulet, distraught at his daughter's predicament and physically prevented from saving her by the courtiers, screams at them: 'Your mothers prostituted themselves to their lackeys! / You're all bastards!' Hugo's political critics claimed that the line contained an allusion to Louis-Philippe's mother, notorious at the time for her affairs with the royal servants. In the absence of any pragmatic motive – Hugo had no political ambitions or associations with the Republican ene-mies of Louis-Philippe – it is difficult to see what he could gain personally from such an inept attack on royalty. But what about Hugo's rejection of the reigning literary codes in France? It is here, in the area of literary debate about genre, versification, dramatic structure and so on that we will find the real reasons for the play's failure to win a regular place in the Romantic repertoire in 1832 and since.

The case concerning dramatic *genre* is simply stated: *Le Roi s'amuse* is not a Romantic drama at all but rather an 'anti-tragedy' which, although it retains all the formal markers of neo-classical tragedy, deliberately over-turns them, in the process making them ridiculous. It was the derision Hugo poured upon the conventions of neo-classical tragedy that, accord-ing to this view, enraged the elite audience in 1832. Demonstrably, Hugo deliberately took each formal element of tragedy, and distorted it. The play appears to be a conventional historical tragedy in five acts and in verse about a glorious King of France; its characteristic rhetorical form is the dramatic tirade, both monological when spoken directly to the audience by the principal characters, or dialogical when it takes the form of alternat-ing diatribes addressed by the characters among themselves; and the uni-ties are, on the whole, loosely respected, with some changes of scene within Paris and with a month passing between Acts 3 and 4. But Hugo took the French neo-classical tragic genre turned it upside down. He deliberately chose an anti-classical hero figure as protagonist. Conventionally the King should be the hero, but here François I, in his various disguises of student and army officer, plays the role of common seducer, profiting from his position to have his royal way with his subjects' wives. An audience seeking an alternative hero to the King, will not find one in Act 1, where Triboulet shows himself as immoral as he is physically grotesque. As the compliant procurer of women for his master and as the courtiers' malevolent enemy, he can hardly be considered a 'hero' in the neo-classical understanding of the term. M. de Saint-Vallier, who has the nobility and who finds himself in the tragic predicament of a neo-classical hero, takes no further part in the action after hurling his curse at Triboulet. (The dramatic symmetry, with the betrayed noble father's outburst preparing the low-born jester's loss of his daughter, is striking.) Nor does Triboulet redeem himself morally throughout the rest of the play. Far from seeking moral redemption, he tries to have his daughter's seducer, François I, murdered by a hired assassin. His paternal love merely conflicts with his moral unworthiness, just as his abject pleading to his enemies for his daughter places him outside the conventions of tragedy, as Ubersfeld explains:

> The aesthetic code of tragedy is accompanied by a code governing propriety whose meaning refers not so much to morality as to aesthetics. There exists a 'moral' aesthetics of tragedy, very different from the moral aesthetics of melodrama, but just as compelling: the tragic hero can, without shame, be cruel or treacherous; he cannot be cowardly or frivolous, nor can he whine. Now it is precisely because the characters of Le Roi s'amuse are living contraventions of the classical code ... that Triboulet's ignoble malevolence, or the King's futile behaviour prevent them from becoming tragic figures. It will come as no surprise to see the public wholeheartedly applaud only once [in 1832] and that is for Saint-Vallier's tirade, a tragic hero who conforms to their expectations with regard to tragedy but who is scoffed at and then disposed of. Such a reversal of tragic characters can only cause a scandal. (RB, 512)

Ubersfeld's analysis once again convincingly explains the public's first reaction to Le Roi s'amuse, but it does little to explain why the play has failed since Hugo's time.

Her later remark that the language in this play reflects the characters' inability to act or to change their destinies takes the problem out of the context of early nineteenth-century squabbles about the overturning by Romantic authors of the conventions of neo-classical tragedy. In fact, Le Roi s'amuse may best be described as a dramatization of rhetorical stasis, with the lack of action producing frustration in all the characters except the King. And frustration is what the audience – unable to achieve lasting sympathy with the principal characters, or to find catharsis in the accomplished action – is likely to feel the play. The only decisive act, i.e., one that produces a change in the unjust political and social situation presented, can hardly be defended on logical grounds. The curse laid upon Triboulet by Saint-Vallier belongs in the world of superstition and folktale. That it forms the 'necessary' cause producing the 'divine' retribution visited upon the unfortunate jester remains unquestioned, however, by Triboulet or by the courtiers present at the confrontation between the vengeful father grieving for his daughter's dishonour and the King's fool and pander. In all other cases, the logic of events depends upon the historical inequalities inherent in the hierarchical nature of French sixteenth-century society, as dramatized by Hugo. Since the King is clearly above the law, his subjects are obliged to stand idly by while he seduces their wives and daughters. Not only above the law, the King enjoys every advantage of youth, beauty, wealth, and power over his less fortunate entourage. M. de Cossé's frustration in Act 1 derives, for instance, from his inability to prevent the King's kissing his wife, even in his presence (1, 2). And Saint-Vallier, powerless to prevent the King from seducing his daughter, cannot obtain justice, even when he accuses the King of his crime; the King reacts by sending him to the Bastille (1, 5; 3, 4). The courtiers, frustrated in their desire to punish Triboulet for his malevolent attempts to persuade the King to exercise his absolute power against them, can think of no better way of avenging themselves on the jester than by acting as procurers for the King (1, 1–4; 2, 5). Triboulet's desire to preserve his daughter from the court's depravity is thwarted in part by his own clumsiness in allowing the King to enter Blanche's garden and by Mme Bérarde's avarice, which the unscrupulous King is happy to exploit. His plan to protect her from the King is frustrated by the love Blanche feels for the young, handsome Francis I (2, 4). But the most dramatic demonstration of frustration occurs in Act 3, scene 3, when the courtiers physically prevent Triboulet from saving Blanche from the King by blocking – with their own bodies – his way to the royal bed. The resulting *mêlée* perfectly illustrates, at the heart of the drama, how paternal love is frustrated by the cynical abuse of royal power and by the subservience of its feudal supporters. In all of these scenes, an audience, unable itself to affect the course of events, of course, must watch the characters' failure to accomplish any meaningful improvement in their position, however merited. On the contrary, the audience must watch as the King, after exploiting to the full the advantages of his person and position, escapes scot-free, thanks to Blanche's self-sacrifice (4, 5). If, as seems likely, audiences seek relief from their frustration, they may well turn with indignation against the playwright.

What remains as catharsis for an audience is mere parody, bathos, and derision. Triboulet's ascent of the throne from which he orders the court-iers to leave him alone with Blanche, *an order which they obey* – as if his tem-porary occupancy of the seat of majesty confers upon him its concomitant powers – parodies the real power structure and value system of the court (3, 4). Similarly, the jester's long monologue of triumph over the 'King's' corpse, provokes derision because the audience is better informed than he; and his discourse then collapses into the bathos attendant upon his pathetic attempts to bring Blanche back to life (5, 4, 5).

Not a single positive result is achieved then by any character's efforts, other than those of the King. And the King, in taking his pleasures, does so in flagrant contradiction of what Ubersfeld has called the 'moral aesthet-ics' of tragedy. Modern audiences who in 1912 and 1965 had the oppor-tunity of seeing *Le Roi s'amuse*, free from the polemics accompanying the Romantic-Classical confrontation characteristic of the 1830s, expressed their own disappointment with the play.[3] It seems probable that their reac-tion derived from the drama's inability to provoke sympathy or to achieve catharsis, being, despite its abundant action, a vehicle that expresses the total frustration of aspiration, whether moral or political. But the story of *Le Roi s'amuse* does not end with the various French receptions of the play. In fact, Hugo's drama inspired at least three dramatic works, each one carefully adapted to fit local social and political preconceptions.

By far the most successful of these, Verdi's *Rigoletto*, premiered at Ven-ice's Teatro La Fenice on 11 March 1851. Verdi had had some difficulty in persuading the Austrian authorities to accept 'a singing hunchback' but, using much the same arguments as those Hugo presented in his Preface to *Le Roi s'amuse*, successfully argued in favour of the Romantic grotesque. Verdi had no problems with the authorities comparable to those encoun-tered by Hugo, however. The reason was simple. By changing the name and rank of King François I to the unspecified Duke of Mantua, presum-ably some member of the Gonzaga family who, by 1851 were forgotten by most of the audience,[4] Verdi took his opera out of the arena where a government could allege that a drama about past royal behaviour was an allegory of the present incumbent's beliefs, actions, or associations. All the other elements of Hugo's play, apart from name changes, remain, and the action of *Rigoletto* is just as cynically dominated by the powerful duke, served by his courtier-procurers and by his unfortunate jester whose daughter he seduces. Hugo's Romantic credo concerning the necessary mingling of sublime and grotesque is fully respected, with scenes of orgy, love arias, and Rigoletto's despair on the riverbank succeeding one another as in the original. All of this has been applauded since 1851, and *Rigoletto* is revived constantly, whereas Hugo's play is virtually forgotten.

Another adaptation of Hugo's drama, much less well known than *Rigo-*

letto, was Tom Taylor's play, entitled *The Fool's Revenge*, in which Edwin Booth starred with great success as Bertucchio shortly before his brother, John Wilkes Booth, assassinated Abraham Lincoln in Washington's Ford's Theatre in 1865. And more recently, Richard Eyre, Director of London's Royal National Theatre, staged there in 1996 *The Prince's Play*. In 1990 Eyre had enjoyed great success directing at the National a production of Shakespeare's *Richard III*, in which the medieval tyrant strutted the stage in a clearly Nazi-inspired, 1930s' fascist uniform. Eyre carefully made all political allusions in the play conform with his condemnation of Hitlerian fascism and of Mosley's English variety. In 1996, however, it was not fascism that Eyre and Tony Harrison, the adaptor of Hugo's drama, chose to attack. Rather, it was the British royal family, in the person of 'HRH' the Prince of Wales, Queen Victoria's eldest son, the future Edward VII. Eyre's production came after a decade of sensational revelations in the British newspapers concerning the sex lives of various members of the British royal family, including most notably, of course, the present 'HRH,' Charles, Prince of Wales, and his estranged wife Princess Diana. The reviewer in the Tory *Daily Telegraph* did not fail to point to the historical parallel: 'As if the Queen didn't have enough on her plate as she celebrated her 70th birthday, the Royal National Theatre has now turned virulently republican.'[5]

In Tony Harrison's verse translation/adaptation, the action of Hugo's *Le Roi s'amuse* is transferred to the late-Victorian London of the Café Royal, of Pall Mall and its exclusive men's clubs, and of West End music-halls, but also to the East End, haunted at the time by Jack the Ripper, whom 'HRH' (the future Edward VII) has already been suspected of being. Hugo's drama of an authoritarian ruler raping the daughter of his hunchbacked jester (in Harrison's version, 'Scotty Scott, the Comic,' a Glaswegian music-hall comedian), is translated into the decadent, *fin de siècle* world of 'fillies and fizz,' or drunken lechery. Hugo's sixteenth-century French courtiers find counterparts in the nineteenth-century British aristocracy when, for instance, Scotty Scott advises the predatory prince on the best method for seducing his courtiers' wives and daughters:

> ... He can get his Garter
> You get both his wife's. A gentlemanly barter!
> Or when he dismisses royal courtiers who would:
> ... charter
> Their own children out to get a Garter.[6]

Scotty is throughout the voice of republican conscience, determined to bring down the monarchy that has destroyed his daughter. Most striking is

Harrison's identification of the present British royal family as the target of the jester's vengeance:

> Once a Windsor's dumped into the Thames
> all dynasties look to their diadems![7]

It is immaterial to complain, as did several London reviewers on the play's opening,[8] that Scotty's identification of 'HRH' with the 'House of Windsor' is clearly anachronistic (the British royal family having adopted the name only in 1917, during a wave of extreme anti-German feeling occasioned by British losses in the First World War). For an audience, the name functions semiotically despite Harrison's rhetorical use of anachronism, and the fallacy remains imperceptible to many, in the absence of a learned footnote.

Although unlikely to disturb the British establishment's reigning icons, Hugo's drama, in this ingenious adaptation, was brilliantly acted by Ken Stott as Scotty Scott, and was imaginatively and excitingly staged by Richard Eyre and his set designer, Bob Crowley. The lavish National production, complete with riverside hovel looking like a stranded hulk submerged in a thunderous rainstorm that flooded the stage, would have delighted Victor Hugo, whose preference for spectacle over recitation informs all of his Romantic dramas. Eyre's production clearly indicates that adaptations that both derive from and generate local relevance are more likely to appeal to modern non-French audiences, for whom French historical personages like François I and his courtiers may well seem too remote to provoke emotional involvement.

LUCRÈCE BORGIA (1833)

The Borgias are the House of Atreus in the Middle Ages.[9]

In December 1832, Harel, director of the Porte-Saint-Martin Theatre, approached Hugo for permission to stage the prose drama Hugo held in reserve. He was able to offer as principal actors two of the most celebrated stars of his theatre, Mlle George, who had just triumphed as Marguerite de Bourgogne in Dumas' drama, *La Tour de Nesles*, and Hugo's favourite Romantic lead, Frédérick Lemaître. After Hugo's reading of the play in Mlle George's apartment in the theatre, Harel suggested, and Hugo accepted, that the play, then entitled *Un Souper à Ferrare* should be called *Lucrèce Borgia* so as to highlight the principal role. (Mme Hugo suggests that Harel wished it to appear thus that Hugo had, in fact, written the drama for the female star of the Porte-Saint-Martin.) Lemaître, after some hesitation, chose the role of Gennaro, rather than that of Don Alphonse d'Este. His biographer explains why: 'Alphonse d'Este,' he said, 'is a sure and brilliant part. Its effects are all concentrated in one act and will carry the actor who plays it. Anybody could make a success of it. Gennaro, on the other hand, is a difficult part. The last scene is especially dangerous with that terrible line: 'Ah, so you are my aunt!' Consequently I chose Gennaro.'[10] The actor's familiarity with his public's sense of the ridiculous enabled him to see that Gennaro's mistaken identification of his mother at the climax of the drama would strike them as hilarious, not so much for the mistake itself, but because of the term 'aunt,' a title, says Mme Hugo, which 'lacks nobility' (*VHR*, 528).

All accounts of the rehearsals, which lasted throughout January 1833, emphasize the collaboration between Hugo and Frédérick as directors. Hugo insisted, for example, that the set constructed for the orgy in Act 5, which he thought looked like a café, should look more like a 'gilded tomb' (*VHR*, 519), since it was there that seven characters would die. Frédérick occupied himself with directing the actors in their roles, including his co-star, Mlle George. Again Mme Hugo provides the details: 'M. Frédérick Lemaître, who had the least need of advice, was the most amenable to the author's suggestions ... He did everything to help his comrades, saying: 'No, that isn't it. Look, try saying it this way' – and giving the right intonation. Sometimes, to show them what he meant, he would act their scene for them, making us regret that he could not play every character in the drama' (*OC*, 4, 1214). Only Frédérick's eccentric ideas on costume, Mme Hugo tells us, did not please Hugo.

The première was Hugo's greatest theatrical triumph, despite some potential disasters. Frédérick, for instance, saved the actors from embarrassment in Act 1, as Baldick tells us: 'Gennaro is supposed to throw away his sash in anger on discovering that it is a present from Lucrezia, and as Frédérick was doing this the sash caught on his sword. Someone giggled, and for a moment the fate of the play hung in the balance. Then, with the presence of mind for which he was already famous, Frédérick drew his sword, tore the sash free, and in a combination of real and simulated fury trampled it underfoot. The audience, quick as all nineteenth-century audiences were to appreciate an ingenious subterfuge, applauded him enthusiastically.[11] There were one or two minor bouts of hissing, such as when the audience realized that Lucrezia was Gennaro's mother in the love scene in Act 1, part 1, scene 4. But the play's suspense gripped them from the beginning of Act 2, when Gennaro risks death at the hands of the jealous Duke, lasting until the climactic scene of matricide at the drama's conclusion.

It was not Frédérick's triumph alone, however. Praise was general for the production, including the sets, particularly the Venetian terrazza with gondolas and view of the city in Act 1 and the final banquet scene. Mlle George had in Lucrezia the most successful role of her career, playing her in the manner of the great classical tragediennes, according to Descotes: 'She conferred on the character the grandeur of the heroines in the classical repertoire. She brought out the two sides of Lucrezia, passing brilliantly from "tender to terrible pathos." She was subtle, feline in her dispute with the Duke to save her son's life, moving in her suffering when she read Gennaro's letter. In Act 2, her gestures and facial expressions showed her terror when she discovered that the culprit was Gennaro, and when she poured the poison for her son to take. The fifth act was her especial triumph. Her entrance produced a great effect: "You are in my house!" The role was to remain one of her best' (DRGC, 251). Later in 1833 Hugo himself confirmed the audience's judgment by one unambiguous proof of his satisfaction: he offered her the role of Bloody Mary in Marie Tudor.

Even the Parisian press was, for the first time in Hugo's dramatic career, mostly favourable. No critics were vehemently against the play, being unwilling, presumably, to take issue with a great popular success. Unfavourable reviewers described his drama as merely a prose melodrama good only for the popular audience at the Porte-Saint-Martin theatre. But Hugo's first-night audience had included many distinguished Parisian theatre-goers as well as Hugo's friends and young Romantic supporters. George Sand, for instance, wrote to Hugo thirty-seven years later to say that, in 1833, she had been so moved by the suspense in Act 3 that she had gripped the hand of her neighbour in the next seat, who turned out to be Bocage, the Romantic actor. And, in her letter on the play's revival in 1870, she wrote to Hugo, still exiled at that time in Guernsey: 'Lucrèce Borgia is perhaps of all your theatre the most powerful and elevated work. If Ruy Blas is successful and brilliant drama, the idea behind Lucrezia is more pathetic, more gripping, and more deeply human.'[12]

So much for the criticism that Hugo's drama was merely a popular prose melodrama. Such a view seems difficult to sustain, not so much because of what Sand saw as the Aeschylean intensity of the tragic events which involve the members of the same noble family. A more convincing proof comes from the play's rejection of the melodrama's conventional happy ending which would see the hero reintegrated into bourgeois society. Hugo in fact wrote three endings, each of which engineers the final anagnorisis quite differently. In the first, Gennaro, after stabbing his mother to death, discovers her identity from the bloodstained packet containing his letters that she carries over her heart. In the second, Lucrezia herself shows him the letters, explains why she had to abandon him (her enemies would have killed him), and, in a great love scene, excuses his act by saying it occurred because of her sin. Hugo preferred to use his third ending, less likely to cause scandal. At the behest of Maffio, his brother-in-arms, Gennaro kills Lucrezia to punish her for poisoning their comrades. Lucrezia has only time to gasp out her relationship to Gennaro as the curtain falls.[13]

One remark made by a Parisian columnist in *La Mode* concerning Hugo's developing politico-social beliefs is less easy to dismiss than the categorization of the play as melodrama, since it describes, albeit hyperbolically, what remained a fundamental ideological principle throughout Hugo's career as dramatist: 'His dramatic system rests on this idea: noble, elevated sentiments [are held by] low-born, poor people, and low, shameful, and criminal sentiments by characters who are the most respected and eminent members of the social order.'[14] The exaggeration, characteristic of political polemic, resides in the neat antithesis between the two 'sides' presented, one being totally bad, the other perfectly good. In fact, to look no further than *Lucrèce Borgia* itself, the play in question in the quoted remark, not all of the low-born characters express noble sentiments. Rustighello, the Duke's henchman, for example, contents himself with expressing his willingness to kill Gennaro and with seeking excuses for his having failed to do so (2, 1, 1; 2, 2, 1). Nor do all the nobles express only low ideas. Maffio, for instance, professes the highest regard for friendship, hardly a shameful or criminal sentiment. That this negative view was expressed by a right-wing newspaper is natural, however, a fact that Hugo's left-wing supporters would see as redounding to his credit, for he was giving a voice to those who, in the history of the French theatre had had (*pace* Molière) little enough attention before Diderot and Beaumarchais. Nevertheless, Hugo's political views would hardly facilitate his conquest of the Parisian theatre, a consequence he willingly accepted. For the moment however, between February and June 1833, Hugo's triumph remained unspoiled. His play earned him some 10,800 francs, an enormous sum for the time and one he would never attain again in the theatre.

All critics commend Hugo for the skill with which he creates suspense in *Lucrèce Borgia*, finding in this skill a principal reason for the play's success. If we analyse the play, we see that this drama ranks first in importance among Hugo's 'fables of identity': from the first scene to the final curtain line, Gennaro remains in ignorance of his real identity. These are plays whose dramatic development depends upon the exchange of information concerning the identity of a principal character or the true nature of a relationship. The exchange takes place (usually at different speeds) both onstage and between the stage and the house. Thus characters may remain unaware of who they are, or to whom they are related, and as a result are unaware of the real nature or probable consequences of their actions, while the audience, better informed thanks to a barrage of dramatic devices, achieves *anagnorisis* long before the characters in question. In such a situation, an audience is easily able to foresee the potentially tragic outcome of actions which, to the characters held in ignorance of all the facts surrounding their acts or identity, seem totally innoccuous or even favourable to their cause. The kind of suspense we are here discussing results from the use of dramatic irony, as we have already seen in a number of Hugo's Romantic dramas. The importance of the devices which create the suspense in *Lucrèce Borgia* demands that we look closely at their functioning.

As I have said, the action of the play is possible only if Gennaro remains ignorant until the final curtain that he is Lucrezia's son. At the same time, the *dénouement* is successful only if the audience realizes, fairly early on, the truth about this relationship. Among the devices allowing for both the creation of suspicion in the audience's minds and the simultaneous maintenance of a state of ignorance in that of Gennaro are various kinds of proleptic irony employed during the exposition. In the very first scene, for instance, we learn from Maffio that, although Gennaro knows neither of his parents, his friends 'do not doubt that he is of noble birth.' And Maffio adds, little knowing how mistaken later events will prove him to be: 'You are lucky enough to be called simply Gennaro, to belong to no one; you don't drag along behind you any of the often hereditary fatalities attached to historic names' (1, 1, 1). Gennaro, in an act that foregrounds the dramatic irony resulting from his ignorance, then goes to sleep onstage while Beppo tells the story of the Borgias, including the news that Lucrezia has had an incestuous child by her brother Jean (1, 1, 1). In scene 2, Gennaro, still asleep, misses a curious revelation made by Lucrezia to her henchman Gubetta. Despite being known for her jealousy in love, and although in Venice to follow Gennaro, the new object of her love, she expresses only satisfaction on learning that he loves someone else, the much younger Fiammetta. Faced with this riddle, an audience may well begin to question the nature of Lucrezia's 'love' for Gennaro. Then in scene 4, when Lucrezia learns from Gennaro that he loves his mother more than her, once again she expresses only satisfaction rather than jealousy, particularly when he reads as proof of his devotion to his mother from one of her own letters to him. And later Lucrezia, having been thus in the happy position of knowing better than Gennaro who it is exactly that he loves, must bear the brunt of his hatred against the 'monster' he knows only as Lucrezia Borgia. At that point, she once more hints, when he declares that his mother is vastly superior to her in moral matters: 'Your mother, Gennaro! You see her differently perhaps from what she is. What would you say if she was only a guilty woman like me?' (2, 1, 6). By this time, enough suspicion of the true relationship between Lucrezia and Gennaro should have arisen in the audience's minds for them to appreciate the multiple ironies caused by the mystery surrounding Gennaro's identity.

If they have worked out this mystery, mistakes made by other uninformed characters will also achieve their effects. The Duke's suspicion that Gennaro is Lucrezia's lover (2, 1, 4), a mistake caused by Rustighello's misinterpretation of Lucrezia's pursuit of Gennaro in Venice, awakens the audience's fear for her at the unjustified accusation. And Gennaro's last mistake concerning the identity of his 'aunt,' the evil woman he intends to kill (3, 3), only tightens the screw of suspense by making the audience fear his hatred for the Borgia poisoner will prove tragic for his mother.

Suspense also rises early in the play, when we are present at the interview between the Duke and Rustighello at which Gennaro's death is plotted with a poisoned cup and drawn sword (2, 1, 1). But the most successful use of dramatic irony in *Lucrèce Borgia* occurs in Act 2, part 1, scene 2. In a passion, Lucrezia demands the instant death of the perpetrator of the insulting *apheresis* which, by suppressing the initial letter of her name affixed to the outer wall of her palace in Ferrara, has turned 'BORGIA' into 'ORGIA.' Throughout the scene, the Duke, like the audience, but for different reasons, savours the irony of a situation in which his ill-informed and impetuous mother digs a grave for Gennaro, the son whose life she is devoted to preserving. When she eventually learns the truth, she finds herself obliged to reverse herself totally and must find answers to every objection raised by the Duke against freeing Gennaro. Thus, for instance, when he mentions the sacredness of a ruler's word, Lucrezia cynically retorts: 'That's good for telling the people,' a tactic which rebounds against her when she tries swearing that Gennaro is not her lover: 'Don't swear,' says the Duke. 'Oaths are good for the people' (2, 1, 4). Once again the audience savours the dramatic irony of the situation, emphasized here by the Duke's sarcasm. So little convinced is he of Lucrezia's good faith that he forces her, in his presence, to pour the poison that Gennaro is to drink. The audience, having received no information about Lucrezia's knowledge and possession of antidotes, fears the worst for Gennaro.

As well as shaping the dialogue, dramatic irony governs other important aspects of the action of Hugo's dramas. In all of his plays, for instance, masks and disguises play a principal role in regulating the strategic exchange of information regarding the true, and false, identities of the characters. The abundance and frequency of such vestimentary devices causes Ubersfeld to call Hugo 'the dramatist of masks' (*RB*, 171, n50), and Jean Gaudon to compare Hugo's use of masks to his affection for dramatic asides, the oral equivalent of a character's act of unmasking (*VHT*, 61–3). In the first act of *Lucrèce Borgia*, set in Venice during the *mardi gras* Carnival at which all the characters either wear or carry masks, thus hiding or exposing their identities at moments chosen strategically by the dramatist, Lucrezia, by removing her mask to weep over the sleeping Gennaro (1, 1,

2), betrays her identity to two black-masked figures who recognize her and assume she is weeping over her lover. Lucrezia's error in unmasking later provokes the Duke's jealous obsession with killing her son. As the annotator of the play in the Massin edition puts it: 'The whole drama is in this heart which needs to be masked and whose tears make the mask impossible' (*OC*, 4, 682). In this case, the cynical use of masks during a carnival to allow for sexual licence between unidentified partners, a custom Jeppo describes as 'Masked face, naked heart' (1, 2, 3), is overturned.

Other means of regulating the exchange of information among characters, while keeping the audience fully apprised of the meaning of events, include characters hidden onstage who listen to 'secret' conversations as a result of which they plan future action. Rustighello frequently plays spy for his master, but nowhere perhaps more sinisterly than in Act 2, part 1, scene 1, when, from his hiding place he listens to the Duke's conversations with Lucrezia and with Gennaro, having previously received instructions to intervene by killing the latter, if the Duke gives him the appropriate signal. A different type of effect, less productive of suspense but more obviously ironic, occurs when Lucrezia, an unseen witness of the conversation between Gennaro and his friends, sees her son destroy the gift she had sent him, upon learning that it came from the hated Lucrezia Borgia (1, 2, 3). (The device illustrates ironically the popular axiom that listeners do not hear good of themselves.) In the case of a character who 'goes to sleep' onstage, as does Gennaro in the first two scenes of Act 1, the audience must decide, on the basis of that character's subsequent ignorance or knowledge of the matters discussed, whether (s)he was merely feigning sleep, that is to say, whether the actor then was 'acting' two roles at the same time. This case of meta-theatrical *double entendre*, in which actions or expressions may be read differently, for example, by characters and audience, informs situations where, according to D.C. Muecke 'the victim say[s] quite innocently or accept[s] in all innocence something which is true in another sense than he imagines' (*CI*, 106).

Muecke also mentions anticipatory and allegorical ironies, which he explains as follows: 'There is a subtler kind of dramatic irony which may be found in Shakespeare and which has recently been noticed in Racine as well. Here the characters unknowingly employ images and allusions that will be actualized in some subsequent scene' (*CI*, 106). One such allegorical incident occurs at the orgy in the final act of *Lucrèce Borgia*, when the five young lords, unaware that they have drunk the poison prepared for them by Lucrezia, suddenly hear, as they listen to Gubetta sing a drinking song, the voices of monks chanting in counterpoint the *De profundis*. The audience has already been alerted in previous scenes to Lucrezia's skill with poisons (1, 2, 1; 2, 1, 6) and to her determination to avenge herself on

Gennaro's five young friends (1, 2, 1; 2, 1, 6) who, in telling him her true identity and crimes against them had turned Gennaro's interest in her into hatred (1, 1, 5). Suspicion is likely to harden into certainty when they hear Gubetta in his song address Saint Peter, the keeper of Heaven's gate, and when the monks enter the orgy singing the chant for the dead. Only the victims remain in ignorance of their fate.

In *Lucrèce Borgia*, Hugo's rhetorical exploitation of dramatic irony culminates in the catharsis provoked by both the revenge plot and by the *anagnorisis* of Lucrezia, tragic victim both of her unsavoury reputation and of her son's perverted moralism. Blinded by his ignorance of his mother's flawed nature, both loving and vengeful, Gennaro is condemned to repeat her bloody act of vengeance which, of course, rebounds against him. Only Hugo's audience gets to anticipate the irony of her fate before the final curtain and, so Hugo hoped, if we are to believe his Preface, to draw a moral lesson from his drama. What exactly this moral message may be, however, remains unclear.

Victor Hugo had another reason besides his theatrical success to remember with affection the production of *Lucrèce Borgia* in 1883 as a period of triumph. It was during the rehearsals for the play that he auditioned and offered the role of the Princess Negroni to a young actress, famous for her beauty but whose reputation was a little soiled by her domestic circumstances. Juliette Drouet, the young actress in question, had been born in Fougères, near Rennes, Brittany, in 1806. At nineteen, she became the mistress of the sculptor James Pradier, bearing him a daughter, Claire, in 1826. Sent by Pradier, without training or protectors, to Brussels to become an actress, she escaped the boards by leaving for Germany and Italy with Pinelli, an engraver. When his financial means ran out, Juliette returned to Brussels where she met Harel, who brought her back to Paris. There she made her debut at the Porte-Saint-Martin theatre in 1830. Renowned as the most beautiful actress in Paris, she was soon surrounded again by admirers, becoming in April 1832 the mistress of Alphonse Karr, journalist and man of letters. Once again she chose badly, at least from a financial point of view. Karr's debts prevented him from keeping her in the style to which she was becoming accustomed, and Polycarpe Charles Séchan, with whom she enjoyed a brief but happy liaison that same year was no more financially reliable. At this juncture, Anatole Demidoff, a wealthy man about town, installed her in a luxurious appartment in Paris, taking her also to Florence to visit his palazzo. On her return to Paris, she was invited by Harel to audition for the role of the Princess Negroni in Victor Hugo's *Lucrèce Borgia*.

On 6 February 1833 Hugo, attracted by her beauty, declared his passion to Juliette. He seems at that point to have been living a celibate life since

Mme Hugo had broken off sexual relations after the birth of Adèle, their second daughter, in 1830. He found in Juliette a mistress who, despite his own infidelities, remained faithful to him for fifty years, until her death in 1883. She acted as his muse, amanuensis, travelling companion, confidante, and lover throughout his life, sharing his exile in Jersey and Guernsey, where she took small apartments or houses near where he lived with his wife Adèle and the children. But all that was far in the future in 1833, and Hugo was to have more immediate problems as he promoted Juliette to play an important role in his next drama.

6. Hugo's Campagin against Social Injustice, 1833–1835: *Marie Tudor* and *Angelo, tyran de Padoue*

In my bedroom I have a portrait of Mary Tudor, Bloody Mary. She was a jealous Queen, a true daughter of Henry VIII, and her bedroom, like her father's, opened out directly onto the scaffold.'[1]

The factors that reduced the success of *Marie Tudor*, at its première on 6 November 1833 seem to have been at least as much personal and sentimental as literary or political. In order to understand why Harel, the director of the Porte-Saint-Martin Theatre, has been found guilty – by such prominent modern scholars of Hugo as Ubersfeld and Laster – of heading a cabal whose aim was to engineer the failure of Hugo's career as a boulevard dramatist, we need to look at the context in which the play was written, rehearsed and performed.

At the end of April 1833, when *Lucrèce Borgia* was still earning impressive receipts at his theatre, Harel suddenly, and without prior consultation with Hugo, took the play off the bill. In the face of Hugo's protests, Harel simply refused an explanation. To Hugo's retort that it was the last of his plays that Harel would produce at the Porte-Saint-Martin Theatre, Harel merely needed to remind him that he had contracted to offer Harel one more play, in return for the extra expenses incurred on the sets and costumes of *Lucrèce*. High words followed, with the upshot being that Hugo found himself challenged by his manager to a duel. Although the matter was smoothed over without violence – Harel replaced *Lucrèce* on the playbill for a time and Hugo did fulfill his contract – the reasons why Harel withdrew Hugo's successful play in the first place are far from clear.

This period of Hugo's career as dramatist is obscured by several personal and professional matters which involved the three couples who should have had a common interest in working together on the various productions in which they were engaged at the Porte-Saint-Martin Theatre. Harel and Mlle George, the manager and female star at this boulevard theatre, counted Victor Hugo and Alexandre Dumas as their most successful playwrights. Among the actresses aspiring to play principal female roles alongside Mlle George (Marie Dorval was to join the troupe at the Comédie-Française in November 1833) were Hugo's new mistress, Juliette Drouet, and Dumas' mistress and future wife, Ida Ferrier. Since February 1833 Hugo had taken Juliette Drouet's dramatic career under his supervision, while Dumas, naturally, wished to better Ida's career prospects at his favourite theatre. As may be imagined, professional jealousies abounded among the three actresses, with Juliette, by far the weakest and least experienced, falling victim to the gibes of her two colleagues and of their allies in the company. Among the three men, Harel was first and foremost a theatrical promoter, just as ready to stage Romantic dramas as circus acts, if they would make money. He clearly saw that Dumas offered not only a better chance of popular successes (Dumas had, after all, already enjoyed three major triumphs) but also found him more manipulable when it came to matters of casting, set and costume design, and more agreeable to cutting production expenses in general. Hugo, on the other hand, with a less successful record of successes to his credit, insisted on imposing his will in all these matters. It is possible that Harel decided to sacrifice Hugo in order to promote Dumas as the principal Romantic dramatist at the Porte-Saint-Martin Theatre. To do so, it is argued by, among others, Mme Hugo and Ubersfeld, he arranged to have *Marie Tudor* fail, and to have Ida Ferrier replace Juliette Drouet in that play. If this was his intention, he was more than half successful: the première of the play was certainly less than a triumph, and Juliette lasted only the one performance, demoralized by the attacks of her colleagues.

Returning to literary matters proper, we can record that Hugo wrote *Marie Tudor* in August 1833, using notes taken in 1829 when he was considering writing a drama about Philip II of Spain. In choosing his subject, he returned (despite the *débâcle* of *Le Roi s'amuse*) to the problems, political and personal, confronted by monarchs in their relationship with their subjects. In *Marie Tudor* he decided to exploit the legendary cruelty that earned the Tudor queen the title 'Bloody Mary.' In this play he would develop, more fully than in any of his previous dramas, a subject that was to form the central axis of all his dramas until *Ruy Blas* in 1838, the problem of social justice. In *Marie Tudor* he emphasizes, for the first time, the inequalities existing between the privileges of noble rank and the social disqualification that humble birth conferred on the popular classes.

Having read his new drama to Mlle George, who expressed her lively approval of a title role to rival that of Lucrezia Borgia, Hugo set about casting the play. For the difficult role of Gilbert, he would have liked to engage Frédérick Lemaître, but Hugo's favourite Romantic lead was also feuding with Harel, finally buying back his contract from him in November 1833. Bocage stepped in but, according to Mme Hugo, displayed so little enthusiasm that after two weeks of rehearsals he still needed constant help from the prompter to stagger through his lines. His lack of professionalism adversely affected the acting of his colleagues, particularly Mlle George, so that Hugo was forced to withdraw the role from him, offering it to Lockroy instead.

Hugo had a different problem in casting the figure of the Jew, an episodic, expositional figure murdered onstage in Act 1 by Fabiani, the Queen's favourite. Hugo wanted Chilly, but Harel disagreed, suggesting other casting changes as well. Hugo held firm, and his stand led to the following exchange, reported by Mme Hugo:

> He [Harel] said to the author:
> 'Be careful, Monsieur, that your play doesn't flop.'
> 'Does that mean, Monsieur Harel, that you will make it flop?'
> 'Understand me, Monsieur, as you wish!'
> 'Well then, Monsieur, you will bring down my play and I will bring down
> your theatre!'   (*VHR*, 542)

Clearly, such a personal conflict between dramatist and theatre manager does not offer ideal conditions in which to cast or rehearse a play.

We can get some idea of Hugo's contribution to the rehearsals of *Marie Tudor* thanks to a set of notes, in Juliette's handwriting, which remain among Hugo's papers at the Bibliothèque Nationale. Ubersfeld, the first to discuss the notes, explains that because of their fragmentary nature they are in most cases difficult to interpret, but they do offer some useful information on Hugo's direction of his plays:

> Hugo is most sensitive to anything concerning staging, so he makes changes and gives precise instructions on gesture ... He notes details of the lighting: '[N]ight should fall on Joshua's entrance.' He is most attentive to any detail of the staging that compromises verisimilitude: 'for the entrance of the first lords, open only one of the double doors – M. Delafosse [Fabiani] should impart his secrets to the Queen more discreetly – Gilbert should speak more quietly to Fabiani.' Hugo is most sensitive to the total pathetic effect of the spectacle; not only does he ask the actors to act with greater intensity: 'Delafosse should appear more bewildered at the beginning of his scene

with the Queen,' but he also insists that the supernumerary players also share in the general emotion: '[A]ll the extras are cold'; 'the onlookers are all icy cold.' (*RB*, 217)

By his 'sensitivity' to verisimilitude and emotional effect, Hugo shows clearly that he understood the rhetorical means best designed to persuade an audience to accept a play's argument.

But Hugo's principal cause for concern during rehearsals involved Juliette. He had cast her in the important role of Jane Talbot, a character who at different moments in the play must express her despair at being betrayed by Fabiani, her repentance to Gilbert for betraying his love, and, at the conclusion, her newly, discovered love for him. Added to this, Juliette had, in the play's long final scene, to hold her own, even triumph over, the formidable figure of Mlle George, as the two women wait to see which of their lovers has been executed. Inexperienced as she was, Juliette was quite unable to fulfil the heavy responsibilities of her role. Nor was she able to bear the attacks of the rest of the cast, jealous of her rapid promotion because of the special relationship she enjoyed with the author. Hugo was quite happy for the confrontation between the two women to be seen as that between a 'gazelle' and a 'tiger,' writing Marie Dorval-type lines in which Juliette, as Jane, could express emotionally her vulnerability in her confrontation with the more violent Queen, played by the most powerful female star of the Romantic drama.

Descotes says of the difficult period of rehearsals: 'Never were backstage quarrels so vicious during one of Hugo's plays; but the disagreements were not frank and open as at the Comédie-Française: machinations developed in an underhand way; and soon, distrust reigned everywhere' (*DRGC*, 254). Tension increased because of an incident which had nothing to do with the preparation of the play but which poisoned the atmosphere even more among Hugo, Dumas, and Harel. On 1 November 1833, less than a week before the première of *Marie Tudor*, an article violently hostile to Dumas by Granier de Cassagnac, a friend of Hugo, appeared in the *Journal des Débats* with whose editor, François Bertin, the Hugo family were friendly, spending part of the summers from 1833 to 1840 in the Bertin château near Bièvres. The article, as well as comparing Dumas unfavorably to Hugo as a Romantic dramatist, accused him of plagiarizing, in both *Antony* and *Christine*, Hugo's *Marion de Lorme*. Literary Paris immediately assumed that Hugo had written the article, or that, at the very least, Granier de Cassagnac was acting on Hugo's orders. Dumas wrote to Hugo expressing his dismay and Hugo's ambiguous reply hardly settled the matter.[2] Whoever was to blame (Mme Hugo blames a compositional error by a sub-editor) the result was to increase pressure against Juliette. It now seems to have been understood that Ida, Dumas' mistress, acting as understudy and so learning Jane's lines, would replace Juliette in case of a disaster on the first night.

Harel almost guaranteed such a disaster by breaking his word to Hugo in the matter of the 250 free passes. Harel had promised Hugo free passes with which to assure that the house would contain an unofficial claque, as at *Hernani*. Just before the première, Harel sent only 50 tickets, which Hugo, furious at the broken promise, returned to him. That any of Hugo's supporters received free passes at all was due, ironically, to Dumas' generosity: he it was who solicited passes for them from Harel. They, for their part, ensured that proceedings began as they should by chanting the *Marseillaise*, an anthem which the bourgeois literary critics of the day saw as being much more subversive and dangerously revolutionary than would be the case nowadays.

All accounts of the première agree that the 'First Day' – for the first time Hugo, in imitation of the Spanish 'Golden Age' tradition, divided his play into 'days' rather than acts – was poorly acted (except by Chilly as the Jew), and the audience received it without great enthusiasm. The next day's reviews would criticize the acting of the whole play, even that of Mlle George, leading Ubersfeld to suggest that the Porte-Saint-Martin troupe did not understand the play. However, Mlle George's appearance, delayed until the opening of the Second Day – a factor surely in reducing the audience's enthusiasm during the exposition – was better received, as Mme Hugo recounts: 'The second-act curtain rose on Mlle George. She was lying on a sofa, dressed in a scarlet robe, her profile to the public; her profile was unblemished, magnificent, imperious, and was set off by a diamond crown. This supremely beautiful woman rising up superbly in her velvet and precious stones, surrounded by splendour, brought the house to its feet in admiration (*VHR*, 545). But the admiration did not last, being replaced with hissing, particularly when this superb Queen actually gave instructions onstage to the public executioner concerning the beheading of her unfaithful favourite, Fabiani.

Nothing illustrates better than this incident Hugo's insistence on totally overturning the neo-classical doctrine demanding the dramatist's absolute obedience to the 'proprieties.' As we have seen, Hugo's Romantic dramas constantly shocked the political and cultural sensibilities of the French audience. Despite the enormous changes that Romantic dramatists had been able to make in public taste – earlier in this very play Hugo presented a murder committed onstage – the sight of a monarch, a Queen at that, actually speaking to the executioner, the crude instrument of her policy, proved too much. That the interview should take place in the Queen's own bedchamber contributed to the scandal, according to Éliette Vasseur, who also points out that this is the first time in the history of the French theatre that such an interview had been dramatized:

> Victor Hugo's obstinacy in keeping this scene despite the fears expressed by his entourage, emphasizes the evolution of his thinking regarding the functions of monarchy: the clemency shown by Cromwell and by Charles V is answered by Mary's vindictiveness and hatred. She herself said earlier to Simon Renard [2, 5]: '[T]he head will speak to the hand.' The union is emphasized still more by the executioner's silence: the hand has nothing to say. Nor is it unimportant that the monarch in this case is a woman. The Queen receives the executioner in front of a bed, the first bed in Hugo's theatre associated with a love scene [2, 1]. The link between feminine sexuality and death counts for as much in Hugo's dramas as do political reflections about the function of the monarchy. (*OC*, 4, 821, n1)

Vasseur's analysis shows clearly why Hugo, over the objections of Harel among others, insisted on keeping the scene.

But a dramatist who makes an adversary of his audience can hardly expect his play to be a popular hit. The final act, Day 3, was greeted with hissing and guffaws, particularly when Juliette, by this time entirely demoralized, according to press reports and critics' analyses, was told by Gilbert to 'Lift up your head, stand up straight and look me in the eye' (3, 1, 7). In her embarrassment and stage-fright, Juliette had kept her head down, muttering her lines and looking, from the back (said the critic in the *Courrier des Théâtres*) as if she had been 'horribly decapitated' (*RB*, 220). Even before the first-night reviews were in, Juliette left the cast in favour of Ida Ferrier.

The overall reception of the play was mixed, with small specialized theatrical papers like *Europe Littéraire* and *Le Vert-Vert*, in favour, and the large-circulation newspapers (the *Constitutionnel*, the *Journal des Débats* and their like) unfavourable. Hugo was accused of the usual errors, everything from having plagiarized Dumas' drama *Christine*, to his lack of historical accuracy, his taste for trivial melodramatic effect, and for low life in all its immorality, crude language, and unseemly behaviour. Ubersfeld, at the end of her detailed analysis of the 1833 reception of the play, concludes that it was Hugo's refusal to kowtow to current cultural and dramatic codes, and his presentation of social, moral, and political positions inimical to the theatre critics' professional beliefs that guaranteed his bad reviews: 'His withdrawal of the grotesque [elements from his dramas] was not enough; his theatre was condemned; it did not belong within the context of what one may call the 'dominant' ideology, and the most typical proof is the (relative) unanimity in opinion, of whatever political stripe. The silent masses had no organ of expression' (*RB*, 233).

Ubersfeld is correct when she distinguishes between press and popular reactions to Hugo's drama. In fact, despite the disasters during rehearsals and first performance, and despite the bad reviews, *Marie Tudor*, without achieving the success of *Lucrèce Borgia*, did find an audience in 1833–4, and has continued to do so since. Between November 1833 and January 1834, the play had 37 performances, as well as one in February and four in March: an honourable success, not a financial blockbuster. Since 1833, revivals have included one in 1873 with Frédérick Lemaître playing the Jew, and most memorably of all, Jean Vilar's production in 1955 with Maria Casarès' triumph in the lead role. Also in the twentieth century, *Marie Tudor* was filmed for the cinema in 1912, has been heard on the radio, and seen – in two different productions, in 1966 and 1975 – on French TV. The 1966 TV version, directed by Abel Gance, is particularly interesting in that it shows how difficult Hugo's ideological and literary positions in that play remained right into our own time. Gance, the great film director, creator of the highly Romantic, almost Dumas-like epic, *Napoléon*, might have been expected to sympathize with Hugo's views on monarchy's relationship to the people. Such was not the case, however, as Gance explained: 'I admit it. I've transformed Victor Hugo's work to make it less black. I have deliberately given it a happy ending. My Marie Tudor, like all the heroines of melodrama, is redeemed at the end, moved by the courage of her victims.'[3] Gance here acknowledges the principal structural difference between Romantic drama, which ends badly for the protagonists, and melodrama with its formulaic happy ending. However, any drama too strong for Abel Gance deserves detailed analysis. Let us look more closely at *Marie Tudor*.

Hugo had written in the Preface to *Lucrèce Borgia*: 'The theatre is a forum. The theatre is a pulpit' (*OC*, 4, 655), confirming both the rhetorical and the didactic function of his dramas. In the Preface to *Marie Tudor* he went further, indicating exactly what his dramas should teach the people about their history, past and present. His ideal drama, he tells us 'would be the past revived for the benefit of the present; it would be history as accomplished by our fathers in confrontation with history as accomplished by ourselves; it would be an onstage mixture of everything that is mixed together in life; it would be riots on the one hand and tender words between lovers on the other, and in those tender words a lesson for the people, and in the riot an appeal to the heart ... To such a drama, which would be for the crowd a perpetual source of instruction, everything would be permitted, because the very essence of the drama would consist in abusing nothing' (*OC*, 4, 754–5). Hugo could make no clearer statement of his belief that the plot's logic should, in order to teach its socio-political lesson, make as powerful as possible a rhetorical appeal to the emotions of an audience. In writing a play about a queen's revenge upon her unfaithful favourite, Hugo claimed in the same Preface to be displaying for the people's edification 'a queen who is [also] a woman. Great as queen. True as woman' (ibid. 754). One can quite reasonably ask what kind of lesson can be taught by a drama which, in the unanimous opinion of Hugo's critics, both friendly and unfriendly, has only the most circumstantial links with the historical period, sixteenth-century England, that it purports to represent.

To discover the lesson Hugo may have had in mind, we need to see the action of *Marie Tudor* as involving not simply royal sexual intrigues, but the theme of social justice, a theme to which Hugo would return constantly, most notably in the theatre in *Ruy Blas*, as well as in his 1862 novel, *Les Misérables*. *Marie Tudor*'s three 'days,' or acts, highlight three different types of injustice or inequality in human and sexual relations, and in all three confrontations injustice triumphs over justice. (We will examine, in its proper place, the exception to this generalization.) The three kinds of injustice concern, in Day 1, the inequality affecting the low-born Gilbert (and therefore also Jane, before her noble birth is discovered) in his dealings with the Queen's ennobled favourite, Fabiani. The second kind of injustice involves, in Days 2 and 3, the Queen's sexual relations with Fabiani, whom she cannot marry because of the difference in their respective ranks. This relationship is complicated by Fabiani's unfaithfulness to Mary, an act which places his life in her power, a power she fully intends, at first, to implement. The third kind of injustice shows, in Day 3, the people used as the naive agents of his policy by a political intriguer and skilful orator, Simon Renard, Simon 'the Fox.'

The unequal confrontation between Gilbert and Fabiani begins in Day 1, when Fabiani insists that Gilbert help him to dispose of the body of the Jew, whom Fabiani has just killed. When Gilbert, who played no part in the murder, refuses, Fabiani has little difficulty in forcing him to cooperate, simply by reminding him of the difference in their social ranks and of its concomitant effect on their respective credibility:

> FABIANI: Believe me, let's get rid of all trace of this. It's more in your interest than mine.
>
> GILBERT: That's too much!
>
> FABIANI: One of us struck him down. I am a lord, a nobleman. You are a passerby, a workman, a man of the people. A gentleman who kills a Jew pays a fine of four sous; a working man who kills one is hanged ... If you denounce me, I'll denounce you. They will believe me rather than you. In any case, our chances are unequal. A fine of four sous for me, the gallows for you.   (1, 7)

Unable to defeat his adversary's authority or logic, Gilbert allows himself to be browbeaten, helping Fabiani dispose of the body. Fabiani, for his part, rewards Gilbert, his social inferior, with a purse of money, which Gilbert after some hesitation, accepts.

But Fabiani has not finished with Gilbert so easily. He announces, and is subsequently able to prove that, as a great Lord, he has had little difficulty in seducing Jane whom, though Fabiani does not know it, Gilbert is about to marry. Gilbert's reaction is violent but despite this extreme provocation, the social inequality of the time prevents him from obtaining satisfaction:

> GILBERT: Curses! My lord, you have dishonoured my fiancée, you are vile! Give me satisfaction.
> FABIANI (*putting his hand on his sword*): Willingly. Where's your sword?
> GILBERT: Damnation! To be working class! To carry nothing, neither sword, nor dagger! I will wait for you at night on some street-corner, I'll bury my nails in your throat to kill you, wretch!
> FABIANI: You? Take revenge against me? You so low, I so high! You're mad! I defy you!   (1, 7)

In fact, so little impressed is Fabiani, the nobleman, by the threats of Gilbert that, compounding injury with insult, he adds that he already had enough of Jane in any case, and contemptuously tosses Gilbert the key of her bedroom. The result for an audience of such an unequal and clearly socially unjust rhetorical confrontation is likely to be indignation.

The confrontation between nobleman and worker does not end there, however, and Hugo achieves catharsis, purging the indignation aroused, by a striking plot reversal in Day 2. Thus Simon Renard seizes the opportunity to use Gilbert's passion for vengeance against Fabiani, who is an obstacle to Renard's plan to marry the Queen to his master, Philip II. He makes Gilbert swear a pact, like Hernani's, by which he offers his life in exchange for vengeance. Gilbert's chance comes in the 'Trial scene' in Day 2, when the Queen, having already had Gilbert condemned to death, asks him to confirm that Fabiani had set him on to assassinate her. The scene takes place before the 'whole Court' assembled in the Queen's apartments:

> THE QUEEN: Following this man's [Gilbert's] declarations, we, Mary, Queen, accuse before the Court of Star Chamber, this man, Fabiano Fabiani, count of Clanbrassil, of high treason and of attempted regicide upon our imperial and sacred person.
> FABIANI: I, regicide! This is monstrous! ... (To Gilbert) Whoever you are, wretch, do you dare assert that what the Queen says is true.
> GILBERT: Yes.

FABIANI: I urged you to regicide?

GILBERT: Yes.

FABIANI: Yes! Always yes! Curses! You can't know, my lords, how false all this
is ... My lords, this man has been paid ...

GILBERT: By you. Here's the purse full of gold that you gave me for the
crime. Your coat of arms and monogram are embroidered on it.   (2, 8)

The tables are turned! Now it is the nobleman whose word is doubted by
all his peers, and the working man is believed because, in swearing to Fabiano's guilt, he condemns himself to death as well. This rhetorical demonstration of the evils of social inequality is rendered all the more striking
because, in each case, the arbiters to whom appeal is made are shown to be
ready to believe the lie concocted by the political schemers, Mary and
Simon Renard. Hugo's cynicism runs counter to the optimistic lip service
paid to social justice by his principal critics. Given our own cynicism about
the good faith shown by governments, security agencies, and financial
institutions, Hugo seems once again to have been ahead of his own time
and, like Stendhal, to have been writing for posterity.

A second type of social injustice, that existing between the sexes, receives
a paradoxical treatment in *Marie Tudor*. Not only is the 'normal' sexual
hierarchy overturned, with the woman virtually all-powerful and the man
dependent upon her whims, but the politically powerful Queen frequently
shows or announces her personal weakness in her dealings not only with
her male ministers but, paradoxically, with her low-born, foreign lover, so
detested by her nobles. Simon Renard expresses throughout the play the
conventional male view on women in power who have fallen under the
influence of a lover: 'Lord Chandos, when a woman reigns, caprice reigns.
Then politics is no longer a matter of calculation, but of chance' (1, 2).
And later he adds to Dulverton in the Tower: 'It's very strange, as you say.
But what do you expect? The Queen is mad; she doesn't know what she's
doing. We can count upon nothing; she's a woman. I ask you, what has she
come here for? Look, a woman's heart is a riddle ...' (3, 1, 2). Mary shows
by her actions that Renard, despite his political and sexual bias, is not
entirely wrong.

At first, convinced of Fabiano's infidelity, she seeks to punish him with
death. Adultery not being a capital offence, she enlists Gilbert's aid in having him judged guilty by his peers who hate him and are happy to avenge
themselves upon the Queen's favourite. She insists that her vengeance be
seen as exemplary, describing with relish to her distracted former lover
every detail of his public execution:

Do I have to hide when I take my vengeance? No, by God! I want daylight, do you hear, mylord? High noon, blazing sunshine, the public square, the axe and the block, crowds in the streets, crowds at the windows, crowds on the roofs, a hundred thousand witnesses! I want people to be afraid, do you hear, mylord? I want them to find it imposing, terrible, magnificent, and I want them to say: 'It was a woman outraged, but it was a Queen who took her vengeance!' My favourite, so envied, this handsome, insolent young man whom I've covered with velvet and satin, I want to see him bent double, terrified, trembling, kneeling on a black cloth, barefoot, hands bound, hooted at by the crowd, manhandled by the hangman. Around this white neck where I placed a golden necklace, I want to fasten a rope. I've seen what kind of effect Fabiani made on a throne. Now I want to see what effect he will make on a scaffold. (2, 7)

Despite Mary's striking use of *hypotyposis*, or visually powerful, vivid description, it is quite possible that Hugo's audience found unlikely a queen's expression of such naked emotion before her assembled court. Unlikely because, even nowadays, despite our experience of the sexual escapades leading to the fall of the House of Windsor, the 'divinity [that] doth hedge a King,' in Shakespeare's words,[4] still remains a superstitiously persuasive notion. Mary Tudor entertains no such desire to keep up appearances, and Hugo's bourgeois audience seems to have found her frankness too hard to take.

Just as Lucrezia digs a grave for Gennaro by allowing her passions to rule her head, Mary further indulges her indignation at Fabiano's betrayal when she gives her instructions to the public executioner, as Vasseur reminded us, next to the bed in which Mary and Fabiani had made love:

THE QUEEN (*to the executioner*): Come here, you. I'm happy to see you. You are a good servant ... It is customary for monarchs of the realm to give you the most splendid present possible when they come to power. My father, Henry VIII, gave you the diamond clasp from his cloak. My brother, Edward VI, gave you a goblet of chased gold. It's my turn now. Until now I have given you nothing. I must give you a present. Come here. (*Pointing to Fabiani.*) Do you see that head, that young, charming head, that head which, still this morning, was for me the finest, dearest and most precious thing in the world? Well, that head, you can see it, can you? I give it to you.' (2, 9)

The Queen's anger and spite should not make us forget that Fabiani remains innocent of regicide, the crime for which he will lose his head.

In view of this primary injustice, the Queen's own frequent lamentations on the sexual inqualites from which even she, as a 'mere' woman suffers, may seem less persuasive. Nowhere is this paradoxical 'weakness' displayed more strikingly than in Day 3, after Mary has changed her mind about having Fabiani killed. She loves him still, and to Simon Renard, who reminds her of her lover's treachery, she cries: 'What difference does that make to me? All men do the same. See, my lord ... see, I know what you're going to say. That he is a vile, cowardly wretch. I know that as well as you do, and I blush for it. But I love him. What do you want me to do? I would love him less perhaps if he were a gentleman ... Besides, I'm a woman. I both want and don't want [him] at the same time. I'm not consistent. This man's life is necessary to mine' (3, 1, 6).

Hugo's concept of love as uncontrollable passion, unconnected with moral esteem for the person loved, must have seemed outrageous to French audiences used to seventeenth- or eighteenth-century writers of neo-classical tragedies about love like Corneille or Voltaire. Classical convention demanded that woman's love go to the hero, celebrated for his qualities both physical and moral. The Romantic notion that love was a fatal attraction, existing independently of the object's worth or lack of it – obviously in 1833 a notion appearing before its time – militated against the audience's easy acceptance of a queen's potentially demeaning relationship with a favourite not her social equal. Looking for some rationalistic control of emotion, Hugo's audience merely sniggered at sexual passion when presented, in Hernani's words in a different context, as a 'force of nature,' rather than as an expression of society's norms. They may also have found disconcerting, in the mouth of a queen, Mary's cynical assertion in the drama's final scene that, because she is more powerful than Jane, she has a better right to save her lover: 'Ah, my love is as great as yours, and my hand is stronger than yours! You will not budge. Ah! Your lover! What do I care about your lover? Are all the women in England going to call me to account for their lovers? Of course I am saving mine as best I can and at the expense of anyone in my way. Look after your own!' (3, 2, 2).

Mary's abuse of her power to change the course of events did succeed, in the first ending that Hugo wrote for the play. Ubersfeld calls this ending, in which Fabiano survives and Gilbert is executed, the 'logical' ending, as opposed to the ending Hugo finally settled for, in which the mens' fates are reversed. This ending she calls 'political,' on the grounds that, being more optimistic, it would cause less offence to Hugo's public (*VHTL*, 1, 1431); however, neither Hugo's logic nor his rhetorical strategy in saving Gilbert seem to have persuaded his audience of the advantages of social justice over dynastic alliance.

The third kind of social injustice dramatized by Hugo in *Marie Tudor* is the kind most likely to be of use to 'the people' and the one that an Estab-

lishment first-night audience, who probably considered themselves superior to the 'the people,' would have found the most subversive. This type of
social injustice depends upon the hierarchy of relationships existing
among the wielders, instruments, and subjects of political power. The feudal pyramid in Tudor England posited the social (and by extension, the
moral) superiority of those at the top: the Queen, then the aristocrats from
whom she generally chose the principal instruments of her prerogative,
along with those ambitious members of the middle classes who allied themselves with and shared the fortunes of the noble families close to the monarchy. These formed the group in power. The working classes – servants,
tradesmen, cannon fodder, etc. – had, in the normal course of events no
means, short of insurrection, of influencing the powerful. Insurrection is
precisely what 'the Emperor's right arm in London' (1, 3), Simon Renard,
a foreigner, and therefore not entirely subject to English power structures,
promotes in order to further his own policy. Lest we be deceived that the
ironically named Renard has any higher aim than power-broking in mind,
Mary herself warns us about him: 'Do you think I don't know that you only
want to bring [Fabiani] down in order to put in his place the Count of Kil-
dare, that conceited Irishman ... And don't talk to me about the Prince of
Spain. You couldn't care less about him! ... Don't, I beg of you, put on that
air of maidenly innocence and good faith. I know about all your plots'
(3, 1, 4).

Furious at his loss of the power to influence the Queen, Renard the
pragmatist changes his discursive strategy by seeking to influence a different audience:

> RENARD: I withdraw, Madam. I spoke for all of your nobles.
> QUEEN: What do my nobles matter to me?
> RENARD (*aside*): Let's try the people. (*He goes out after bowing humbly.*) (3, 1, 4)

Four scenes later, the result of Renard's implied (offstage) efforts to
foment rebellion are heard, as the mob surrounds the Tower, eventually
forcing Mary, despite her decision to save her lover, to agree to his public
execution. This is the first time in Hugo's dramas that the people, hitherto
powerless and absent (except in *Cromwell*) from the dramatic action,
directly changes the course of political events. The Queen tries, by the last
minute substitution of Gilbert, to overturn the sentence passed by the Lord
Chancellor on her lover, but once more Renard spots the trick and 'justice' triumphs: Fabiano is beheaded for a crime, regicide, of which he is
not guilty. Or, as Renard puts it, in the final curtain-line: 'I saved the
Queen and England' (3, 2, 2), meaning, presumably, from popular revolt
and civil war. Rather than being optimistic, as Ubersfeld sees it, such an

ending is more likely to strike modern audiences as cynically ironic, a factor which also greatly reduced its chances of convincing Hugo's contemporary audience.

Mention must be made of the extraordinary special effects by means of which Hugo dramatizes the opposition between Queen, ministers, and people in the Third Day of *Marie Tudor*. In order to suggest the revolt by the populace, sound and lighting effects first warn of coming events, as the stage directions indicate: '*For some moments, a distant tumult, confused shouting is heard. The light fades*' (3, 1, 7). Then, one scene later: '*The tumult outside has grown louder. Night has fallen almost totally. Death threats, torches, the sound of a marching crowd. The clash of arms, shots, horses stamping*' (3, 1, 8). From a balcony, Renard harangues the noisy (offstage) crowd, promising them Fabiani's death. The climax of this dramatic confrontation between royal and popular power is accompanied by a spectacular scenic effect, when the Queen shows Jane the whole of London, joyfully illuminated at the prospect of her favourite's imminent execution:

> QUEEN: Hatred against Fabiani is proud, radiant, triumphant, in arms and victorious, at court and among the people; hatred has filled the streets with men, it mouths cries of joy; hatred is haughty, arrogant, all-powerful; hatred has lit up a whole city around a scaffold! Love is here, two women in mourning in a tomb. Hatred is there!
>
> *Violently, she pulls aside the white backdrop which, as it opens, reveals a balcony and, beyond, as far as the eye can see, the whole of the City of London brilliantly illuminated against the night sky. What can be seen of the Tower of London is also lit up. Jane stares in amazement at the dazzling spectacle whose reflection lights up the whole theatre.*   (3, 2, 2)

Such a spectacle must have recalled only too vividly to Hugo's Parisian audience the street rioting, barricades, and military repression of recent insurrections in 1830 and 1832. That Hugo fully intended his audience to view such scenes with unease is proved by his Preface: the need to achieve social justice is the lesson he expected his drama to teach. However, even the audience at the Porte-Saint-Martin Theatre, more popular in character than the establishment élite at the Comédie-Française, seems to have found the lesson unacceptable.

ANGELO, TYRAN DE PADOUE (1835)

> Bring together in a single plot entirely involving emotion two grave and distressing figures, woman in society, woman outside society; that is, in two living types, all women, the whole of womanhood ... Place the blame where it

> belongs, that is on men, who hold the power, and on social custom, which is
> absurd. (*OC*, 5, 267)

As Hugo made clear in this extract from the Preface to his next play, he
was continuing to pursue the theme of social justice in his dramas, choosing this time to examine woman's role in a male-dominated society. In
Angelo, he wrote two central female roles, probably having in mind the star
of the Comédie-Française, Mlle Mars, and Marie Dorval, the former star of
the popular Porte-Saint-Martin Theatre. Dorval, at the Comédie since
November 1833, had in February 1835 appeared with great success in
Alfred de Vigny's Romantic drama, *Chatterton*. By promising Hugo such a
cast, Jouslin de La Salle, Taylor's successor as manager of the Comédie-
Française and a man not unfavourable to the young Romantic dramatists,
had little trouble convincing him to abandon Harel.

Hugo composed his new play, originally entitled, *Padua in 1549*, in eight-
een days (2–19 February 1835) and signed a contract with Jouslin on 24
February stipulating not only the production of *Angelo*, but also revivals of
Hernani and *Marion de Lorme* within the same year. Jouslin was not to
honour this contract and Hugo would be forced to sue the Comédie-
Française once again.

When he read his new play to Mlle Mars, Hugo, having informed her
that Marie Dorval, her new rival at the Comédie would play one of the principal parts, gave her the choice of roles. Mme Hugo, no friend of the star
actress, fictionalizes the incident, attributing to Mlle Mars the following
reasons for her decision:

> She reflected, turning the matter over in her mind for a long time and said:
> 'Well, all things considered, I choose Thisbe.' This is how she arrived at her
> decision. She didn't say: 'Which of the two roles suits me best?' She asked
> herself: 'Which will be worse for Mme Dorval?' The author has probably
> written Thisbe for her. Thisbe is an actress, a busker, a kind of shameless
> beggar, with an actor's slovenliness and cynicism; the role is certainly made
> for Mme Dorval. She shall not have it; she shall play the other one. With her
> fishwife's voice and manner, and her bohemian looks, she'll be ridiculous
> as a great Venetian lady, a patrician. Let's be sure to leave Catarina's role to
> her. (*VHR*, 548–9)

Whether Mme Hugo was right or not in her surmise, Mlle Mars' intuition
in fact proved correct. By casting herself against type, she awakened new
expectations among her claque of supporters at the Comédie, and played
Thisbe, the actress-courtesane with great success; except, of course, in the
view of Mme Dorval's counter-claque. When, after Mlle Mars withdrew

from the role, Dorval did play Thisbe in March 1836, Hugo at least believed that the play lost some of its effect, since Thisbe's emotional outpourings became more predictable (*VHR*, 567).

As might be expected, given the clash of egos involved, the rehearsals preceding the première of *Angelo* on 28 April 1835 were stormy. The accounts we have tell, for instance, of attempts by Mlle Mars to upstage Mme Dorval's dramatic exit: 'I want to die praying. For you, Sir' (3, 2, 10), and to ensure for herself exclusive top billing, with her rival's name relegated to supernumerary status. She was more successful in imposing her Parisian costume, fashionable in 1835, on the Renaissance Italian courtesan. She once again wore the 'Muscovite,' or 'coolie-style' hat she had insisted upon for her role as Doña Sol.

As well as defending Mme Dorval from the spite of her colleagues at the Comédie, Hugo also had to make major changes to the text during rehearsals. Principal among these was the suppression of three whole scenes forming the first part of Day 3. The scenes involve the meeting of a group of spies and paid killers in a broken-down hovel, the abduction of Reginella, and the murder of Homodei by Rodolfo. Jouslin was able to convince Hugo that his unrestrained use of grotesque scenic elements and action in Saltabadil's hovel in Acts 4 and 5 had caused the failure of *Le Roi s'amuse*. Hugo agreed, and so substituted in *Angelo* a classical-style narrative to advance the plot between Day 2 and the second part of Day 3. Hugo's betrayal of the position he outlined in the Preface to *Cromwell* where, as we saw, he denounced such undramatic devices as narrations by characters of actions occurring 'in the wings,' as it were, leads Ubersfeld to declare *Angelo* a 'compromise' drama, one adapted with success in mind at the expense of Hugo's Romantic principles (*DR*, 139). Hugo carefully kept the suppressed section among his manuscripts and Sarah Bernhardt restored it in her 1905 revival of *Angelo*. Since then, the play has been performed in its complete version.

One aspect of Hugo's direction of *Angelo*, his insistence that the actors in his dramas behave with less physical restraint onstage than was the case in neo-classical tragedy, is illustrated by Marvin Carlson: 'Hugo's Angelo used furniture in an unusually informal way. Angelo leaned frequently on the backs of chairs or sat on their arms while at one point in Act 3 Catherine "leans against the edge of a table as if sitting" – a pose unthinkable earlier in the century.'[5] An even more innovative element of the staging of *Angelo*, as Carlson remarks, is another use of furniture, or rather its displacement, to advance the dramatic action: '... *Rodolfo enters Catarina's chamber. She is sitting in an armchair down left and he brings another chair from upstage to sit next to her. Upon hearing a noise in the corridor he climbs out onto the balcony to hide while she retires to her bed upstage. Thisbe, who enters, recognizes from the changed posi-*

tion of the chairs that an assignation has taken place, without any dialogue neces-sary to make the point.[6] Once again, Hugo's innovations in stagecraft were followed by later producers in the 1830s.

At the première, there were two distinct audiences inside the Comédie-Française: the supporters of Mlle Mars and those of Mme Dorval. Day 1 went to the neo-classical actress whose Thisbe, Mme Hugo tells us, 'was applauded at every word in the scene involving the key, all her lines were razor-sharp in their effect, her supporters were ecstatic, saying: "She's so charming, so ravishing! No one else can speak lines like that"' (*VHR*, 558). In Day 2, Mme Dorval, whose *claque* of young (and, by 1835, not so young) Romantics was 'shushed' by the more numerous bourgeois supporters of her rival, needed to surpass herself to gain applause. Happily, this she was able to do and, in Mme Hugo's estimation, she completely eclipsed the neo-classical star of the Comédie: 'The entire Act was an ovation for Mme Dorval; her success had erased that of Mlle Mars; Mme Dorval was pro-claimed a great actress. The difference was noticeable between [Mlle Mars'] studied, well researched, but artificial, skin-deep acting style and that of Mme Dorval, [which was] so natural, inspired by the situation, and whose effects arose out of her very soul – the difference between premedi-tated and spontaneous talent, between truth and convention' (*VHR*, 559). In the end, both sets of spectators were satisfied, calling back both actresses for repeated curtain-calls, as the Register at the Comédie-Française records. The première was a triumph. *Angelo* was also a financial success for Hugo and Jouslin. There were 36 performances before it was taken off in July 1835.

Analysis of *Angelo*, and particularly, of the 'battle of the sexes' it drama-tizes rhetorically confirms that it is no exaggeration to speak of male-female relationships in the play as a 'battle,' nor to claim that social injus-tice, between the sexes and between rich and poor, forms the play's princi-pal theme. In his Preface of 7 May 1835, Hugo describes the subject of *Angelo* as the subordination to men of two archetypical women, the wife and the courtesan: 'Show these two women, who in their persons encapsu-late all, often generous, always unfortunate. Defend one from despotism, the other from contempt. Teach what trials the first's virtue resists, what tears wash from the other her contamination ... Next to these two women, place two men, the husband and the lover, the monarch and the outlaw, and summarize in them by many secondary plot devices all of the regular and irregular relationships that men may have with, on the one hand, women, and on the other, with society' (*OC*, 5, 267–8).

The need for 'many secondary plot devices' explains the complications in the drama's action, which includes the device known by narratologists as the 'closed room,' and which is necessary for the *dénouement* in Day 3. The explanation and control of its entrances and exits necessitates a whole act of exposition (Day 1, 'The Key'). Hugo also creates a character-catalyst, whose function it is to precipitate the violent confrontation between the men and women in question and thus to engineer the rapid resolution of their love-hate relationships. Homodei, member of the secret Venetian Order of Ten, murderer, spy, and spurned suitor of Catarina, the wife of Angelo (absolute ruler of Padua) drives the plot by his jealousy of Rodolfo, Catarina's chaste lover. Also jealous of Rodolfo's love for Catarina is Thisbe, the low-born actress envious of the privileges society lavishes upon the high-born wives of its ruling élite.

Other devices of plot and language necessary to provoke the drama's didactic conclusion include some of the tools of melodrama, particularly keys, secret doors and passages, poison and counter-poison, and a gallery of rogues, as cretinous as they are deadly. In addition, the set of *Angelo* rivals in complication the one Hugo had used in Acts 4 and 5 of *Le Roi s'amuse.* Frederick Burwick offers a plausible explanation for Hugo's preference for such spatial complexity: 'Hugo was partial to a décor of hidden passages, reversals of on-stage and off-stage events, and above all to a dynamic interaction between character and stage setting ... Setting participates in dramatic action ... Thus "local colour" should not only convince us of the historical period and place, it should also reveal the motives, lusts, ambitions of the inhabitants.'[7] Angelo's palace, with its secret passages, hidden doors and wall cavities admirably suggests the atmosphere of intrigue and violent double-dealing that Padua's *podesta* maintains in order to keep his power.

The principal tool of the melodramatic *anagnorisis* here (like the baby's shoe that allows her mother to recognize La Esmeralda as her long-lost daughter in *Notre-Dame de Paris*) is a crucifix which, in *Angelo*, also supplies the title to Day 2, in which Thisbe, the woman of the people, shunned by polite society, confronts Catarina, untouchable wife of the city's powerful ruler. The crucifix also represents the means, as outlined rhetorically in Hugo's Preface, of redeeming and pardoning society's evils: 'Finally, above these three men [Angelo. Rodolfo and Homodei], between these two women, place ... the god who died on the cross. Nail all of this human suffering to the back of the crucifix' (*OC*, 5, 268). The recognition scene (2, 5) represents the first of the drama's principal peripeteia. Thisbe arrives in Catarina's chamber determine to denounce to Angelo Catarina's love affair with Rodolfo. Angelo, although he does not love his wife, personifies Venetian society's belief that the deceived husband has the right to punish his guilty wife, even with death. But Thisbe suddenly notices on the wall a crucifix. Hugo's exposition has already prepared the dramatic reversal which forces Thisbe to change from vengeful proletar-

ian to compassionate supporter of Catarina against Angelo's wrath. Thisbe
speaks to Angelo:

> THISBE: You know who I am, a working girl, an actress, a thing you caress
> today and break tomorrow ... Well, as worthless as I am, I had a mother ... A
> poor woman with no husband who sang folksongs in the public square at
> Brescia ... One day, it seems that, unknown to her, one song contained
> something offensive to the lords of Venice ... A senator passed by ... Off
> with that woman to the gallows! My mother kissed me; a tear fell on my
> forehead. She took her crucifix from her neck and allowed them to
> attach the garotte in its place. I can still see the crucifix. In polished copper.
> My name, Thisbe, crudely scratched on the base ... But the senator was
> holding the hand of a young girl, his daughter probably, who was sud-
> denly moved to pity ... She threw herself at the senator's feet, and wept so
> many tears from her beautiful eyes that she won my mother's pardon ...
> When my mother was untied, she took her crucifix – my mother – and
> gave it to the lovely child saying: 'Madame, keep this crucifix; it will bring
> you luck.'
>
> ANGELO: ... What will you give this woman when you find her?
>
> THISBE: My life, if she wants it.   (1, 1)

Hugo thus bases his reversal on an argument whose credibility depends
upon our accepting that it is out of gratitude that Thisbe is saving Catarina
from Angelo's anger. Influenced by this appeal to our emotions, we accept
(or not) that Catarina will owe her life to Thisbe's mother and her good-
luck charm. Consequent upon this position are the propositions that
because Thisbe cannot avenge herself on the woman whom Rodolfo loves,
and also because she herself cannot have Rodolfo, she therefore chooses to
die at his hands. In all cases dramatic verisimilitude depends upon our vulnerability (or lack of it) to Hugo's appeal to fairly conventional, if hyperbolic, Romantic emotions.

To render more interesting the lesson taught by the events onstage – to
sugar the pill, as it were – Hugo includes various hints and clues to intrigue
the audience. The reason is that the drama, as he says in the Preface to
Angelo, should be both entertaining and didactic, for it is by touching an
audience, by appealing to their emotions and sensibilities, that he proposes to convince them of the social and sexual injustice existing both in
sixteenth-century Venice and in nineteenth-century Paris: 'It goes without
saying that artistic requirements should first of all be entirely satisfied.
Curiosity, interest, amusement, laughter, tears, constant observation of
everything in nature, expressed in wonderful style, drama must have all

that, otherwise it would not be drama; but to be complete, it must also desire to teach, even as it desires to entertain' (*OC,* 5, 269).

Particularly striking as a rhetorical means of exciting an audience's literary curiosity and interest is Hugo's systematic use of allegorical onomastics in *Angelo.* Among the eleven names he gave to the drama's characters, five add ironic resonance to the onstage events by triggering intertextual echoes of other fictional universes. In all five cases, the characters' names are ironically misleading: Angelo is no more an angel than is Shakespeare's sexual harasser in *Measure for Measure*; Thisbe, unlike Ovid's virginal heroine, the tragic victim of her own mistaken inference concerning the death of her suitor Pyramus in the *Metamorphoses,* is the courtesane who, unwilling to live without the man she loves, forces Rodolfo to stab her to death; Rodolfo, is not only the Romantic lead – to be later glorified by Eugène Sue among others, and parodied by Flaubert – but is also a double murderer; Homodei is not, as his name would have it, a 'Man of God,' but a spy and worse; and Orfeo, neither poet nor musician, is a slow-witted cutthroat. In addition, the drama numbers among its *dramatis personae* an usher called Troilus (Troilo in Italian), and a policeman called Virgil (Virgilio). By transporting in imagination spectators able to spot such allusions between the fictional universes inhabited by the non-ironical namesakes of his characters, Hugo's allegorical references intermingle sublime and grotesque, high and low, security and menace.

In *Angelo,* Hugo develops his theme of woman's unjust treatment at the hands of men and society by demonstrating that, despite the equally unjust conditions separating poor women from their wealthier sisters, they share a common interest which should make them allies. He does so by showing Thisbe's conversion – thanks to the crucifix, both melodramatic tool of *anagnorisis* and symbol of divine redemptive justice – which leads to her achievement of a final solidarity with Catarina against Angelo. Hugo carefully avoids idealizing Thisbe, and so making her a rhetorical personification of the trials of virtue. By having her choose death by her lover's hand, he shows her dying for love rather than to promote social reform.

In the first emotionally-charged confrontation between women in *Angelo,* Thisbe, the courtesan opposes Catarina, the wealthy, protected wife of the *podesta,* or tyrant, of Padua:

> THISBE: The *podesta*'s mistress holds in her hands the *podesta*'s wife ... An actress, a theatre girl, a clown, as you call us, holds in her hands, as I just said, a great lady, a married woman, a respectable woman, a woman of virtue! Holds her in her hands, in her nails, in her teeth! Can do what she wants with this great lady, with this high, gilded renown, and will tear it to pieces, reduce it to shreds, to scraps! Ah, great ladies, I don't know what's

going to happen, but what is certain is that I have one of you under my feet!
And I will not let her go!   (2, 5)

Sure that Catarina is Rodolfo's lover, Thisbe, in the name of the women of
her class, declares her intention to avenge what she describes as the hypocrisy of respectable wives. She does so discursively, by means of an antithesis
opposing the sexual roles that social class imposed upon women:

> THISBE: You are no better than than we are, ladies! What we say aloud to a
> man in full daylight, you mumble shamefacedly to him at night. Only the
> hours are different! We take your husbands, you take our lovers. It's a fight.
> Very well. Let's fight! Ah, fakery, hypocrisy, treachery, apes of virtue, false
> women. No, by God! You are not as good as we are! We don't deceive any-
> one! You deceive society, your families and your husbands. You'd deceive
> God Himself if you could! Oh, the virtuous veiled ladies who go by in the
> street! They go to church ... Go right up to them, tear off their veils. Behind
> the veil there is a mask, behind the mask, a lying mouth! Oh, it's of no
> matter. I am the *podesta*'s mistress, and you are his wife, and I shall ruin
> you!   (2, 5)

It is this vehement and vituperative condemnation that the crucifix
reverses; because of Thisbe's emotional debt of gratitude to Catarina she
must suppress her class hatred, and in so doing she discovers instead the
common interest binding them together as victims of male dominance.
She implies the reason for her belief in gender solidarity when, speaking of
the young girl who had saved her mother, she declares her intention to
seek out her benefactor in order to come to her assistance. There is no
question that she will need assistance, because, according to Thisbe's
enthymeme, 'she is a woman now, and consequently unfortunate' (1, 1).
The crucifix has reminded her that woman's universal lot is suffering, thus
making redundant the syllogism's general premise ('All women are unfortunate').

In her final conversation with Rodolfo, Thisbe also recounts how the
child or woman without other resources than her own body becomes the
victim of men: 'Do you really think that I ought to cling to life? Think
again! As a child I was a beggar. And then, at sixteen I found myself without bread. I was picked up in the street by some great lords. I fell from one
gutter into another. Hunger or orgies! I realize what they tell you: "Die of
hunger, then." But I have really suffered!' (3, 3, 3). Clearly sentimental,
her appeal smacks also of hyperbole. Her punishment for such pathetic
exaggeration will, however, be exemplary: she will die on her idol's dagger.

Catarina, as the *podesta*'s honoured wife, suffers from no such disadvantages. But Hugo sympathetically points to the inequalities existing when marriage is merely a strategically-planned transfer of daughter and funds between noble families. When Angelo, his family honour wounded by Catarina's (unconsummated) love for Rodolfo, tells his wife he has condemned her to death for her transgession, Catarina denounces the sham of marriage for money or increased power:

> I really despise you! You married me for my money, because I was rich, because my family owns rights over the water in Venice's reservoirs. You said: 'That's worth a hundred thousand ducats a year. Let's take the daughter.' And what kind of life have I had with you for five years? You don't love me. But you're jealous. You keep me locked up. You have mistresses; that's allowed. Everything is allowed to men ... Oh, one needs to have suffered like me to understand the fate of women ... Truly, we are in an execrable country! It is an abominable republic in which a man can walk with impunity over an unhappy woman, as you do, sir! And in which other men say to him: 'You do right; Foscari killed his daughter, Loredano his wife, Bragadini ...' (3, 2, 8)

The nice logical balance between Angelo's unjust denunciation and Catarina's chaste relationship with Rodolfo shows Hugo designing his emotional appeal so as to arouse an audience's indignation. Once again dramatic irony has empowered this appeal. However, Hugo's belief in the didactic power of his dramas did not, paradoxically, extend to any desire on his part to make them political tracts having as their direct aim the immediate reform of such social abuses. He nonetheless states clearly his position on these abuses.

Angelo's male jealousy completes the reversal in Thisbe's feelings toward Catarina. The two women stand together to thwart Angelo's vengeance, and Thisbe both administers the narcotic that will save Catarina and provides for her flight with Rodolfo. The final dramatic irony occurs in the drama's last scene (3, 3, 3), completing the contrast between the generous gestures of the women and the unjust behaviour of the men. Rodolfo arrives, like Gennaro in the final scene of *Lucrèce Borgia*, determined to murder the woman he imagines has betrayed him. He believes that Thisbe has denounced Catarina to Angelo and has connived at her murder. Better informed, the audience is likely to regard Rodolfo's decision as scandalously irrational and so to condemn it as one more proof of male abuse of the power society gives men over women. Earlier, in 3, 2, 6, despite the terror her imminent death inspires in her, Catarina had 'protected' Rodolfo from the knowledge that Angelo intended to murder her. Now, to lessen Rodolfo's guilt at killing her, the dying Thisbe blames herself: 'You did nothing. I am responsible. I wanted to die. I forced your hand' (3, 3, 3). Offering her lover an easy conscience as well as escape from Angelo's ven- geance in Padua and life with Catarina thereafter, Thisbe once more exemplifies woman's self-sacrifice to her male exploiters. In Hugo's 'battle of the sexes,' women inevitably fall victim to men.

The press reception of *Angelo* never attained the virulence of the attacks made on *Marie Tudor*. The main complaints concerned the play's lack of historical verisimilitude, and its lack of originality compared to the dramas, Romantic and otherwise, appearing in Paris since 1828. To the first attack, Hugo reacted by publishing in 1837, along with the text of *Angelo*, a curious set of extracts from the 'Statutes of the Inquisition of the [Venetian] State' dated 16 June 1454, and unearthed by Napoleon's soldiers when they over- ran the Republic in 1797 (*OC*, 5, 346–9). The statutes lay down the rules concerning the maintenance by Venice of a system of state espionage on its subjects; they also spell out the state's duty to employ assassins to remove its enemies, to suborn bishops and to use poison as a tool of state policy. No one has established the historical accuracy of these extracts and so they remain rhetorically ineffective as guarantors of the play's historicity. Hugo attempted no answer to press criticisms that his work lacked originality, feeling no need, presumably, to defend his literary reputation in this regard.

He did react strongly, however, when it became obvious that neither Jou- slin de La Salle nor Védel, his successor as manager of the comédie, had any intention of honouring the contract signed in February 1835 stipulat- ing the revival of *Hernani* and *Marion de Lorme*. Hugo waited more than two years before bringing his suit for damages to the Commercial Tribunal of the Seine on 6 November 1837. The trial centred on Hugo's loss of earn- ings occasioned by the Comédie's failure to meet its financial obligations to him as one of the authors who entered into agreements with the com- pany. Hugo's lawyer, Paillard de Villeneuve, had little difficulty in proving statistically that no financial losses accrued from the performance at the Comédie of Hugo's plays. On the contrary, compared with the receipts earned by even the state-funded theatre's favourite star, Mlle Mars, Hugo's dramas, *Hernani* and *Angelo*, had consistently outperformed them finan- cially. He also pointed to the gross disproportion between the number of performances accorded annually to the convential, 'well made' bourgeois productions of Casimir Delavigne and Scribe, when compared with those given to all 'new' (i.e., Romantic) dramatists. This time Hugo succeeded. The court ordered Védel to pay Hugo damages of 6,000 francs, and to revive *Hernani, Marion*, and *Angelo* within five months. On Védel's appeal- ing the verdict, the Cour Royale de Paris decided, on 12 December 1837, that Hugo's case was indeed proved, but ordered Védel to pay a reduced sum of 3,000 francs, given the Comédie's poor financial health. The court also refused to extend the period within which Védel was to have Hugo's dramas performed. Even after total victory, Hugo was never to get full satisfaction from Védel or from the State theatre. But, maintaining throughout the affair that his enemy was never the Comédie itself, he willingly abandoned his right to damages in 1838. *Hernani* was performed six times in both January and February 1838, with Mme Dorval enjoying a great personal success. *Marion de Lorme* received six performances in March. Hugo cancelled the daily fine incurred by the Comédie's delay, and on 24 February abandoned to Védel his claim for the sum of 1,350 francs adding: 'On my side, I will appreciate any efforts the Comédie makes to forget the past' (*OC*, 5, 1132). He also thanked the actors of the Comédie for performing his plays, again cancelling on 6 March a debt of 2,400 francs owed to him by the theatre. Finally, on 20 August, recalling that the Comédie still owed him 18,000 francs for its failure to revive *Angelo*, he gave up all claim to the damages due him.'[8] So much, then, for the allegations often heard about Hugo's 'avarice' concerning contractual agreements involving his literary works.

7. Social Justice as Erotic Aspiration; 'An Earthworm in Love with a Star': *Ruy Blas*

> Let M. Victor Hugo make no mistake about it: opposition to his plays owes more to his politics than to his dramatic system; people bear him less of a grudge for scorning Aristotle than for insulting kings; the disputes over his works in both the theatre and in the newspapers are animated more by party spirit than by [literary] doctrine, and he will always find forgiveness more easily for imitating Shakespeare rather than Cromwell.[1]

Hugo's next dramatic venture necessitated a change of theatre: having quarrelled with Harel at the Porte-Saint-Martin and having successfully sued the Comédie-Française, he could hardly expect, had he so wished, to see a play of his performed sympathetically at either theatre. Fortunately, his reconciliation with Dumas after their temporary misunderstanding during the rehearsals of *Marie Tudor* in 1833 predisposed him to accept his colleague's offer to co-direct the new 'Second Theatre of France.' This idea – to provide a venue in which the plays of young successful Romantic dramatists could be performed – was the brainchild of Dumas' old and Hugo's new friend, Louis-Philippe's son, the Duke d'Orléans and his wife, Helen of Mecklenburg, a great admirer of Hugo's work. Since neither Dumas nor Hugo wished to manage the new house, which was to be called the 'Renaissance Theatre,' they asked Anténor Joly, director of the Parisian review *Le Vert-Vert*, and an enthusiastic supporter of the Romantic drama, to assume the task. They secured the preferential right to perform comedies, tragedies, and dramas, and, with some difficulty, that of adding to them musical interludes as well as that of performing musical comedy. They did not manage to secure a government grant, however, nor could they obtain the right to employ actors already engaged in other Parisian theatres. This meant, for instance, that some of the stars of the Romantic drama, notably Marie Dorval, Bocage, and Mlle George, would be unavailable for the opening in November 1838. But Frédérick Lemaître, Hugo's first choice for his new drama, was free and was to triumph in *Ruy Blas.*

Hugo wrote the drama in July–August 1838, after an intensive period of reading to deepen his knowledge of the history of Spain in the seventeenth century. As usual, he supervised the casting of his play, delighting Lemaître by offering him the name-role. Lemaître, famous since his enormous popular success as Robert Macaire for his ability to play swashbuckling grotesques, had assumed without enthusiasm that he would be playing Don César de Bazan, just such a character. Casting the Queen caused Hugo some loss of sleep. Juliette naturally felt that she had some claim on Hugo's female roles. Mlle Ida, Dumas' mistress, and Atala Beauchêne, Frédérick's mistress and dramatic protégée whom he had caused to be engaged by Joly, also felt they had a right to roles at the Renaissance Theatre. Finally, Mme Hugo intervened. Believing Juliette incapable of playing the Queen, she ensured that the role went to Atala, under her professional name, Louise Beaudouin. Saint-Firmin, a tenor rather than a dramatic actor, was to play Don César de Bazan not entirely with success, and Alexandre Mauzin would be the 'satanic' Don Salluste.

Hugo directed the rehearsals of *Ruy Blas* more closely than those of any other of his dramas, designing sets, choosing the costume designer (his friend, the painter Louis Boulanger), personally advising the actors on their line-readings and gestures, and blocking out their movements onstage. Rehearsals continued as the interior of the theatre was being renovated around them, giving rise to three incidents reported in all accounts of Hugo's dramatic career. The first involved a large iron bar which crashed down upon the seat which Hugo had just left in order to climb onstage to show two actors how he wanted them to move during their dialogue. Hugo's professionalism seems in this instance to have saved his life. The second incident concerns Joly's desire to dispense with the footlights. He believed that, because they emphasized theatrical artifice, they made the actors less human, and that footlights were in any case unnecessary, because in the model he had drawn up for the Renaissance Theatre, the stage was lighted from above. Hugo took exactly the opposite point of view, and his reason underscores the distinction he made between the Romantic drama and 'real' life:

> The model presented a new system: the overhead lamps, positioned on struts concealed in the wings, illuminated [the stage] from above, like the sun; one would no longer be in the theatre but in the street, in the woods,

in a bedroom. M. Victor Hugo opposed the removal of the footlights; he answered that the crude reality of such a performance would run counter to the poetic reality of the play, that the drama was not life itself, but life transfigured into art, that it was therefore right that the actors should also be transfigured, that they were so already by their white makeup and rouge, that the footlights transfigured them all the more, and that the line of light separating the house from the stage formed the natural frontier between the real and the ideal [worlds]. (*VHR*, 579–80)

The footlights stayed, thus helping to distinguish Hugo's rhetorical view of symbolic history from contemporary reality.

Hugo's use of lighting effects to enhance dramatic illusion at the expense of mimetic realism produced experimental scenes in which darkness partly obscured, partly revealed, as in Acts 4 and 5 of *Le Roi s'amuse*, or in Act 4 of *Ruy Blas*, onstage events. Frederick Burwick situates Hugo's lighting effects within the logic of the Romantic exploitation of individual subjectivity: 'Of particular significance on the Romantic stage is the use of optical effects in representing the subjective and the supernatural. Hugo emphasized *chiaroscuro* effects on stage and preferred to use light to emphasize shadowy darkness. Instead of a "realistic" setting with "natural" overhead lighting, Hugo would create stark effects with angled light, hand-held lanterns, and torch or candle processions.'[2] Among such scenes which produce powerful emotional effects are Triboulet's discovery of his dying daughter by lantern-light, the ritual processions of courtiers in *Hernani* and *Ruy Blas*, of monks singing the *De profundis* in *Lucrèce Borgia*, and the entry of the Inquisition in *Torquemada*.

As vigilant to provide optimal conditions for the spectators as he was to protect theatrical illusion, Hugo also rejected another innovation proposed by Joly. Since the new theatre was not situated on the 'boulevard du Crime' and would therefore draw most of its spectators from the fashionable, not the popular public, the manager suggested that he should provide for its wealthier patrons more luxurious seating, with individual seats rather than benches in the orchestra pit. Hugo's stand on this matter shows him defining what he believed to be the ideal audience for his dramas:

M. Victor Hugo replied that fashionable society would have the orchestra stalls, the balconies and the boxes, but that he intended that the popular spectators should keep their places, that is to say [the benches in] the pit and gallery; that they were the real public, lively, impressionable, without literary prejudice, just what was needed for an art that was free; that they were perhaps not the public that went to the Opera but that they were the public that went to the drama; that these spectators were not used to being cooped up and isolated in boxes, that they were never more enthusiastic, intelligent, and content than when they were crowded closely together, and that, for his part, if they took away his pit, he would take away his play. (*RBL*, 1, 102)

The remark is interesting because it shows Hugo once more insisting that the Romantic drama is to be a popular drama, accessible to the whole French public, unlike the learned, or more properly, the quasi-learned, genre favoured by the state-assisted theatres and by the members of the literary and political Establishment who frequented them. Hugo in fact aimed, by his dramatic rhetoric, to influence the whole Parisian theatre-going public.

On 8 November 1838, the evening of the première of *Ruy Blas*, the renovations to the Renaissance Theatre were still not complete. The fashionable audience found the lack of heating most disconcerting: they were obliged to watch the play in their furs and overcoats. Although few of Hugo's supporters from the 'battle' of *Hernani* in 1830 were present, the play's first three acts were well received. Until, that is, Don Salluste's humiliation of Ruy Blas, his valet now become Duke of Olvedo, favourite of the Queen. Don Salluste's trick in dropping his handkerchief, which Ruy Blas must pick up, drew whistles. And Act 4, the invasion of Don Salluste's safe house by the grotesque aristocratic vagrant Don César, was also found wanting partly because the audience judged that Saint-Firmin lacked the panache necessary to bring off such a virtuoso performance.

The principal reason for the drama's success at its première was the performance of Frédérick Lemaître as Ruy Blas, the 'earthworm in love with a star' (2, 2), a naive, though flawed hero. His antithesis, the cynically corrupt Don Salluste, recruits him to destroy the Queen's reputation in revenge for Salluste's being sent into exile for seducing, making pregnant and subsequently refusing to marry one of the Queen's ladies-in-waiting. As Hugo intended, the French audience found extremely distasteful the humiliation by Don Salluste of Ruy Blas, the rapidly maturing hero, who has just brilliantly demonstrated his ability to diagnose Spain's political ills and even, as the Queen's Minister, to begin their reform. As Hugo calculated, in obeying his master's offensive order to close a window, Frédérick's dramatic skill drew applause rather than catcalls: 'But after Mauzin [Salluste] had given the order to close the window, he heard the audience burst into applause. He turned round towards Frédérick and saw him standing motionless, very pale, hesitating, and weeping real tears' (*DRGC*, 323). Frédérick, whom the popular audience identified with the vagabond thief Robert Macaire, had, when he played one of Hugo's exalted popular heroes, the inestimable advantage, for Hugo, of personifying the Romantic hero. His ability to suggest the combination in the same character of sublime and grotesque traits, of heroism and raffishness, eradicated from Lemaître's portrayals of lovers, for example, any cloying sentimentality. The latent violence he was also able to unleash served him well in Act 5 of *Ruy Blas*. Mme Hugo tells us that Lemaître 'dominated' the final act: 'His manner when he tore off his livery, when he went to bolt the door, when he slapped the sword down on the table, when he said to Don Salluste: '... Look!/For a man of intelligence, you really surprise me!,' when he came to ask the Queen's forgiveness, when he drank the poison, all of this was great, deeply felt, magnificent, and the poet [Hugo] had the rare joy of seeing brought to life the character he had dreamed of' (*VHR*, 582).[3]

We have another view of Frédérick's performance in Act 5, this time from the poet Théodore de Banville, only fifteen when he saw *Ruy Blas* in 1838, and clearly fully persuaded to sympathize with Hugo's protagonist: 'I can still see Frédérick in the last act when he rises to punish Salluste. His head raised and threatening, lightning flashing in his eyes, his great head of hair dishevelled; he had discovered an absolutely beautiful, heroic physical stance: his arm thrown back, he held straight out the sword of vengeance and I still remember the indignation, grief, barely contained fury, and contemptuous pity that accompanied this line: 'You dare – your Queen – a woman to adore!' I also remember how gently, in a phrase so musical that its notes might have been written down, Ruy Blas sighed after drinking the poison: 'Sad flame, be extinguished!' (*VHT*, 150). The star's triumph ensured an enthusiastic word-of-mouth that, in its turn produced a solid financial success. *Ruy Blas* ran for fifty performances before being taken off when Frédérick left the company at the end of May 1839.

The press reaction, which Joly judged 'good' (*RBL*, 1, 107), could only be so rated by a nineteenth-century theatre manager accustomed to the ferocity of the politico-literary partisanship that characterized theatre reviewing at the time. Those who criticized the drama after seeing it – unlike Balzac and Sainte-Beuve, who in their correspondence state that their distaste for the play prevented them from actually watching a performance – found much that was wrong with it. The play's political dimension, Hugo's return, that is, to the theme of social justice, offended critics of the far Right as well as the Liberals. The Queen's relationship with a lackey offended contemporary ideas, literal and figurative presumably, about good breeding and about the decorum that should characterize royalty's dealings with commoners. Act 4, almost entirely given over to the comic relief deriving from Don César's sudden and totally unprepared re-entry into a dramatic action that his blunders would make tragic, drew frequent indignant criticism of a moralizing nature. Hugo's preference for 'symbolic history' over historical accuracy, a preference which, he believed, would produce lessons about contemporary events, did not convince many drama critics. And Gustave Planche, in yet another personal attack on Hugo, speculated that the author of *Ruy Blas* must by now have gone completely insane, writing: 'Either *Ruy Blas* is a wager against common sense or it's an act of madness.'[4]

The press condemned Hugo on two political counts: 1) they accused him of offending public decency by linking his lackey with the Queen of Spain and 2) they rejected his concern for the Spanish people whom Ruy Blas describes as starving because of the Grandees' greed and lack of political honour. Planche, for example, combined righteous indignation and voyeurism in his comment on the Queen-lackey theme: 'A Queen in love with a lackey, this is the subject chosen by M. Hugo. Eighteenth-century marquises had themselves bathed by their lackeys explaining that a lackey is not a man; M. Hugo has discovered that a lackey possesses, for the Queen of Spain, the stuff of a lover' (*RB*, 342). Asserting without proof that the public shared his reaction, Planche also expressed his scandal at the Queen's association with a 'Minister' prepared to suffer the humiliation that Ruy Blas' master inflicts upon him in Act 3: 'This scene aroused amazement, shudders of indignation in the auditorium ... To obey such insulting orders, you need to be a coward, a madman ... Ruy Blas is resigned to his own degradation as if he wishes to hasten the accomplishment of the vengeance prepared by Don Salluste ... The cup of Absurdity overflows' (*RB*, 343).

The charge of absurdity was also levelled by the Parisian press at the dual aspect of Hugo's hero, man of the people on the one hand, Minister of integrity and chaste suitor of the Queen on the other. And they are joined by at least one modern critic, W.D. Howarth, who also critizes the Queen-lackey love affair on the grounds of historicity and verisimilitude (*SG*, 184), while at the same pointing to a number of literary sources and historical instances that Hugo might have adduced. Such examples involved records of just such liaisons between royal ladies and commoners. Hugo explained in a note to the published text of *Ruy Blas* that in his conception, historical fact was to be used to guarantee the credibility of fictional events: by defining time and setting – for in a play they can do no more – authentic details allow for imaginative reconstruction of the past (*OC*, 5, 775–7).

Formalist critics like Frederick Burwick, however, absolve Hugo from any real desire for historicity by reminding us of the inevitably illusionist nature of all dramatic representation, and particularly of the Romantic drama: 'For Hugo, the paradoxical nature of stage illusion implicated and, depending on the playwright's skill, replicated the essential antagonism confronting all social, political, and religious ideals in the real world. His "history plays" pretend no fidelity to actual historical events. He uses history as a psychological moment to explore possible motives and actions. Hugo is especially concerned with dramatizing the opposition of the practical and the imaginary and his stage settings provide for a contest between orthodox and radical interpretations of history.'[5] Historical accuracy therefore takes second place to the Romantic drama's philosophical or poetic 'truth' which may well teach us allegorical lessons about contemporary political situations and personages. As Hugo himself wrote in November 1838: 'The small details of history and domestic life must be scrupulously studied and reproduced by the poet, but only as a means of increasing the reality of the whole, and to spread to the darkest corners of the work that general and powerful life in the midst of which the characters are truer and the catastrophes, consequently, more poignant' (*OC*, 5, 775–6).

It was Hugo's poetical belief in the 'general' (rather than the 'particular') truth of historical events that allowed him to dispense with historical accuracy as rhetorical need dictated. Less important to him were the historical constraints preventing Ruy Blas' rise in seventeeth-century Spain, than was the character's allegorical value as a man of the people personifying the aspirations of those like him in nineteenth-century France to ascend the social scale. Naturally, the dangers to the established minority of such a lesson were obvious, as their newspapers revealed and as another poet, Théodore de Banville, realized: 'What amazement, what a shudder of fear when Frédérick appeared, "a flunkey in red livery and galloons," and when the livery, as worn by him, truly looked like the purple of some god in exile, as he cried out: "That man! The King! I am jealous of him!" But the drama did not continue without whistling, for the fortunate ones with large bellies were saying to themselves, not without cause: "What will become of us if the starving are allowed to say they are hungry, and if we allow them to erect their ladders to climb into our heaven?"' (*PVH*, 143–4). Hugo's use of his dramas to spread his hatred of social injustice explains the violent attacks he received from the Parisian press, weighted then as now in favour of the political 'haves' rather than the 'have-nots.'

Analysis of *Ruy Blas* demonstrates the centrality to the play of the theme of social reform. The class war exists in the play at two levels: both at the formal (or 'psychological') as well as at the symbolic (or political) level. Viewed formally as characters involved in a drama, Don Salluste, Ruy Blas, and the Queen represent a fairly conventional logical triangle in French theatre: the master, defeated by the woman he has tried to dominate, obtains his revenge by tempting his valet into seducing her and so ruining her reputation. But in *Ruy Blas* the woman in question is not some fictional marquise but the Queen of Spain. The drama then takes on symbolic meaning and so rhetorical power. Any such attempted seduction must be seen within the context of seventeenth-century Spanish history. In case any doubt should remain on this score, Hugo's Preface to the play explained its meaning, if viewed as a document illustrating the 'philosophy of history.' Seen thus, Don Salluste and Don César, two representative Spanish noblemen, personify opposite reactions – respectively, the corrupt will to power and wealth, and the descent into dissipation – to the decadence into which Spain and her empire had fallen at the end of the seventeenth century. As Hugo declares antithetically: '[T]he first half of the Spanish nobility would be summarized by Don Salluste, and the second half by Don César' (*OC*, 5, 672). In such a context, Ruy Blas' place becomes quite clear, as Hugo resolves the conflict by introducing him as the synthetic personification of Spain's democratic future:

> If we continue our examination of the Spanish monarchy at this period [around 1695], beneath the nobility divided thus, and which might up to a point be personified by the two men just mentioned, we can see something great, something dark and unknown moving, in the shadows. The people. The people, who possess the future but not the present: the people, orphaned, poor, intelligent and strong; positioned very low down, aspiring very high; bearing on their backs the marks of servitude and in their hearts a premeditation of genius; the people, valets of the great lords and, in their abjection and wretchedness, in love with the only figure in this society in ruins who represents for them authority, charity and fecundity. The people is Ruy Blas.' (*OC*, 5, 673)[6]

It is within this philosophico-historical logic that we are justified in seeing Ruy Blas' suicide and concomitant failure to arrest Spain's slide into decadence as indicating Hugo's pessimism concerning the people's ability to govern, both in seventeenth-century Spain and in nineteenth-century France.

Hugo accompanies his rhetorical interpretation of the historical significance of his play with the disclaimer that such an interpretation is not the only one possible, adding that there are at least three 'subjects' in the play: 'The philosophical subject of *Ruy Blas* is the people aspiring to rise to greater heights; the human subject is a man's love for a woman; and the dramatic subject is a lackey's love for a Queen' (*OC*, 5, 674). It is the complications in the parallel and simultaneous development of these three subjects (combining appeals to emotion and to reason) that best illustrate Hugo's skilful use of the devices most characteristic of the Romantic drama.

As usual he employs the dramatic tools borrowed from the melodrama. Each of the three male characters employs a disguise to change his identity or to conceal himself at strategic points in the dramatic action. Disguise is accompanied, in the case of Ruy Blas, by a change of name when, in Act 1, he assumes the identity of his friend and 'brother,' Don César de Bazan. In fact, Ruy Blas changes his skin so often that it is difficult to assign to him a firm identity. In Act 1, we learn that his life as an idealistic student has ended that very day when he assumed the livery of Don Salluste's valet. By the end of the same act, however, Salluste, partly by dressing him in his own cloak, has already successfully passed him off to a group of court grandees as his own cousin, Don César. The irony of such an impersonation is obvious, of course: if a commoner can so readily and with so little help, assume the identity of a Spanish grandee, what exactly is it that comprises the social, intellectual, or moral superiority claimed by the members of the over-class?

Meanwhile, Don César himself, by stealing and putting on the Count d'Albe's doublet, prepares his own arrest in Act 4. Don Salluste goes into exile at the end of Act 1, returning in Act 3, at the high point of Ruy Blas' prestige when, as Minister of the Crown, his manservant basks in the Queen's admiration of his political vision of Spain. Dramatic irony heightens Don Salluste's return in disguise – the audience watches him listening to Ruy Blas' naive lyrical outpourings – as Hugo's stage direction makes clear: '*Several moments before [the end of Ruy Blas' monologue], a man enters by the door upstage, muffled up in a huge cloak, wearing a hat trimmed with silver. He comes slowly forward towards Ruy Blas without being seen by him, and at the very moment that Ruy Blas, ecstatically happy, raises his eyes to heaven, this man suddenly puts his hand on his shoulder. Ruy Blas turns round as if startled out of sleep; the man allows his cloak to fall open, and Ruy Blas recognizes Don Salluste. Don Salluste is wearing flame-coloured livery with silver braiding, like that of Ruy Blas' page*' (2, 4).

Not only does the livery – the iconic sign of the interchange in their roles – suggest the ambiguity, collusion, indeed the virtual doubling, of Salluste the master plotter and Ruy Blas the hitherto willing pawn in his game, it also marks the climactic peripeteia of the plot. In fact, Hugo had originally planned to open *Ruy Blas* with this dramatic confrontation which reverses forever Ruy Blas' situation.[7] Having arrived at the height of his power and prestige, having conquered the Queen's esteem, as she has just shown in Act 3, scene 3, Ruy Blas sees his world crumble at the touch of Don Salluste's hand on his shoulder. And it is the Romantic use, or Shakespeare-like abuse, of the devices of disguise and change of identity that makes the reversal possible. Only in Act 5, by re-assuming his lackey's livery and proclaiming his name and social condition ('My name is Ruy Blas, and I am a lackey!' [5, 3]) can he save the Queen from Salluste's plot and take his vengeance on his 'master.' As the dissatisfied critics' remarks show, Hugo's contemporary audience was less convinced by the valet's humiliation than by his vengeance, which seems to have offended no one.

No less striking as an example of Hugo's use of a peripeteia based on *anagnorisis* is the process, in Act 2, scene 3, by which the Queen learns the identity of the unknown admirer who, at the risk of injury and arrest, climbs into the grounds of the palace to bring her flowers each day. As she ponders the latest development – a piece of bloodstained lace she found three days earlier on the spike-topped palace wall – a delegation with a letter from the King is announced: '*The group enters with great solemnity. The Duchess first, then her ladies. Ruy Blas remains upstage. He is splendidly dressed. His cloak covers his left hand, hiding it. Two pages, carrying the King's letter on a golden cushion, come forward and kneel down in front of the Queen*' (3, 3). Ruy Blas, in his disguise as King's messenger, delivers the King's note, whose flatness ('Madame, it is very windy and I killed six wolves') recalls Louis XVI's famous diary entry on 14 July, 1789 ('Nothing today').[8] The Queen has no difficulty in recognizing the handwriting in the King's letter, but not knowing that the messenger is also the King's amanuensis, asks to speak to Ruy Blas, who tells her that, three days earlier, he had left Madrid to attend the King.

Inserted within the recognition scene is one of dark comedy. Don Guritan, an aged courtier hopelessly in love with the Queen, in order to discourage Ruy Blas in whom he scents a dangerous rival for her affections, informs him that part of his [Ruy Blas'] duties as her equerry consists in holding open the door to her chamber when the King goes at night to fulfil his conjugal duties. This news is too much for the lovesick, injured Ruy Blas, who faints. What follows – dialogue, asides and stage directions – illustrates the skilful combination in Romantic drama of speech in various voices, along with mime and action:

> *He falls exhausted into an armchair. His cloak falls open, revealing his left hand wrapped in a blood-covered bandage.*
> CASILDA: Good Lord, Madame, he is wounded
>   In the hand!
> QUEEN: Wounded!
> CASILDA: He's fainting!
>   Quick, let's get some smelling salts!
> QUEEN: (*searching in the front of her dress*)
>   I have a flask containing a liquid ...
> *At this moment her eye falls on Ruy Blas' right cuff. (Aside.)*
>   It's the same lace!
> *At the same moment she takes the flask from her bosom, and with it, in her confusion,*

*the piece of lace hidden there. Ruy Blas, who does not take his eyes off her, sees the lace
leave the Queen's bosom.*
RUY BLAS: Oh!
The Queen and Ruy Blas look at each other in silence.
QUEEN: (*Aside*)   He is ... !
RUY BLAS: (*Aside*)   Next to her heart!   (2, 3)

The recognition scene is all the more effective because, earlier in the act,
Hugo had been careful to inform the audience fully of both the identity of
the Queen's admirer and her attitude towards him. This example of dramatic irony confirms once again Hugo's skill in its use and his acceptance
of the logic of inference and implication on which it rests. And, if dramatic
irony is a particularly successful Hugolian dramatic technique, so is his
'Shakespearean' incorporation into Act 4 and elsewhere of the grotesque,
a principal characteristic of the Romantic drama.

We have already seen the black comedy that Don Guritan introduces into
Ruy Blas. His role as farcical victim, providing comic relief continues in Act
2, which ends with the Queen' sending him on a frivolous errand to Austria
in order to prevent him from killing her young admirer. Both Don César
and Ruy Blas himself also personify different aspects of the grotesque in the
play. Ruy Blas, with his allegorical name, half noble, half commoner, illustrates Hugo's use of oxymoron as a device revelatory of character. He carries in his lackey's soul a combination of high thoughts and sincere feelings,
a combination grotesquely out of keeping with his social status. He is also
the hero whose tragic flaw – his love for the Queen makes him an uncomprehending but compliant accomplice to the blackening of her reputation
– prevents him from accomplishing the great promise that his political
analysis of Spain's social ills demonstrates. Arriving just as Spain's noble
Ministers are engaged in dividing amongst themselves for their own profit
the 'spoils,' their helpless country, Ruy Blas harangues them in a speech of
some one hundred lines, beginning 'Bon appétit, messieurs,' in which he
compares their self-interested machinations to the appetites of beasts of
prey. Exploiting to the full the figures of vehemence – most notably sarcasm, imprecation, reproaches, derision, prophecies and threats of
retribution[9] – the new Minister displays both his contempt for cynical aristocratic *Realpolitik* and his desire to aid the underclass:

                    O honest ministers!
Virtuous counsellors! This is the way
You serve, servants who pillage the house!
So you have no shame and you choose the time,

The dark time when a dying Spain can only weep!
So you have no other interest here
Than that of filling your pockets and decamping afterwards!
In the face of your declining country, may you be branded
As grave-diggers who rob her in her tomb!   (3, 2)

But Hugo has deprived the speaker of *ethos*, which is to say rhetorical authority. And so the harangue appears grotesque in the mouth of a lackey disguised as a Minister of the Crown, wearing robes borrowed from Don Salluste and an identity from Don César de Bazan. Hugo's oxymoron both empowers and defuses Ruy Blas' rhetorical power.

But Ruy Blas is not the only paradoxical character in the drama. Don César, the comically grotesque nobleman who has wasted his inheritance and is forced to survive by living among thieves and cut-throats, nonetheless possesses a moral characteristic which gives him, for a moment at least, a generosity that probably explains why audiences offer him their sympathy. Tempted in Act 1 by Don Salluste with money – his pressing need and besetting vice – Don César, unlike his friend Ruy Blas, rejects utterly any plot against a woman, without even ascertaining the victim's identity. His refusal earns him exile, enslavement to pirates, and the risk of death. But, Hamlet-like, he escapes his captors and returns intent upon a reckoning. Act 4 is entirely devoted to the second grotesque rise and fall of Don César, down-at-heel pícaro and man of honour. Don César's 'resurrection,' thanks to a series of misunderstandings involving his 'sharing' the same name with the house's newly powerful occupant, Ruy Blas, allows him to satisfy all his appetites. He begins by obtaining food and drink, then receives money, is offered an assignation with an unknown lady, and finally wins a duel by killing Don Guritan. Don César thus reacquires all the attributes of the Spanish grandee, only to lose them again when Don Salluste re-appears.

Scenes 2 to 5 of Act 4 present a delicious parody of some of the best-known scenes in French comedy. Misunderstandings pile up because no one thinks to question Don César's behaviour. His name causes his interlocutors to imagine that he is the owner of the house and the paramour of the lady whose duenna arrives to arrange the evening's rendez-vous. But when he becomes the innocent victim of Don Guritan's wrath, both men are comically misinformed. Don Guritan is enraged when Don César claims merely to be himself – Don Guritan is seeking revenge against Ruy Blas whom he knows as Don César – and Don César himself imagines that his evening meeting is with Don Guritan's wife. Their dialogue rapidly takes the form of a comic *stichomythia*:

> DON CÉSAR: I have just arrived from the strangest countries.
> DON GURITAN: You have arrived, my dear sir? Well, I have arrived
> From even farther than you!
> DON CÉSAR (*beaming*):   From what famous shore?
> DON GURITAN: From yonder, in the north.
> DON CÉSAR: And I, from way down
> In the south.
> DON GURITAN: I'm furious!
> DON CÉSAR: Is that right?
> I'm in a rage!
> DON GURITAN: I've covered twelve hundred leagues!
> DON CÉSAR: And I, two thousand ...
> DON GURITAN: I was tricked, sir!
> DON CÉSAR: And I was sold!
> DON GURITAN: I was practically exiled!
> DON CÉSAR: I was practically hanged!   (4, 5)

The farcical nature of this scene between two interlocutors each determined to cap his adversary's statements clearly identifies it as an example of Hugo's Shakespearean taste for comic relief in the midst of tragedy. Naturally Act 4 produced some of the most negative comments from critics of the play in 1838. Modern audiences, however, are likely to judge that it contains some of the drama's most comically ambiguous moments.

But tragedy returns in Act 5, when Don Salluste attempts to ruin the Queen's reputation by recalling Ruy Blas to his lackey's function and by tempting the Queen with the offer of flight and subsequent happiness with the man she loves. Since his return to Madrid, Don Salluste has already reminded Ruy Blas of the social reality that their respective ranks imply:

> Know your place. I am most generous, most soft-hearted,
> But, what the devil! A lackey, humble or genteel,
> Is but a vase into which I pour my whims.
> One does what wishes, my dear, with people like you.
> Your master, according to the plan that moves him,
> At his pleasure disguises you, at his pleasure unmasks you.
> I made you a lord. That's an odd role for you,
> For the moment. You have the whole suit of clothes,
> But, don't forget, you are my valet.
> You are courting the Queen by chance,
> Just as you would stand as footman behind my coach.   (3, 5)

No clearer statement could be made of the constraints placed by social class upon Ruy Blas' conduct.

Such constraints, and his acceptance of them, explain his subjection to Don Salluste in Act 5 until, seeing the Queen manipulated and threatened with disgrace by her enemy, the worm turns, or, more properly, the lackey proclaims his status and, rejecting subjection to a 'monster,' proceeds to take action that falls outside polite society's constraints:

> Listen, whatever his rank,
> My lord, when a traitor, a crooked, double-dealing rogue
> Commits certain rare and monstrous acts,
> Nobleman, working man, every man has the right, when he goes by,
> To come and spit his sentence in his face,
> And to take a sword, an axe, a knife! ...
> By God! I was a lackey! What if I turn executioner?   (5, 3)

Even the manner of Don Salluste's death becomes the material of social comment for, when his master asks for a sword to defend his life, Ruy Blas sarcastically points out the social impropriety of such a request:

> DON SALLUSTE: A sword at least!
> RUY BLAS: Marquis, you're joking!
> Master? Am I a gentleman?
> A duel? For shame! I am one of your servants,
> A flunkey in red livery and galloons,
> A rascal to be punished and whipped – and a killer!
> Yes, I'm going to kill you, my lord. Do you understand?
> Like a wretch! Like a coward! Like a dog!   (5, 3)

This incident defines *Ruy Blas* as a post-Revolutionary drama. In Molière's *Don Juan*, in Beaumarchais' (or Mozart's) *Marriage of Figaro*, the servant was never able to punish his master for his transgressions. But rather than Molière's or Beaumarchais' plays, it is Hugo's own *Marie Tudor* that this scene most vividly recalls. In his earlier drama, Gilbert, the working man, despairs at not possessing the right to bear arms and the ability to engage Fabiani in a duel. In contrast, *Ruy Blas* shows the man of the people exacting revenge precisely by refusing his noble would-be opponent the right to a sword. The social inferior thus breaks one of the social restraints imposed by the *ancien régime*, whether in Spain or France.

But in Hugo's dramatic world the people's revenge can only be self-defeating. Ruy Blas must die for his transgression or he, in his turn, risks becoming another Don Salluste. The allegorical hero's suicide at the end of *Ruy Blas* is the measure of Hugo's political pessimism in 1838. Despite his criticisms of the manifest social injustices perpetuated by the French political system, he refrained in *Ruy Blas* from preaching violent revolution, presumably believing the people inadequate to the task of governing France. Revolution would come to Paris in 1848, but by that time Hugo's career as Romantic dramatist was all but over.

8. Hugo Abandons the Romantic Drama: *La Esmeralda, Les Jumeaux,* and *Les Burgraves*

Victor Hugo's output for the stage had been slowing down since 1836. No more would he produce, as in that *annus mirabilis* 1832, two plays in a single year. If he had entertained the ambition of dominating the French theatre by occupying at the same time the stage at both the Comédie-Française and at the Porte-Saint-Martin, by 1836 he had abandoned this ambition, for he was producing fewer plays and the intervals between them were growing longer. As we have seen, between June and September 1832, he wrote two dramas, *Le Roi s'amuse* in verse, and *Lucrèce Borgia* in prose. Then, after a twelve-month interval he wrote the second of his prose dramas, *Marie Tudor*, in August 1833. He waited eighteen months before composing *Angelo*, his next prose drama, in February 1835. But almost three and a half years were to elapse before he completed his next verse drama, *Ruy Blas*, which opened in 1838. And *Les Burgraves*, the last play he wrote before his exile, would appear only in 1843, after an even longer gap of four and a half years.

Nor was he any longer writing his dramas with Mozart-like ease and sureness of hand, or like Shakespeare, who 'never blotted out a line,' according to Ben Jonson at least.[1] In Hugo's papers we find, increasingly, alternative beginnings and endings, and variant scenes for his dramas. It is true that, from *Marion de Lorme* onwards, his manuscripts occasionally show him hesitating, unsure of his way, but his uncertainties appear with greater regularity with *Marie Tudor*. For that play, for instance, he wrote a whole first act but, dissatisfied, he then set it aside before beginning again. Whether or not, as Descotes suggests, he did so because he wanted to create a more important role for Juliette Drouet, we do not know, for Hugo gives almost no information about his creative processes. What we can say, is that the new first act hardly improves the exposition of *Marie Tudor*. Between 1834 and 1839, he also began and abandoned a number of dramatic projects, another sign of unaccustomed hesitation on his part. His manuscripts contain notes on a possible drama entitled *Mme Louis XIV* about the wife of Scarron the poet. (As Mme de Maintenon, she became the last of the Sun King's female consorts.) Such a topic, that of a great monarch forced to take second place to one of his subjects, would clearly have possessed great interest for Hugo. But it was to another uncompleted drama, also concerning Louis XIV, that Hugo devoted the greatest proportion of his unproductive time and energy in this period, and that, in August 1839, he abandoned late in Act 3. In *Les Jumeaux* (*The Twins*), he dramatized, as we shall see, the legends surrounding the 'Man in the Iron Mask.'

Study of the critical attacks on Hugo the dramatist between 1833 and 1835 suggests that his hesitations and falling dramatic output were caused in part by the enmity of critics like Désiré Nisard and Gustave Planche, both violently opposed to the Romantic drama, particularly when written by Hugo. Nisard, for instance, who in 1834 published a study of the poets of the Roman decadence, also wrote an all-out assault on the Romantic drama. The following short extract gives some idea of the virulence of Nisard's criticisms: 'The third branch of facile literature is the drama which one might say is written on getting up from dinner, between [visits to] a theatre manager and some celebrated actress, on the end of a drinks table, perhaps – goodness knows! – on the actress's naked shoulders ... ; the drama flanked by its theories and presumptuous prefaces condemns for the sins of stupidity and ignorance whoever does not fall down in admiration of it ...' (*RB*, 239). Even Hugo, despite his confidence in the validity and seriousness of his literary endeavours, must have entertained some doubts on reading such an attack, from an acknowledged literary critic, spread over two numbers of the *Revue de Paris* in December 1833. No longer was Sainte-Beuve ready to defend him either, for by now the personal rift between the two men had solidified into both private and professional enmity. For the first time since 1830, the year of *Hernani*, Hugo completed no drama in 1834; such halts were to be repeated over the next nine years, which would see him finish only two more dramas, *Angelo* (1835), *Ruy Blas* (1838), and the epic melodrama, *Les Burgraves* (1843).

LA ESMERALDA[2]

Nothing illustrates better that Hugo's dramatic talent was, if not drying up, then at least flowing more sluggishly, than the problems he encountered in adapting *Notre-Dame de Paris* into the opera named after that novel's heroine, *La Esmeralda*. The novel appeared in March 1831, the same month that Hugo's future collaborator, Louise Bertin, saw her opera, *Fausto*, produced at Paris' Théâtre-Italien. She was the daughter of François Bertin, founder of the *Journal des Débats*, with whom, as we have seen, the Hugo family entertained friendly relations. Out of friendship, Mme Hugo tells us, Hugo agreed to write the libretto for an opera. He had already refused such an offer from Meyerbeer to adapt his novel to the operatic stage. The first lines that Hugo contributed to the collaboration date from September 1831, but the opera would not be staged until 14 November 1836, at the Académie Royale de Musique. It is true, of course, that the work progressed intermittently, with the composer requesting lines of different lengths to fit the music – the libretto contains lines of five, six, seven, and eight syllables as well as occasional alexandrines – and, in his libretto, Hugo also had to modify his novel, changing particularly its ending, to meet his collaborator's demands. As ever for Hugo, censorship was a problem too. The Catholic Church placed *Notre-Dame de Paris* on its Index of Condemned Books in November 1834; so when the libretto went to the censor in January 1836, a change of title was imposed, as was removal throughout of the word 'priest' – Dom Frollo being Esmeralda's sexually obsessed would-be lover. However, in publishing the libretto – which was on sale on the first night – Hugo retained the original text, and the singers, complaining of poor memories, performed in some instances the banned words.

Berlioz conducted the orchestra during the rehearsals in October-November and Liszt prepared a piano transcription of the score which was published in 1837. Berlioz wrote of the opera and its reception:

> The main parts – Phoebus, Frollo, Esmeralda, and Quasimodo – were taken respectively by Nourrit, Levasseur, Mlle Falcon and Massol – in other words by the best actor-singers at the Opéra.
>
> Several numbers, including the big duet for the Priest and the Gipsy in the second act, a ballad, and the extremely striking aria for Quasimodo were loudly applauded at the dress rehearsal. Nevertheless, this work by a woman who had never written a line of criticism, who had never been guilty of attacking anybody nor of praising anybody insufficiently, and whose sole crime was that she belonged to a family that owned a powerful newspaper whose political views were detested by a section of the community – this work, though greatly superior to many ephemeral pieces that are successful or at least tolerated, failed utterly and catastrophically.[3]

Other commentators were less categorical in declaring the work a 'catastrophic' failure, but it was taken off after six performances and it remains unknown nowadays, with only Quasimodo's 'Aria of the bells' existing on disk. Once again, Hugo's political enemies, or the enemies of his friends, were responsible in part for causing the failure of a dramatic work in which he had a hand.

LES JUMEAUX

Between 26 July and 23 August 1839, Hugo wrote almost three acts of what is, along with *Torquemada*, his blackest drama, *Les Jumeaux* (*The Twins*). His interest in the legends surrounding the mysterious political prisoner who in the seventeenth century was moved around from prison to prison in France had been aroused when he read Voltaire. In the *Dictionnaire philosophique*, as well as in *Le Siècle de Louis XIV*, Voltaire, who had himself spent two periods of imprisonment in the Bastille, presented the hypothesis which nineteenth- and twentieth-century writers of historical fiction would later exploit: namely, that the 'Mask' was the twin brother of Louis XIV, incarcerated for life by French ruling authorities from Mazarin and the Queen Mother to Louis himself, in order to prevent civil war and the possible division of France. Hugo's reason for considering such a subject was, like Voltaire's, political and philosophical. If, the Voltairean hypothesis went, divine Providence could produce such an historical anomaly or *aporia* as two equally legitimate heirs to the French throne, what then are we to make of political claims concerning Louis XIV's legitimacy, guaranteed as it was by a political crime? Or alternatively, what credence should we give to claims by supporters of the Bourbons concerning the 'divine' right of Louis to rule, or by believers in the benevolence of a 'divine Providence' which thus proved itself capable of playing such tricks on hapless royal rulers and their bewildered subjects? It was this politico-philosophical complexity that made *Les Jumeaux* even more compelling to Hugo as the subject for a verse drama on seventeenth-century France than his projected play, *Madame Louis XIV*, about the aged Louis XIV's taking second place, chronologically speaking, for his wife's favours to Scarron, the scrofulous poet.

In the almost three acts of *Les Jumeaux* that he did complete, Hugo produced a grotesque picture of seventeenth-century France, a kind of 'downside' or 'dark side' of the 'Great Century.' Act 1 presents a mysterious figure, initially called simply 'The Man,' who exchanges his rich clothes for the mummer's garb of Guillou-Gorju, a mountebank, thief, and charlatan. Guillou-Gorju and Tagus, his fellow pickpocket, strolling player, and fairground barker, gull the bourgeois patrons gawking at their show of patent medicines while also relieving them of their watches, wallets, and other valuables. Among the passers-by in the Saint-Germain Fair on the Place de Bussy, several noblemen discuss the misdeeds of Mazarin, the young King

Louis XIV's Minister, guilty, among many other political crimes, of outlaw-
ing for plots against him one Jean de Créqui, who, fifteen years earlier, had
unknowingly seduced his brother's wife. She had subsequently given birth
to their incestuous child, Alix de Ponthieu. Also in the square, accompanied by his men, is Master Benoit Trévoux, Parisian Chief of Police, come
to arrest Guillou-Gorju for thieving and general charlatanry. 'The Man,'
who in his mummer's costume is identical to Guillou-Gorju – a reflection
at the vestimentary level of the theme of identity between the royal
brothers[4] – is able, thanks to his quick-witted exploitation of chance-gained
evidence, to turn the tables completely on his adversary, finally blackmail-
ing the Chief of Police into complicity to defeat justice. The noblemen
return, the Man reveals himself to be Jean de Créqui and promises them
help in their projected revolt against the civil authorities, just as he promises his help, on her arrival, to his daughter, Alix de Ponthieu, to free the
Mask, with whom she is in love.

As may be seen from this summary, Hugo omitted few opportunities in
Act 1 to blacken the 'Great Century,' perhaps in answer to his own critics
who constantly quoted to him the acknowledged superiority of the French
neo-classical authors of the Age of Louis XIV. Civil strife, police inefficiency
and dishonesty, unpunished popular crime, even incest among the nobility
– all these things produce a general atmosphere of corruption and political discontent that pervades the events presented or discussed. What he
may have omitted in Act 1, he supplies in Acts 2 and 3. We meet the Mask,
pathetic victim of his mother's decision to have him locked away for life in
favour of his twin, Louis XIV. In accordance with some historical authorities, Hugo represents Anne of Austria, the Queen Mother, as married to
Mazarin, Cardinal and First Minister of France. (In the part of the drama
he completed, she does not get to play what in his notes Hugo called the
drama's 'great scene' in which she as mother fails to recognize her
unmasked son, confusing him with his more fortunate brother, the King.)
Count John, as Créqui is called now, and Alix rescue the Mask from his
prison in the château de Pierrefonds.

Act 3, set in Créqui's fictional former home, the significantly named
Plessis-les-Rois, presents onstage the sixteen-year-old King Louis XIV, whom
both his mother and Mazarin manipulate for their different ends. The
Mask is on stage, hidden from his enemy's view, when Mazarin, old, sick,
and exhausted, but at the height of his political power and with a vision of
Europe that Hugo was fully to espouse, begins a long soliloquy on the
theme of government and its responsibilities. The manuscript comes to an
end in mid-line, without resolving the problems implied by the Mask's freedom, the unlikely happiness of the lovers, and Mazarin's, or worse, the
Queen Mother's intervention. Hugo simply wrote at the bottom of the

manuscript: 'interrupted on August 23 [1839] because of illness,' and stopped there.

The reasons advanced for Hugo's leaving the drama uncompleted are many and diverse. That he was really ill seems likely. Hugo suffered frequently from an ocular disorder brought on by excessive reading, and the disease had recurred in August 1839. But a passing eye problem fails to explain why he never returned to Les Jumeaux once recovered. It is also true that he left soon afterwards for his annual trip with Juliette, this time to the Rhine, but again, why did he not complete the play after his holiday? Biographers of Hugo have pointed to the extraordinary resemblance of the relationship between the brothers in Les Jumeaux and that between Hugo and his own brother, Eugène, who had died in 1837 after fourteen years locked away in the Charenton lunatic asylum. Eugène's malady, they point out, had worsened dramatically the night of Hugo's marriage to Adèle. Does the theme of incest in Les Jumeaux represent an allegorical comment upon Hugo's sexual guilt in marrying a woman his brother also desired? Does the theme of the royal twins, one the favoured idol of his country, the other incarcerated for life by his own family, allegorize Hugo's guilt at his own success and his brother's tragic fate? No sure answer suggests itself but, given these disturbing similarities, coincidental or otherwise, Hugo may well have preferred not to complete a subject he found too painful, or too revealing.

Someone did complete Les Jumeaux, however. The drama, published in its incomplete form for the first time only in 1933, was performed by Jean Serge – who fashioned an ending from the sketches and fragments Hugo left of Act 4, as well as from Alfred de Vigny's poem, La Prison – at the Festival of Carcassonne in 1970. Ubersfeld, who has edited Hugo's manuscript additions to the incomplete drama, gives this account of one possible ending, which Serge seems to have used:

> Two sheets of paper attached to the manuscript allow us to conjecture how the play would have continued: Mazarin sees the Mask and locks him up; the Queen arrives, who mistakes him for the King, but then [the Mask] makes her recognize him; [maternal] love scene. Probably the Mask is disguised in the King's clothes and passes for him. Act 4 would probably have had a scene between the Queen and Count John, then between the Queen and [Count] Brézé, who proposes to kill Mazarin. The next scene would present some character hired to murder the Mask, but the idea would arise that someone else might be killed and substituted for the intended victim. Thus Alix, like Blanche in Le Roi s'amuse, could give her life for the Twin. A scene between the Queen and Alix. Act 5 would see the reversal of this situation: Count John, who holds the Mask captive, comes to

claim his daughter and the Queen her son. Apparently, the exchange takes place and the Mask goes back to prison. (*VHTL*, 2, 969)

Such an ending would confirm Hugo's darkly pessimistic view of the history of France's 'Great Century,' with reasons of state justifying crimes against individual liberty and family ties. We shall never know, of course, how Hugo would, in fact, have ended the drama, but we possess enough of it, in my view, to make plausible both Serge's version and our conclusion concerning Hugo's pessimism.

EPIC MELODRAMA: LES BURGRAVES

> For some time now, the theatres have been going through a crisis whose duration remains unknown. The public has become totally indifferent, and authors seem to be striving to outdo each other in maintaining the public in its dreary slumber. How could we know, ten years ago, that this would be the outcome to which the new drama would bring us?[5]

It is significant that this lament should have appeared, in April 1841, in the review whose editor-in-chief, François Buloz, had become administrator of the Comédie-Française in 1838. Buloz it was who approached Hugo in August 1841 for a new drama for performance at the Comédie. Hugo, just elected to the French Academy in January of that year, promised to have his new play ready for him by 15 February 1842, but it was in fact March 1843 before *Les Burgraves* was ready for performance.

During the five years since *Ruy Blas*, the theatre-going public had seen major changes in the Parisian dramatic scene, including the rise of a new star at the Comédie, one who did not act in the successful Romantic dramas of the day, preferring to play the great tragic heroines of Corneille and Racine, eventually triumphing as Phèdre in 1843. Rachel Félix was capable, like Mlle Mars before her, and Sarah Bernhardt thirty years later, of enormously increasing the receipts at the state-funded Comédie by her sole presence in the cast of a classical tragedy. As a result, critics have frequently assigned her a major role in causing the demise of the Romantic drama. Also held partly responsible was François Ponsard who, in 1843, staged his Republican tragedy in the classical style, *Lucrèce*, at the Odéon. The roles of Lucretia and Brutus were played by Mme Dorval and Bocage, the former stars of the Romantic dramas of Hugo, Vigny, and Dumas. In fact, as Maurice Descotes points out, by 1843, 'the great generation of Romantic actors was becoming extinct' (*DRGC*, 337), with the result that when Hugo did complete *Les Burgraves*, he was to have difficulty casting the principal roles.

It seems to have been easier for Rachel than for Ponsard to turn back the clock to classical techniques, however. While she, as the new star of the Comédie-Française, was able to recycle the tricks used by the classically-trained actors at the School of Declamation, Ponsard as a new playwright not only needed Romantic actors to impersonate his ancient Roman characters, but also found himself drawn to imitate the forms of the Romantic drama. Théophile Gautier pointed to this generic influence in his review of *Lucrèce*:

> We were very surprised by the performance. We were expecting a purely classical work and our expectations proved quite happily to be mistaken. The past does not begin again and, even in the most deliberate pastiche, modern life always slips into some nook. Unity of place is not respected in *Lucrèce*, since the action moves from Collatia to Rome. Brutus is a character from the [Romantic] drama, if ever there was one, because strict tragedy does not permit the combination of sublime and grotesque ... The abuse of local colour, for which the poets of the new [Romantic] school were reproached so much, is pushed very far by M. Ponsard, and his style, frequently free and lively, does not possess that holy horror of the concrete term [*mot propre*], [or] that academic taste for periphrasis which distinguishes authors of the classical school. (*HADF*, 3, 48)

While Pousard adopted some of the features of the Romantic drama into his 'classical' play, Rachel totally abandoned the style its actors had developed. Trained by Samson, an old actor long at the Comédie-Française who presented her there as his protégée, she reverted to the old ways of the state-funded house. As Descotes tells us: 'First of all her teacher instructed her in some indispensable traditions. She learned that an actor who knows his business does not come onstage just any old way: he "looks round the assembled public, and favours them with a half-smile"; next, he waits for complete silence, and then he raises his arm. Entrances like this were the opposite of the tumultuous entrances of Frédérick [Lemaître] or Marie Dorval' (*DRGC*, 330). Descotes also explains how Rachel's method of preparing a role was classically inspired: 'We know also how Rachel worked. She did not *feel* the role right away, like Dorval: she copied it out, looked for and took note of the lines in which the characters betrayed themselves; then, she composed, prepared, and moderated each role in its ensemble. For an hour or more, she made every effort to decide upon a line's intonation, using her lips and tongue. A role was first and foremost for her an object requiring long study' (ibid.). It is little wonder that Alfred de Vigny, for whom the emotional Marie Dorval represented the ideal female actor, commented: 'Rachel can express scorn and irony, but her talent lacks love' (ibid., 331).

While these changes in dramatic taste, which would work against Hugo's new play, were occurring in Paris, Hugo himself was changing in his attitude towards the Romantic drama. His manuscript drafts show him moving increasingly away from drama towards the epic as he prepared *Les Burgraves*, and the Preface to the play also indicates clearly his return to that most classical of dramatists, Aeschylus, whose *Oresteia* trilogy Hugo was in some measure to attempt to imitate. Like Aeschylus' trilogy, Hugo's three-part play would end in expiation and reconciliation between 'avenger' and guilty party. *Les Burgraves* would thus be the first of his plays written since 1830 to end, if not entirely happily – after all, Guanhumara dies, as we shall see – but at least without the deaths of either of the principal characters or of the young lovers. Moreover, the happy re-establishment of the imperial family's dynastic stability indicates an ending more appropriate to melodrama with its reassuring, if naive, political optimism. Also, produced just three years after Napoleon's ashes were brought back to France from Saint Helena to be eventually deposited in the catafalque in Les Invalides, Hugo's new drama would present the epic legend of the German Emperor Barbarossa's even more remarkable 'return' from the dead. Thus the oxymoron 'epic melodrama' best describes the true generic make-up of *Les Burgraves*.

But the clearest reason influencing Hugo to write an epic melodrama set in the thirteenth century in a castle on the Rhine among the bandit 'burgraves' or feudal barons, was his new-found passion for Germany, which he visited with Juliette in 1838, 1839 and 1840. From these trips he brought back enough material to publish in 1842 *Le Rhin*, partly based on his letters to Mme Hugo written during his travels which show him meditating upon, among many other Germanic myths and historical events, the legendary Emperor Barbarossa's campaigns against the bandits infesting the Rhine. In fact, as he explained to friends, when they asked him why he had chosen as the principal characters of his play Barbarossa and Job, men in extreme old age (the Emperor is 92), Hugo gives us a rare glimpse of his creative imagination at work:

> [He] explained that, during his travels on the Rhine, wandering through ruined citadels and dreaming of making one of them the scene of a tragedy, he had immediately thought of the great enemy of the Burgraves, Frederick Barbarossa, an epic, remote figure, more real perhaps in poetry than in history. Right there and then, the legend of Barbarossa's mysterious appearance after his death came to mind. Wouldn't it be fine to resuscitate for his work the imperial ghost? Except that by that time Barbarossa was of course an old man, and so, in order to place him in in a later milieu, he would have to show him rediscovering survivors of his own age, bound to him by ancient sentiments of love or hatred. (*OC*, 6, 545)

What Hugo does not say is that, by making the action of *Les Burgraves* depend upon events that occurred in the lives of the principal characters some seventy years before the play begins, he would be forced to have recourse to long narrative passages by witnesses or story-tellers to fill in the missing details. This reduction of the staged action went directly against the aesthetic principles for the Romantic drama he had laid down in the Preface to *Cromwell*, and considerably reduces the action shown onstage. His reliance on the techniques of epic storytelling, on diegetic accounts of actions long since forgotten by the play's protagonists, replaces their mimetic re-enactment, losing in the process much of their emotional impact.

After meditating upon his subject until August 1842, Hugo began composition, completing the drama between 10 September and 19 October. The Comédie-Française accepted the play without difficulty, but would do little to aid Hugo in casting its roles. More than any of his earlier dramas perhaps, *Les Burgraves*, because of the difficulties deriving from its epic, legendary, and, it must be said, largely undramatic qualities, required actors of quite exceptional ability. Unfortunately, none of his first choices for the principal roles were in the troupe at the Comédie. Hugo wanted Frédérick to play Job, but this was impossible, said Buloz. Mlle George was the obvious choice to play the old hag, Guanhumara, a witch determined to force Otbert into patricide; this too was impossible as she was not a member of the troupe. Rachel herself, who had been present at Hugo's reading of the play to the assembled members of the Comédie, refused the role, fearing it would age her in her public's eyes (in 1843 she was 23). So Hugo was forced once again to compromise. As the three Titans, or giants, Job, Magnus, and Barbarossa, he chose MM. Beauvallet, Guyon, and Ligier, of whom only Guyon was tall in stature, an unfortunate fact commented upon by, among others, Frédérick himself. As Guanhumara, Hugo first chose Mlle Maxime, newly elected to the troupe, but then withdrew the role after thirty-two rehearsals, expressing himself dissatisfied with the actress's performance. At this late juncture, Hugo tried to engage Mme Dorval, but the troupe refused to elect her to their number, so he finally settled on Mme Mélingue, recruited specially from the Porte-Saint-Martin theatre. Thus Mme Mélingue represented his fourth choice, after Mesdames George, Maxime and Dorval for this central role. There is disagreement concerning the performances given by Hugo's cast. In a note to the text added on publication, Hugo expressed complete satisfaction with the production as prepared by the Comédie and complimented highly all the principal roles (*OC*, 6, 650–1). Without adducing any evidence, Ubersfeld, however, writes that the play was 'performed less than indifferently by actors who visibly did not believe in it' (*DR*, 152).

The première took place at the Comédie-Française before the most distinguished audience Paris had to offer. Lyonnet gives the following list of notables:

> In the stage boxes, the sons of Louis-Philippe. Here and there, Lamartine, Balzac, Vigny, Dumas who has interrupted the writing of *The Three Musketeers* to come, Alfred de Musset with Émile Deschamps, the latter's brother, Antony, the translator of Dante and, straight from Dr Blanche's surgery, Gérard de Nerval.
>
> Here are Michelet, Quinet, Méry, Alphonse Karr, Arsène Houssaye, Paul Lacroix, Hector Berlioz, Louis Boulanger, Eugène Delacroix, Ary Scheffer.
>
> In the balcony: Frédérick Soulié ... Casimir Delavigne, pensive and sickly. In the boxes, George Sand, Mme de Girardin, Louise Bertin who had composed the music for *Esmeralda*, the pale Princess Belgioiso. The theatrical world is represented by Frédérick Lemaître who had been Ruy Blas, by Bocage who had played Didier, Rachel come to see how Mme Mélingue will act the role of Guanhumara that she refused, Mlle Mars who had been Doña Sol, Mlle George who had played Lucretia Borgia, Mme Dorval who had been Marion de Lorme ...
>
> What a house! Among the critics: Th. Gautier, Jules Janin, Jules Sandeau, Hippolyte Lucas, Cassagnac, Édouard Thierry, Charles Magnin, and all the rest of less importance. Only Sainte-Beuve was absent, which did not prevent him from commenting severely on the play in the *Revue Suisse*. (*PVH*, 156–7)

It seems probable that it was this distinguished audience's experience of Romantic dramas that reduced their enthusiasm for Hugo's epic melodrama. Indeed, Jean Massin, who can hardly be accused of being anti-Hugo, describes the première as 'one of the blackest failures in theatrical history' (*OC*, 6, 547).

The performance itself does not seem to have caused the flop. A few minor accidents produced derisive laughter. Part 1 opens in the portrait-gallery of Job's castle, with the portraits turned to the wall; the audience, imagining some error by a set dresser, found it amusing, particularly since they had to wait several scenes for an explanation. One critic, in the *Coureur des Spectacles*, never very favourable to the Romantic drama, nevertheless seems to have been right in pointing out the obvious disproportion between the human actors and the legendary, or epic quality of their roles, a quality that endangers the dramatic illusion by confusing mythic and human characters: 'The actors playing in *Les Burgraves* suffered the effects of the indecision that remains concerning the genre of the work. If they had been convinced that it was a comedy, a tragedy, a

drama with the necessary conditions, or even a melodrama openly identified as such, but heightened by its style, they would have adapted their
acting in consequence'.[6] The rhetorical problem of genre is central both
to the understanding and to the appreciation of Hugo's last drama
before his exile, and so it is to the work's generic conventions that we
turn first in our analysis.

The process by which Hugo's interest was moving away from the dramatized clash of characters and principles on one of the great Parisian stages
and towards the imaginary world of legendary and epic allegorical heroes
and heroines – a process that was to culminate in the great poetic cycle he
called *La Légende des siècles* (1859) – was already well advanced in 1842–3. As
we have seen, the practical and material problems involved in having his
plays successfully produced in Paris may well have turned Hugo back
towards epic poetry which, in its printed form, allowed him to express his
ideas persuasively without the conflicts and disappointments associated
with the theatre. In fact, reference to Hugo's plays written after his exile
from France in December 1851 serves to situate *Les Burgraves* within his
dramatic career in a new way. Rather than being the last Romantic drama,
it thus becomes the first of the verse epics, melodramatic and otherwise,
which he published after *Ruy Blas*.

What Hugo meant by the terms 'legendary' and 'epic' drama becomes
clearer if we examine the Preface he added to *Les Burgraves* on the work's
publication in March 1843. More than one contemporary critic welcomed
the text as an explanation of what the dramatic performance had left mysterious. The Preface itself is interesting not as an explanation of the meaning of Hugo's drama but rather as a rhetorical commentary on his way of
approaching his subject. He begins by explaining the analogy with Aeschylus and his world that had influenced him to append the subtitle 'trilogy'
to his drama:

> In Aeschylus's time, Thessaly was a sinister place. Giants had lived there in
> an earlier age; now, there were ghosts ... ; for Aeschylus and his contempo-
> raries ... [Thessaly] was the terrifying battlefield where the Titans had
> fought against Jupiter.
>
> What fable invented, history sometimes repeats. Thus ... there is today in
> Europe a place which, making all due allowance, is for us, from the poetic
> viewpoint, what Thessaly was for Aeschylus, that is, a battlefield both memo-
> rable and prodigious. As you will have guessed, we mean the banks of the
> Rhine. There, as a matter of fact, six centuries ago, other Titans struggled
> against another Jupiter. These Titans were the Burgraves; this Jupiter was
> the Emperor of Germany.' (*OC*, 6, 567–8)

Throughout the Preface, Hugo insists upon the triple thematic and formal nature of his drama. This triplicity explains, for instance, both his choice of setting and to some extent of the characters who, as Aristotle recommended, are members of a single ruling family:

> Reconstruct in thought, life-size and in all its power, one of the castles where the burgraves, the equivalent of princes, lived almost like kings ... Show in the citadel the three things it contained: a fortress, a palace, a cavern; in the citadel, thus opened in all its reality to the astonished eye of the spectator, install and cause to live both together and at odds with one another four generations, grandfather, father, son, and grandson; make of this family the total, living symbol of expiation; place on the grandfather's head the sin of Cain, in the father's heart the instincts of Nimrod, in the son's soul the vices of Sardanapalus ... In this way place before all and make visible to the spectator the great moral ladder of racial degradation which should serve as a living example eternally raised up before the eyes of everyone. (*OC*, 6, 570–1)

The tripartite action of *Les Burgraves* opposes, as in allegorical melodrama, the fatalistic principle of vengeance, personified as she informs us, by Guanhumara: 'I am murder and vegeance. I am bloodlust!' (1, 4), to Providence in the shape of the Emperor Barbarossa. His clemency brings to an end the feud existing between himself and Job, his bastard brother who had tried, seventy years earlier, to murder him and steal Ginevra whom they both loved. The subject's trilogical form developed in his mind as follows, Hugo tells us:

> What the author wished to place and describe, at the climax of his work, between Barbarossa and Guanhumara, between Providence and Fatality, was the soul of the old centenarian burgrave Job the Accursed, a soul which, on the edge of the grave, combines in its incurable melancholy three sentiments for his house, Germany and his family. These three emotions gave to the work its natural divisions. The author therefore decided to compose his drama in three parts. ... The first part might be called *Hospitality*, the second, *Patria*, and the third, *Paternity*.[7]
>
> The divisions and form of his drama being decided, the author resolved to write on the work's frontispiece, the word *trilogy*. Here as elsewhere, trilogy signifies only and essentially a poem in three cantos or a drama in three acts. (*OC*, 6, 573)

Although Hugo's re-reading of Aeschylus had greatly increased his respect for the classical form of the *Oresteia*, it does little to explain what he actually meant by the generic shift in his performed works from tragic drama to epics that end happily.

Modern critics like Jean Massin see *Les Burgraves* as an 'epic amplification of the myth of *Hernani*' (*OC*, 6, 556), in which Otbert concludes the same Faustian pact with Guanhumara that Hernani made with Don Ruy Gomez. The pact, which occurs in both drama and melodrama at a moment of climactic change in the destiny of an Emperor (the election of Charles V in *Hernani*, and in *Les Burgraves* the succession to Barbarossa of his grandson, Frederick II of Hohenstaufen), illustrates the epic quality common to both dramas. (The principal structural difference between the two plays, a difference ensuring that *Hernani* remains a Romantic drama, is the tragic ending of the protagonists.) Massin also suggests that Hugo's interest in medieval German history reflects his hopes for a modern united Europe – hopes he expressed also in the Preface (*OC*, 6, 574–5). Hugo himself underlined the vastness and diversity of the ingredients from which he composed his drama: 'Thus history, legend, story, reality, nature, the family, love, naive customs, wild faces, princes, soldiers, adventurers, kings, patriarchs as in the Bible, manhunters as in Homer, titans as in Aeschylus, everything offered itself up at the same time to the author's dazzled imagination in this vast picture to be painted, and he felt himself irresistibly drawn towards the world he was dreaming about (ibid., 572). But, whether from modesty or otherwise, Hugo then goes on to say that the work as projected in his imagination attained only a much inferior form in actuality. Better, as a statement of the epic vision presented in *Les Burgraves* seems Jacques Seebacher's summary: 'An infinite mirror of cascading paternities and powers, the play exaggerates Aeschylean heights and the Shakespearean grotesque ... [This] final tumble of three old bandit kings before Barbarossa, timeless Emperor of a universal Germany, results both because of and in spite of a sorceress, a maker of pacts and an agent of fatality' (*PF*, 307). The melodrama as thus envisaged by Hugo and Seebacher does attain an epic grandeur with dimensions stretching far beyond the Venice of *Angelo* or the Paris of *Le Roi s'amuse*, for instance. But can such an epic subject succeed onstage, played as it was in 1843 by classically trained actors, albeit with sets by Ciceri?

The answer in 1843 was clearly in the negative and, if we put aside the easy reasons proposed by critics – the cabal organized by Mme Maxime to punish Hugo for stripping her of the role of Guanhumara (*PVH*, 154), or the interference of Halley's comet, which made one of its periodic appearances during the run of Hugo's drama (*TF*, 586–7) – the real one seems to derive from the kind of 'shorthand' that Hugo employed in the writing of the play which, as we shall see, goes directly against some of his most cherished dramatic principles. Let me explain what I mean by Hugo's 'short-hand.'

By 1842, when he began the composition of *Les Burgraves*, Hugo had already written eight Romantic dramas, one melodrama (*Amy Robsart*), and the libretto for *La Esmeralda*. There is no doubt that he had honed his dramatic technique well during the eleven years between *Cromwell* and *Ruy Blas*. *Les Burgraves* represented a major change for him in terms of its geographical setting and time period: it was his first drama set in Germany and in the Middle Ages, in this case the thirteenth century. The onstage events emphasize the epic, legendary, and heroic dimensions of theme and characters. So fascinating (or overwhelming), in fact, was the subject that the dramatic techniques necessary to its unfolding as an articulated onstage action had to take second place. The effects of thematic decisions like, for instance, the timing of the action – seventy years after the events causing the love-hate triangle involving Fosco, Donato, and Ginevra, i.e., the future Job, Barbarossa, and Guanhumara – meant that this essential pre-dramatic action had to be reported by means of narratives and conversations among characters long after the events they describe and even, in some cases by 'messengers' who were not themselves present when Fosco, after attempting to kill Donato, sold Ginevra into slavery. (Hugo originally wrote a Prologue in which the pre-dramatic action would be explained, but changed his mind, incorporating into Part 1, particularly into Karl's monologues in Part 1 Scene 2, the drama's most essential expositional elements.) The resulting narrative monologues – called 'tunnels' in French theatrical parlance because they are long and one can see only with difficulty their eventual outcome – replace dramatic action on the stage in *Les Burgraves*. They are substitutes for action, performing a purely thematic function, that of narrating and explaining the significance of earlier events. This schematic shorthand reduces the possible emotional involvement of spectators, who become no more than interpreters of events they learn about at second (even third) hand, rather than participating in them as they unfold on stage.

Another example of Hugo's dramatic shorthand or merely sketched action in *Les Burgraves* involves his abuse of the technique of *anagnorisis*. The astonishing number of recognition scenes – a constant motif, albeit one used more sparingly in Hugo's earlier dramas – reveals the schematic nature of the device in this play. Almost no one among the principal characters is who (s)he seems. The members of the love-hate triangle formed by Fosco, Donato, and Ginevra lose their Italo-Corsican names and identities, becoming Job, Barbarossa, and Guanhumara, with each change producing a dramatic reversal necessitating adjustments in an audience's apprehension and appreciation of events onstage. Barbarossa's identity introduces a further complication. He first appears as an aged beggar seeking Job's hospitality, before revealing himself to be the Emperor of Germany returned from the dead. Otbert, the Hernani-like young soldier, alias Yorghi Spadaceli, turns out to be George, the youngest son of Barbarossa, stolen by gypsies while still a baby. A single reversal through *anagnorisis*, may well prove relatively unproblematic within dramas like *Marie Tudor* or *Lucrèce Borgia*, but when multiplied, such dramatic reversals, which hinge upon instant changes of identity and therefore of dramatic fate, may well appear contrived.

The third element of dramatic shorthand employed by Hugo in *Les Burgraves* was also imposed by the epic dimensions of the plot. The notion of verisimilitude that inheres in epic or legend is far removed from that which informs the drama, where events occur before the spectators' eyes. Howarth points out that the kind of mythological or legendary world created by Tolkien or Mervyn Peake (he might have added all the authors of the multiple versions of Arthurian Romance, at least since Malory) 'can be more easily realized in the novel or the epic poem, than in the theatre' (*SG*, 338). One is forced to agree with him when epic convention replaces dramatic verisimilitude in *Les Burgraves*. The climax of the plot presenting Barabarossa's defeat of the Burgraves occurs in Part 2, scene 6, for example, after the old beggar has revealed himself to be the Emperor, come to punish the Burgraves for their crimes. Logic is upon Magnus's side when he asks sarcastically how Barbarossa intends to carry out his threat:

> I am amazed at you!
> Where are your men? Where are the Imperial forces?
> Will we soon hear the trumpets sound? ...
> Here you are nothing.
> It is my father who is feared here; he is loved.

As the Burgraves surround Barbarossa with raised swords, ready to kill him for his temerity in entering their stronghold alone and unarmed, a single word from Job, the Emperor's inveterate enemy, is sufficient not only to save his life but to consign all the Burgraves, including Job's own son Magnus, and grandson Hatto, the reigning lord of the fortress of Heppenheff, to prison. This total reversal in the fates of everyone concerned in the dramatic action – with the possible exception of Guanhumara – occurs abruptly, without any preparation and is accompanied by only the starkest 'shorthand' explanation of Job's motives:

JOB
Sire, my son Magnus has spoken the truth. You are

My enemy. I it was who, as a soldier, angrily
Raised my hand against your majesty.
I hate you. But I wish Germany to exist in the world.
My country is bowed down, overcome and in deepest shadow.
Save her! I fall on my knees in this place
Before my Emperor whom God brings back to me.   (2, 6)

On hearing Job's command, the Burgraves drop their swords, free their prisoners, and allow themselves to be chained up and herded off to the dungeons. Nor are they even mentioned again in Part 3. Even in a medieval *chanson de geste* involving the epic exploits of legendary leaders like Roland and Oliver, or in the romances telling of the adventures of King Arthur's knights, such disdain for the logic of action and its consequences would seem arbitrary. In a Romantic drama it would clearly be out of place, as the reception given by its first audience seems to suggest. Even in this, Hugo's first epic melodrama, it may well seem unconvincing.

But *Les Burgraves* is unconvincing not only on the grounds of verisimilitude. When completed by the play's final peripeteia, Barbarossa's offer of clemency to his old enemy Job – despite the latter's attempt to murder him and despite the kidnapping of his fiancée, Ginevra – produces an ending more appropriate to melodrama or Shakespearean comedy, with all dramatic tension resolved and lovers united, ready to 'live happily ever after.' Thus the symbolic figures achieve their optimistic finale: Otbert is revealed to be George, youngest son of the Emperor; Barbarossa confers upon his newly-discovered youngest son the hand of the resuscitated Regina (no longer, happily, victim of Guanhumara's spells and potions), and the Emperor forgives Job his transgressions. Thus does the melodrama restore the Imperial family's dynastic destiny. The only jarring note in this utopian resolution is Guanhumara's suicide, accomplished by drinking one of her own concoctions, because her plotting has failed. All that remains is for Barbarossa to announce the happy vision of a future time which will replace the mythic times of old:

I leave to the world a sovereign.
A moment ago, over yonder, the imperial herald
Has just announced that the princes in Spire
Have elected as Emperor my grandson Frederick.
He is truly wise, free from hatred, and from error.
I leave him the throne and I return to solitude.   (3, 4)

When compared to the tragic endings of all of Hugo's dramas from *Hernani* to *Ruy Blas*, this distribution of prizes and rewards for services rendered – a dramatic convention more appropriate to comedy – may well seem unpersuasive to a modern audience expecting *Les Burgraves* to conform to the constraints Hugo had earlier imposed on his Romantic dramas. Analysis of the logic of plot and incident in *Les Burgraves* forces one to conclude that by 1843 Hugo had returned to the melodramas of his youth.

But one modern theatrical director has managed to present a vision of *Les Burgraves* which, according to some spectators at least, did allow the play to transcend Hugo's dramatic 'shorthand.' So great were the changes necessary in Antoine Vitez's 1977 production of Hugo's epic melodrama in Ivry that some spectators wondered, however, whether he sacrificed too much to the modern taste for purely symbolic or cerebral drama. Ubersfeld, however, responded enthusiastically to the production: 'He gives of the play an image not historical but purely metaphorical. His Burgraves are five tramps lost in old age and poverty, in a universe whose ruins they personify and, sitting on a staircase, they re-enact the fable of the collapse of a world. This 'indirect representation' disconcerted some, but gave to the text a dimension other than picturesque and anecdotal' (*DR*, 170–1).

This post-Beckettian, metaphorical, view of Hugo's play disconcerted, among others, Arnaud Laster, who, while sympathizing with Vitez's general intention, points to several flaws in the production. Vitez exaggerated beyond measure the drama's grotesque element, making it, according to Laster, a 'mockery of the work.' He used only five actors for the drama's 27 roles, giving the role of Guanhumara to a man, Pierre Vial. But it was Vitez's imposition upon the actors of a style of diction that, in Laster's opinion, grossly deformed the meaning of the play's alexandrines, which the critic holds principally against this production:

> Convinced of the need for a pause on the rhyme and of a scansion based upon it, he made the actors speak the text as if it were a classical play, by Racine, for example, without taking account of *enjambement*, or rather, counting on fidelity to the older form of diction to show up the dislocation achieved by Hugo. The result was that the primary meaning of the discourse was broken, analogous to that which, according to Vitez, occurs in dreams: '[S]ingle words are understood but sentences remain obscure or rather we get another, hidden, terrible, meaning from them.' In brief, as Jacques Seebacher wrote in admiration, the drama seemed to be both 'acted and mocked by a group made up of lunatics, students, tramps, the physically handicapped, the mentally infirm: their disabilities drive the action and their antics provide suspense.' One can imagine ... the confusion felt by the spectators, most of whom were not familiar with the play. (*PF*, 307)

Laster concludes that, rather than contributing to making the play better known, Vitez's production further fostered the myth of its unperformability.

Mention of Vitez's respectfully mocking production inevitably recalls the parodies inspired by *Les Burgraves* in 1843. As usual, Henry Lyonnet offers the best account of them, adding that few works have so inspired the parodists (*PVH*, 165). The simultaneous presentation onstage of four generations of the same family, the collection of old men and women invited laughter, he says. The first, *Les Hures-graves, a Parody in Three Acts in Verse against les Burgraves* were performed at the Palais-Royal only days after the première of Hugo's drama. Hugo had called his play a trilogy. Dumanoir, Siraudin, and Clairville, authors of *Les Hures-graves*, or 'Tousled-headed lords,' called theirs a 'trifouillis' or 'mess,' the three (muddled) parts of which were entitled, 'The Tricentenarian,' 'One of the Four Beggars,' and 'The Cleaned-up Cellar.' Barbarossa becomes 'Old-Nice-Face,' 250 years old; Job is 300; Asinus, his son, is 107; and Alto, his grandson, is 60. Guanhumara appears as Coinavieura, a two-hundred-year-old fortune teller (played by a man), and Otbert, now called Gobelair is still the lover of Regina, now called Raisina. Other contemporary parodies included *Les Buses-graves*, by M. Tortu Goth, as well as *Les Bûches-graves, Pièce de Résistance Served at the Comédie-Française.* Perhaps more entertaining would have been *Les Barbus-graves*, or *The Solemn [Grey]beards*, by Paul Zéro, in which Job is Victor Hugo, Magnus, Alexandre Dumas, and so on.

Whatever may have been his reasons, the fact remains that after the failure of *Les Burgraves* in 1843, Hugo's dramatic output became reduced, until 1854 at least, to a number of fragments (*OC*, 6, 1003–1098). Later on, however, he did complete two plays to which he gave the name, 'drama.' One was written in 1866, in prose; it was set in Paris in the nineteenth century, and entitled *Mille Francs de récompense (One Thousand Francs Reward)*. The other, written in 1869, in verse, was set in Spain and Italy in the fifteenth century and was entitled *Torquemada.* They were his final Romantic dramas and it is to them that we shall turn now.

9. Hugo's Theatre after 1843: *Le Théâtre en liberté*; Return to the Romantic Drama: *Mille Francs de récompense* and *Torquemada*

'I prefer my plays badly performed rather than not performed at all.'
(*VHTL*, 2, iv)

EXILE FROM THE THEATRE

After the failure of *Les Burgraves* in 1843, a number of events conspired to distract Hugo's interest from dramatic production. On 4 September of that year, the death of Léopoldine, his eldest daughter, drowned in a boating accident in the Seine near Villequier with her husband of six months, brought to a temporary stop the flood of publications Hugo produced in a normal year. He attempted to forget his grief by entering political life, becoming in 1845 a Peer of France, a rank admirably suited to launch him on a political career in the Government of Louis-Philippe. When the latter fell, in the Revolution of February 1848, Lamartine, head of the new Republic's Provisional Government, offered Hugo the Education Ministry, a position he refused out of loyalty to the deposed royal family. Elected as a deputy to the National Assembly, Hugo initially supported Louis Bonaparte, the former Emperor's nephew, when he was triumphantly voted President of the Republic by the French people on 10 December, 1848. But Hugo openly opposed Louis Bonaparte's imperial ambitions and, after the *coup d'état* in 1851 by which the President suppressed the Republic in favour of his 'Second Empire' Hugo was forced into exile. He went first to Brussels, then to Jersey until 1855, and finally to Guernsey, living there from 1855 until the disastrous defeat of French forces by the Prussians in 1870 led to the fall of the Second Empire. For nearly twenty years, Hugo thus had no access to the Parisian stage. The Imperial censorship banned his dramas written before 1851, and he could hardly hope to see any new ones staged in France. For the first time he considered mere publication, rather than performance, as their logical form. In 1859, for instance, he wrote: 'Since my [dramatic] repertoire has not been produced in Paris for eight years, the theatre is clearly closed to me; I am resolved therefore to publish my plays' (*VHTL*, 2, 921). The only exceptions to the Imperial ban on the performance in Paris of Hugo's plays during this period, were the following: through an oversight of the censor, *Marion de Lorme* was performed four times at the Comédie-Française in 1852 ; *Hernani* enjoyed spectacular success at the Comédie-Française during the Great Exhibition of 1867; and *Lucrèce Borgia* had a similar success at the Porte-Saint-Martin in February 1870, amid Bismarck's final manoeuvrings to involve France in a war with Prussia.

It is not accurate to say, however, that during the twelve years between 1843 and 1855, Hugo abandoned all interest in writing for the theatre – an activity to which he had devoted a considerable percentage of his working life since at least 1827. Between 1843 and 1851, he worked on at least seventeen projects, fragments of which may be consulted in the Massin edition of his works (*OC*, 7, 515–96). Between 1851 and 1853, however, his manuscripts contain no dramatic writings, as he moved from France to Brussels and then to Jersey. Then, in January 1854, an event occurred that confirmed in Hugo the central role dramatic composition occupied in his creative life. The event was the visit to Jersey of a troupe of travelling players, there to perform *Ruy Blas* before an audience that included the assembled Hugo family. Hugo rehearsed the leading actor, Besombes, in his role, and arranged that ticket prices in the pit were low enough that all French exiles in Jersey could afford to attend. They did not miss the political allusions in Hugo's drama, reinterpreting and even adding to them in the light of their own experience of political tyranny. Hugo's conclusion from the experience shows that his innate love of theatrical performance, far from dead, was to lead him to further dramatic composition: 'The performance of *Ruy Blas* revealed a side of me which I had believed entirely imperceptible. I found the performance painful. The desire to work in the theatre has overcome me again, and I suffered at the thought that I am totally prevented from doing so. Bonaparte would make any performance impossible' (*OC*, 9, 1494). Despite this practical constraint on performance, Hugo was soon at work on a new one-act comedy in verse, *La Forêt mouillée*, the manuscript of which bears the date 14 May, 1854. After the move to Guernsey, and in the more settled conditions that his purchase of Hauteville House made possible, Hugo devoted himself increasingly to dramatic composition, producing in the next nine years some thirty fragments of projected comedies, sketches and dialogues, many of which he would incorporate into the works making up *Le Théâtre en liberté*.[1]

In 1864 he finally published his long projected meditation on the dramatic author to whom, more than to any other, he owed his conception of Romantic drama. *William Shakespeare* arose, despite Hugo's lack of English, both from his experience of attending performances of the plays, and also from his sympathetic reading of the translation that his son, François-Victor, had completed of Shakespeare's works between 1856 and 1863. Conceived originally as a preface to his son's translation, the work had grown in the writing to become an immense contemplation on art and theatre. From 1859 until its completion in 1869, Hugo also researched for his final Romantic drama, the life and times of the Grand Inquisitor Torquemada, whom, as we shall see, he was to make the symbol of his hatred of religious oppression.

All of these threads seem to have come together in the period 1865–7, when he wrote four plays which form the first 'volume' of the collection usually referred to as *Le Théâtre en liberté* (*Theatre at Liberty*). The two verse comedies, *La Grand'mère* (written 18–24 June 1865), and *Mangeront-ils?* (18 January–27 April 1867) feature the light, fairy-like vein typical of most of the plays in this collection. But the two prose plays, the four-act drama, *Mille francs de récompense* (written 5 February–15 April 1866), and the one-act comedy *L'Intervention* (7–14 May 1866), are both set in nineteenth-century France and both deal with a subject new to Hugo's theatre: money, and the conflicts produced by the bourgeois characters' lack of it. For the first time Hugo dramatizes the lives not of kings, nobles, ministers, and jesters, but those of the class to which the vast majority of his audience belonged.

There is little agreement among the editors of the group of plays that Hugo left at his death for posthumous publication. *La Forêt mouillée* is excluded from *Le Théâtre en liberté* by both of the most recent editors, Jean Massin and Arnaud Laster, although included by Paul Meurice, Hugo's literary executor, in the 1886 edition, the basis for the first 'official' edition of the complete works, called the 'Imprimerie Nationale' edition, in 1911. *Torquemada*, on the other hand, although published separately in 1882, three years before Hugo's death, now figures among the plays forming the *Théâtre en liberté* in both modern editions. Massin and Laster explain that their decisions to include in *Le Théâtre en liberté* the last drama Hugo published separately in his lifetime were taken for structural reasons. Hugo had apparently intended to publish his last plays in two volumes, the first of which was to have as its organizing principle the paradoxical theme of the 'Power possessed by the Weak.' Massin places in this first volume the four plays mentioned in the preceding paragraph, all of which end happily thanks to the intervention of some character believed – by the other characters or by society in general – to be of little worth or consequence. Massin then goes on to argue that volume 2 of *Le Théâtre en liberté* should therefore contain the four plays, all written in 1869, which show the *powerlessness* of the Weak to defend themselves against the Great (*OC*, 14, 423). These plays are *L'Épée*, *Les Deux Trouvailles de Gallus*, *Torquemada*, and *Welf, castellan d'Osbor*. Despite several objections to be made against such a grouping, which does not entirely respect Hugo's own published intentions, its generic logic does reflect Hugo's move from optimistic comedies to pessimistic dramas in his final theatrical works. As will be seen, *Mille Francs de récompense*, which Hugo several times called a 'drama,'[2] has the same kind of bitter-sweet ending as had his previous melodrama, *Les Burgraves*, but without the latter's ambition to achieve epic status. *Torquemada*, on the other hand, plunges us unequivocally back into the world of blood and heretic-burning of the Romantic drama, notably *Marie Tudor*.

One final matter calls for explanation, before we turn to analysis of Hugo's last full-length dramas: the ambiguous title of *Le Théâtre en liberté*. Hugo insisted that three of the short, one-act plays, *La Grand'mère*, *L'Intervention*, and *La Mort de la sorcière*, (first title of *Mangeront-ils?*), as well as *Margarita*, the first of the *Deux Trouvailles de Gallus* 'could be performed on our existing stages.' But he felt constrained to add: 'The others are playable only in that ideal theatre that everyone has in the mind' (*VHTL*, 2, x). So, despite his insistence on performability, one cannot but compare them to Musset's collection of intimate dramas, entitled *Un Spectacle dans un fauteuil*, written in 1833–4 to be read rather than performed. More suggestive of Hugolian rhetoric is a second remark, about liberty, that Hugo made in a planned Preface to the collection: 'The theatre can be free in two ways, with regard to the government which combats its independence with censorship and with regard to the public which combats its independence by whistling. Whistling may be either right or wrong. Censorship is always wrong (*OC*, 14, 429). As we have seen, Hugo had suffered sufficiently from censorship, both in the period of his greatest success, 1830–38, and during the Second Empire, to have earned the right to make such a remark. In his two final dramas, he will criticize bourgeois society's exploitation of the poor and organized religion's abuse of humanity's credulousness: in both plays, society's victims either sacrifice or lose their liberty.

MILLE FRANCS DE RÉCOMPENSE (1865)

This prose work is a hybrid, combining the principal element of the bourgeois melodrama – the family's reintegration into contemporary society –

with that of the Romantic drama, namely the tragic fate of the protagonist. The action, which develops the Romantic theme concerning the ambiguity of the exceptional individual's relationship to bourgeois society, is set at Carnival time in Restoration Paris. The subject is the sacrifice of his liberty by Glapieu, ex-thief and therefore outlawed[3] by the capitalist society of the day. He intervenes, generously and against his own interest, in order to save from poverty and prison for debt and false pretences, Major Gé-douard, an honest former soldier of Napoleon and to help the Major's family. The other 'side' in the antithesis between idealism and self-interest is the bourgeois society that condemns him. Its greed is represented in the play by its passion for gambling, whether on the Stock Exchange or at the bawdy-house tables, and it takes as its motto, 'Money makes money.' The axiom is stated by its most cynical and hypocritical representative in the play, Rousseline, archetypical melodramatic villain, the would-be seducer of the innocent heroine, Cyprienne, in the form, 'If you want to make money, don't give the impression you're poor' (1, 4). And the theme of disguise, or deception for profit, returns constantly, triggering the dramatic devices of *anagnorisis* and dramatic irony that, as we have seen, characterize Hugolian dramaturgy. Rhetorically, then, rather than returning to the tragic Romanticism of *Hernani* or *Ruy Blas*, Hugo melodramatizes an ideology involving grasping villains and pathetic victims. The resulting hyperbolic emotional appeal and logical stylization suggest the naive optimism of Pixérécourt's *Coelina*. But the punishment meted out to the selfless hero recalls the naturalistic determinism of Henri Becque's 1882 cynical comedy, or 'comédie rosse,' *Les Corbeaux.*

As in *Les Burgraves*, Hugo disregards his own condemnation, in the Preface to *Hernani*, of narrations of events occurring offstage. In *Mille Francs*, several characters explain the elaborate pre-dramatic action necessary to the plot's logic, to its complications, and to the happy ending that Glapieu's self-sacrifice makes possible. Thus we are told, rather than shown, that about seventeen years before the Parisian carnival we see onstage, Cyprien André had departed for the Napoleonic wars leaving behind Étiennette pregnant with their daughter, Cyprienne. On his return, with mother and daughter lost, he has risen through financial speculation to become the lonely millionaire Baron de Puencarral. As usual in Hugo's dramas, name-changes lead to complications: confusions arise over the identities of both André/Puencarral and of Edgar Marc, Cyprienne's lover, whose surname may be used also as a first name, thus delaying Glapieu's recognition of him until the final *dénouement.*

Glapieu, whose original, allegorical name in the manuscript was Gladieu (i.e., *Glaive de Dieu* [Sword of God]), resembles other Hugolian outsiders capable of both acts of great humanity and exceptional exploits. Such characters include Jean Valjean and Gavroche in *Les Misérables*, and Airolo in *Mangeront-ils?* In *Mille francs*, Glapieu is at once the ironic commentator on the absurdities of both society and of art and also the principal manipulator of events, only rivalled in this role by Rousseline, the villain he must defeat in order to save the two generations of lovers, Cyprien-Étiennette and Edgar-Cyprienne. That the hero's manipulations are themselves treated with typical Hugolian irony becomes clear when, in attempting to help Cyprienne's lover, Glapieu succeeds only in getting him arrested and accused of theft. Jean Massin sees this incident as illustrating 'the law of Hugolian drama: the young hero is destroyed by the character trying to save him' (*OC*, 13, 397, n14).[4] Despite this failure, however, Glapieu is able to make good his early vow. 'Well then, good people, I'm going to look after you' (1, 4), he had said, proving himself later to be as good as his word. He saves from drowning Edgar who, in despair at losing the last of his employer's 4,000 francs at the gambling den in Act 2, had flung himself into, the Seine. Glapieu thus wins, indirectly, the eponymous 'One thousand francs reward' offered by Puencarral, Edgar's employer. Finally, it is Glapieu who, like Sherlock Holmes, presides over the final unravelling of the plot's complicated logic of cause and effect before the principal characters assembled at the Palais de Justice for Edgar's trial for theft. Unlike Sherlock Holmes, however, it is equally Glapieu, who, by his explanation, incriminates himself and who is led off to the prison-hulks in Toulon harbour. Glapieu's fate deprives *Mille Francs* of the happy ending of comedy, or of the conventional Pixérécourt-style melodrama. His sentence, like Valjean's exemplary five years' imprisonment for stealing a loaf of bread in *Les Misérables*, expresses Hugo's pessimistic view of contemporary capitalistic society, given over to speculation and profiteering.

Equally black is Hugo's depiction of the arch-representative of Restoration society, Rousseline, financial agent of Puencarral, and oppressor of the poor. Rousseline specializes in seizing and auctioning off the furniture of indigent families, and he intends to use his position as director of bailiffs to blackmail Étiennette into consenting to his sexual exploitation of her daughter, Cyprienne. But even this standard melodramatic figure, hypocrite, toady (to Puencarral), and thief – the dramatic equivalent of Thénardier in *Les Misérables* – has a 'Hugolian' reason for his cruelty: 'I am all emotion [he says]; and I have a heart, an abyss. I love money? No, I love me. I want to be loved; I want to be loved by women. By fair means or foul I intend to be loved. Watch out if I am not! I never forgive a snub. Being bald and ugly makes my blood boil. Against whom? I've no idea. Oh, what enormous pleasure to punish whoever scorns you, to chastize whoever finds you old and ridiculous' (3, 1). However odious his actions, Rousseline's motivation – lack of love makes him vicious – remains totally comprehensible within the emotional economy of Hugo's dramas which include among similar obsessive revenge-seekers for love's slights, Don Ruy Gomez de Silva, Homodei, and Don Salluste.

In contradistinction to the play's rhetorical schematism with its emphasis on the villain's role and on his reason for oppressing his victims, is Hugo's insistence on the ambiguities and misunderstandings produced by Restoration society's confusion of reality and appearance. Disguises – masks, false noses, fancy dress costumes, and veils – as well as name-changes, changes of identity, of career, and even of ways of life complicate throughout the play the exchange of information among the characters and between them and the audience. Such ambiguity-creating agents operate with particular frequency and emphasis in Act 2, set on the Quai des Ormes on which stand both a theatrical costumier's shop and the bawdy-house-cum-gambling-den in which the Carnival reigns. The atmosphere, that of *Mardi gras*, the feast of fools when the world turns upside down, is set by the song sung by an appropriately anonymous masked character at the beginning of the act:

> Brandy! Brandy!
> Jesters and wise men, put on your costumes.
> Ten-franc masks, two-cent masks.
> God made the world, I forgive him.
> Brandy! Brandy!
> While the dead sleep on,
> Pagans, Christians, let's enjoy ourselves.
> Venus laughs, Eve gives us the eye,
> Each offers us her apple.   (2, 1)

Masked mulatto ladies in low-cut dresses, claiming provocatively to be 'better than white women,' enter the Ball, while in the costumier's shop Barutin, a deputy from the National Assembly, disguises himself as a Turk. He does so in contrast to Tancrède de Pontresme, a playboy disguised as a chivalric knight who learns that the following day, Ash Wednesday, first day of Lent, season of fasting and abstinence, he must change one disguise for another, becoming a magistrate in the real world of the Palais de Justice. Such ironic confusions between ritual or professional disguises – the latter of which include, as Pascal said, the magistrate's red robe worn to impress the criminal with the judge's authority – and the masks, dominoes, and false noses assumed for the Carnival call attention to the frivolity undermining bourgeois society's claims to justice and responsibility.

Circling around the Carnival is Glapieu, in rags despite the falling snow, without money to enter the 'real,' i.e., the Carnival world of food and drink, of anonymous sex and high-stakes gambling. Only after saving Edgar's life and winning the 4,000 francs reward offered by Pontresme – the key to entry into bourgeois society – can Glapieu satisfy his hunger and obtain shelter from the cold. That he does so ironically – asking at the costumier's shop for 'the costume of an honest man' (2, 4) – should not surprise us. And, when Hugo, in a later stage direction, describes the previously ragged Glapieu, on his entry into Puencarral's new mansion, as being 'dressed in black, with a white tie, white shirt, boots, bowler hat in hand. Grotesquely correct in appearance' (3, 2), we can see that Glapieu's very appearance combines the sublime and grotesque aspects characteristic of the Hugolian Romantic hero.

Hugo obviously felt that, without such heavy emphasis, his criticism of contemporary society's vagaries risked passing uncomprehended by his readers. That, at least, is the conclusion underlined, for instance, by Glapieu's final speech before the new magistrate, the ex-playboy Pontresme, ready now in his new reincarnation to enforce the rigour of the law against the thief who has incriminated himself in order to help the threatened family and to save Edgar from prison. Despite his good intentions, Glapieu admits that, as a previous offender, the law must condemn him: 'I am Glapieu the recidivist, I tell you. A recidivist can only recidive. I stand condemned. I tried to do good. But what's that to you? It's very difficult to do a good deed. I've done more damage than anything else. A good deed botched is punished. So I'm confessing [my crime]. Fortunately there's still time to mend what's been broken. I am the thief, the real thief. I know what will happen to me. [For breaking] into a house at night where there were people, Toulon for twenty years. We'll speak no more about it. It'll never be cleared up. The truth always ends up by being unknown.' (4, 6) Maybe Jean Massin is right when he declares Glapieu's final speech, the 'height of sarcasm' (OC, 13, 419, n8), but we should remember that, rhetorically speaking, sarcasm is merely the hyperbolic form of irony, being characterized by the obviousness peculiar to any form of overstatement.

But Mille Francs possesses another less ideologically simplistic device which, according to Arnaud Laster at least, has recommended it particularly to modern theatrical producers. (Its first dramatic production was in 1961 at the Théâtre de l'Ambigu by La Comédie de l'Est, directed by Hubert Gignoux.) Glapieu's role as ironic chorus, who comments upon rhetorical or theatrical devices, gives to Hugo's drama a meta-theatrical or Brechtian quality, in which distancing is achieved by the questioning of the theatrical illusion itself. In such a case, Romantic 'suspension of disbelief' expands to integrate such illusion-breaking devices as references to the author or his works, or direct addresses by a character to the audience at the expense of the drama itself. Illustrating the first category are incidents like the one in Act 2, scene 2, when Glapieu replies to the playboy Pontresme's use of Parisian street language: 'Sir, I'm not a man of the world; I don't speak slang.' Hugo's extensive use of slang in *Les Misérables*, published four years earlier, had created a critical controversy in Paris. Similarly, Glapieu's derogatory remarks concerning the alexandrine, by far Hugo's favourite poetic metre, would have been seen by Parisian audiences or readers (had there been any in 1865) as an example of *chleuasmos*, or irony turned by Hugo against himself: 'I find that policeman tiring ... And then, what an alexandrine he is! He is handsome, I admit, but what monotony of movement! No variety ... A bludgeon. False majesty. Decidedly, deep down, I'm hostile to all governments' (2, 2). As Laster points out, such a remark is all the more savoury coming in *Mille francs*, the last of Hugo's plays in prose.

Also deconstructive of the dramatic illusion are some of Glapieu's asides addressed to the audience. One can contrast this kind of aside, which resembles, for example, addresses to the camera made, in close-up, by modern film actors – Tony Richardson's film of Fielding's *Tom Jones* contains many good examples of the technique – with the more functionally 'psychological' kind. The latter is illustrated by Rousseline, in the conventional role of the parodic villain of melodrama speaking his thoughts aloud in a monologue 'overheard' by the audience (3, 1), according to mimetic convention. In *his* asides, however, Glapieu deconstructs the plausibility of remarks made by other characters, or, by seeming to usurp the role of author, or director, of the play, he shatters before spectators' eyes the dramatic illusion itself.[5] In the first case, Glapieu's remark remains within the logic of conventional dramatic presentation. By his ironic comment on Rousseline's overblown rhetoric, he reveals the profiteering financier to be a hypocrite:

> ROUSSELINE: France has rediscovered the way to honour and the source of public happiness by following the white panache [of Louis XVIII].
>
> GLAPIEU: Another metaphor that's long been walking the streets. (1, 4)

This example introduces the kind of Brechtian distancing that first attracted Hubert Gignoux to perform the play in 1961. In the same vein are the sceptical remarks addressed by Glapieu to the audience about the version he has just recounted of his own life and imprisonment for theft: 'That's my story. You don't understand it. Neither do I' (1, 1). And Glapieu's role as onstage 'director' of the action shows him, perhaps for reasons of verisimilitude, rushing the drama towards its *dénouement* to make for a quick ending: 'No delays,' he urges; 'I'm [deliberately] cutting things short' (4, 6).

Gignoux's view of the Brechtian nature of Hugo's drama, while restricting, has been influential. He saw the drama's modernity as deriving from
'the mockery it poured upon bourgeois justice, the dialectical opposition
between the old soldier of Year I [of the Revolution] and the Restoration
profiteer, the criticism of the clear consciences of bankers, the demonstration of the virtues and of the powerlessness of the people, in short all the
elements of a strongly demystifying denunciation' (*VHTL*, 2, xiii). Later
productions of the play – by Arlette Téphany in 1979, by René Loyon at the
Palais de Chaillot in 1985, and by the Comédie-Française in 1995, all of
which have employed Gignoux's *mise en scène* – have also emphasized its
Brechtian overtones. And, in *Les Nouvelles Litteraires*, Gabriel Marcel, the
Existential philosopher and dramatist, wrote in his May 1961 review of
Hugo's 'subversive' drama on the absurdity of the French criminal justice
system: '[This play] not only prefigures the France of *Crainquebille* [a 1904
short story by Anatole France], but more directly and curiously certain
aspects of Anouilh's theatre, and even, in some ways, Brecht's *Threepenny
Opera.*'[6]

Mille Francs de récompense entered the repertoire of the Comédie-
Française in 1995; it is the thirteenth of Hugo's dramatic works to be so
canonized.[7]

TORQUEMADA (1869)

Hugo did not return overnight to historical drama, and that he did so at all
was due to his taste for Romantic paradox. As early as November 1854,
while still in Jersey, Hugo asked how it was possible that a religious system
such as Christianity could produce political oppression and violent death.
The question led him to pose the case of Tomás de Torquemada, the
Dominican monk appointed in 1483 Grand Inquisitor in Spain, and in
1492 responsible for the expulsion from that country of all Jews who
refused baptism, some 170,000 people in all. His name has become synonymous with the *auto-da-fé* and the *quemadero*, during which, Hugo claims,
heretics were burned alive in enormous stone statues set up in the public
squares of Spanish cities by order of the Holy Office. In 1854 Hugo posed
the paradox of Torquemada thus: 'Torquemada caused to be burnt alive
some 400,000 people ... Torquemada tried to save humanity from hellfire
in the wrong way [*faussement*] by burning it in this world. He was a man of
total conviction. As well, this same Torquemada, aged ninety, wore an iron
skull-cap on his head to escape assassination; he wore a hair shirt in self-
imposed poverty. If, in fact, this man had really saved humanity from eternal damnation, as he believed, by a few hours of torture, Torquemada
would really be one of humanity's benefactors' (*OC*, 9, 1498). Hugo's mix-

ture of respect for and horror at Torquemada's beliefs mirrors the paradoxical nature of Torquemada's 'solution' to the Christian problem of Hell.

The passage just quoted also illustrates Hugo's attitude towards historical accuracy. As we have seen, he believed it to come second to symbolic 'truth' in order of importance. Torquemada in fact died in Avila in 1498, at the age of seventy-eight, and modern estimates of the number of his victims fall far short of the 400,000 cited by Hugo in 1854.[8] In 1868, the year before he wrote *Torquemada*, Hugo had occasion to state once more his position concerning the historicity of the personages and events he presented in his dramas and novels. Writing to Albert Lacroix, publisher in 1869 of *L'Homme qui rit* (first title, *Par ordre du roi*), Hugo defined the paradoxical blend of historical material and fiction in his works, soon to include *Torquemada*:

> The historical novel is a very good genre, since Walter Scott practised it, and the historical drama can be a very fine work, since Dumas made his name thanks to it; but I have never written either historical dramas or historical novels. When I depict history, I never have historical characters do anything but what they did, or might have done, given their natures, and I involve them as little as possible in what is, properly speaking, fiction. My method consists in depicting true things by means of invented characters.
>
> All my dramas, and all my novels which themselves are dramas, result from this way of seeing, [which is] good or bad, but in any case suited to my way of thinking.
>
> *Par ordre du roi* will therefore be the true England, depicted by means of fictional characters. The historical figures, [Queen] Anne, for instance, will be seen only in profile. As in *Ruy Blas*, *Les Misérables*, etc., interest will focus only on characters resulting from the historical or aristocratic environment of the time, but created by the author. (*OC*, 14, 1254)

Hugo's astonishing blurring of Aristotle's historical versus fictional categories ('what they did' being confused with what they 'might have done')[9] fully explains, for instance, his attitude towards the anachronisms and historical inaccuracies in *Torquemada*. In fact, Torquemada and Saint François de Paule never met, as they do in Part 1, Act 2 of Hugo's drama, but then neither did Elizabeth I ever meet Mary Queen of Scots, although Schiller arranged such a meeting in *Maria Stuart*. And Rodrigo Borgia, when Pope Alexander VI, never encouraged the Spanish Grand Inquisitor to indulge in the mass burning of heretics, as he does in the same Act of Hugo's play. But to Hugo, such details were unimportant, because he believed it necessary to sacrifice fact to 'philosophical' interpretation, to offer fictional *exempla* as historical accounts. He stated his position clearly in a projected Preface to *Torquemada*, his final drama involving historical characters: 'There is a relationship [in the play] between Borgia and Torquemada. Hence, [there is] an anachronism in this drama. Although the following proposition may sound bizarre, we believe it to be true: in art, the philosophy of history must come before history itself. Facts are subservient to ideas. If they are incomplete, the philosopher's duty is to complete them. From reality's obedience to the ideal, [which is] the aim of art, results the supreme truth.' (*OC*, 14, 696–7). With such porous categories, little wonder that *Torquemada* fits so well into the kind of 'symbolic' history Hugo had included in all his earlier Romantic dramas.

In Act 1, for instance, an unnamed Dominican monk, considered crazy by the Augustinian monks in whose convent he has been interned, is subjected to a formal Inquisition into his heretical beliefs. The interrogation takes place at the entrance to a tomb, in which, if condemned, he will be buried alive. When he refuses to retract, the action onstage becomes as gripping as any scene in Hugolian Romantic drama:

BISHOP:　　　　　　　　Monk, obey. I order you
　　　　To obey.
MONK:　　　　No.
BISHOP:　　　　　　　Go down one step.
The monk descends one step into the vault.
　　　　　　　　　　In the name
　　　　Of Christ, retract.
MONK:　　　　　　　　No.
BISHOP:　　　　　　　　　　Descend.
The monk descends another step.
　　　　　　　　　　　Abjure.
MONK:　　　　　　　　　　　No.
BISHOP: Descend.
The monk descends a third step ... Only his head is out of the grave.
BISHOP:　　　　　　　　　　　　Think again.
　　　　You will be extinguished down there like a torch without air.
　　　　Hunger. Thirst. Dying is horrible.
MONK:　　　　　　　　　　　It is beautiful.
BISHOP: Descend.
The monk disappears completely underground.
MONK'S VOICE *from the grave*:
　　　　　　　　I am at the bottom.
BISHOP:　　　　　　　　　　　Place the slab on top.
MONK'S VOICE: Do it.

At a sign from the bishop, two monks slide the the slab over the entrance to the stairs. At the last moment, as they are closing it completely, they stop, leaving only a tiny air hole. The bishop bends over the opening.

BISHOP: By Jesus Christ! By the ring of Saint Peter!
                  In a moment it will be too late, you will be in the dark.
                  Do you retract?
MONK'S VOICE: No.
BISHOP: Go then in peace!
The two monks slide the slab until the sepulchre is completely closed.   (1, 1, 7)

And so they leave Torquemada to die.

Obviously, Hugo by this extraordinary scene accomplishes several things. There is little doubt that the fate of the unnamed monk must gain him the audience's sympathy, just as his firmness of principle, extending to burial alive for his beliefs, may well gain their admiration. And his fanaticism along with that of the bishop, ready to administer such barbarous justice, prepare the audience to accept the logic of subsequent events in a Spain subjected to the Inquisition's laws. But once the monk is revealed to be Torquemada, any rhetorical *ethos*, or authority gained by his steadfast behaviour, is likely to disappear, and such sympathy as Torquemada had received is likely to dissipate quite quickly – all the more so, as Hugo makes no further attempt to persuade audiences of Torquemada's good character, admirable qualities, or rhetorical plausibility. On the contrary, by his actions Torquemada proves himself to be a religious fanatic. Saved from the grave, for instance, by the two young lovers, Don Sanche and Doña Rose, Torquemada expresses his gratitude and swears to repay them (1, 1, 8). His opportunity occurs in the last act when he finds the lovers who, having escaped from imprisonment by King Ferdinand, remain in mortal danger. Torquemada's fanatical belief that his interpretation of symbols and symbolic acts outvalues human life will force him to abandon logic for contentious or polemical definition, called *horismus* by the ancient rhetors. So he claims that he intends to 'save' his benefactors from hellfire by burning them at the stake.

He makes his decision as the lovers recall how they had saved him from a living grave:

DOÑA ROSE (*to Don Sanche*): And you said: There is a man in the earth!
          Let's save him. But the stone was too heavy, alas!
DON SANCHE: Rose, an iron cross was quite nearby ...
DOÑA ROSE: You tore it out.
A shock of terror passes through Torquemada ...

TORQUEMADA: Oh heaven, they're damned! ...

A cross torn up!

A major sacrilege! Fire, eternal fire

Opens up beneath them! They are beyond salvation. Great
God! ...

A cross! – It comes to the same thing. Let's save them. – In the
other way ...

Don't worry.

Yes, I'll save you!   (2, 3, 4)

The salvation Torquemada offers them presents itself onstage by means of
the following stage direction in which once again Hugo shows his skill at
the creation and staging of the kind of symbolic confrontation in which his
dramas excel. (The lovers are on a terrace from the back of which, out of
sight of the audience, a flight of steps leads up from the garden): *During
the lovers' ecstasy, upstage, behind and below the top step, appears the tip of a black
banner. The banner rises slowly until it can be seen in its entirety. In the centre there
is a skull and two bones in the shape of a cross, white on a black background. It gets
bigger as it approaches. – Don Sanche and Doña Rose turn round, petrified. – The
banner continues to rise. The monk's hood of the banner-bearer appears as do, at
right and left, the cowls of two lines of penitents in white and black robes'* (2, 3, 5).
Just as Don Ruy Gomez's horn summoned Hernani and Doña Sol to their
deaths, so does Torquemada's Inquisitorial banner call to theirs Don
Sanche and Doña Rose. And it does so with this spectacular visual effect
which reverses the vertical movement of Torquemada's descent into the
tomb. As well as exhibiting Hugo's skilful use of the setting, the scene also
emphasizes the ingratitude of the religious fanatic. The Grand Inquisitor
thus repays with death the gift of life he received from his young rescuers.
The result is that at the end of Hugo's final drama, Torquemada stands as
unconditionally condemned for his religious fanaticism as did Don Salluste for his political corruption at the end of *Ruy Blas*.

Despite the spectacular nature of these scenes in *Torquemada*, however, it
is difficult not to agree with Laster when he declares that 'the play of which
he [Torquemada] is the anti-hero marks a kind of apogee of pessimism'
(*VHTL*, 2, viii-ix) in Victor Hugo's work. Certainly, Hugo's optimistic belief
in progress was shaken by his wife's death in 1868, by his daughter's
sudden departure in 1863 for Canada in search of Pinson, the Englishman she believed to be her fiancé, and by his own eighteen years of exile
from France. Even so the viciousness, cynicism, and egoism of the other
principal characters in the drama are likely to seem, to many readers or
spectators, both stylized and hyperbolic.

King Ferdinand and Queen Isabella suffer most from what by 1869 had become Hugo's contempt for royalty and, it must be said, for Christianity. We meet that most Christian King, Ferdinand of Spain, as he arrogantly declares to his minister, the Marquis de Fuentel: 'I have as my law / To be above anything that can be imagined. / Nothing touches me. I am the King' (1, 1, 2). Then in a speech extraordinary for its cynicism and hypocrisy, made as it is between his performance of two decades of the rosary, the King gives his view of the relationship between himself and his chief minister:

> Spare me the boredom of your 'devotion,' my dear.
> To you I am difficult to understand, just as you are to me.
> I play the good prince and you the honest man.
> Deep down we are full of bitterness toward each other;
> I detest my servant, you hate your King.
> You would murder me if you could, and I
> Will have your head cut off one day.
> Except for that, we're good friends. (Ibid.)

Cynical about his minister's loyalty, Ferdinand castigates even more bitterly his Queen, exposing the sham of their life together:

> And my wife, that immovable monster! I am
> The slave of her days, the prisoner of her nights ...
> Side by side, we are all-powerful and dejected.
> When we touch we become colder. God sets
> On some wild and tragic mountaintop ...
> Two masks, two fearsome nothings, the King,
> The Queen; she is fear, and I am terror ...
> The man of marble next to the woman of bronze! ...
> I'm not even sure that she's not dead. (Ibid.)

The King then returns to his rosary, which allows Gucho, his sinister jester, who will later, out of fear of the Inquisition, betray the lovers to Torquemada, to question the reality behind Ferdinand's religious observances:

> Mummery!
> That's how this King will end. A callous hypocrite,
> He believes in nothing; but what chaos in his dark soul!
> When he say a paternoster, he becomes imbecilic.
> Then he yields to the Pope, he respects the papal synod. ...
> *Making the sign of the cross.*

Amen! He is a libertine, a hypocrite, devious,
A liar, cruel, obscene, an atheist, and a Catholic ...
The King puts his rosary back in his belt. (Ibid.)

It is worthwhile noticing, when listening to, or reading this denigration of
Spain's most Catholic King, that the jester's name, Gucho, contains the letters making up Hugo's own name rearranged anagrammatically: his use of
this onomastic figure presumably indicates some sympathy with Gucho's
anti-monarchist position. Ferdinand is also ready to drag Doña Rose from
the cloister for his own sexual gratification (2, 1, 4) and, once convinced by
Fuentel that Torquemada's power is greater in Spain than his own, the
King first suggests bribing the Grand Inquisitor with money or sex, before
proposing to have him murdered (2, 2, 2). So Hugo uses both the logic of
plot, and speeches made by the King and his associates to demonstrate the
character's role as one of the drama's cynical villains.

When Queen Isabella appears in Part 2, Hugo carefully emphasizes her
pride, avarice, and double-dealing. She attends the interview granted to
the Spanish Chief Rabbi, come to ransom, with 30,000 golden crowns, the
hundred old Jewish men to be burnt in the public square of Seville, and to
plead that his people be not banished from their homes and country. As
Hugo's stage directions specify, during the interview both King and Queen
show interest only in the money:

> *The King and Queen stare fixedly at each other without saying a word.*
> *Motionless, silent. Finally the Queen looks down, considering the money on*
> *the table.*
> QUEEN: Thirty thousand golden marks.
> KING: Thirty thousand golden marks. ...
> QUEEN: My mind is troubled.
>   Sir, suppose we say a paternoster?
> *She takes up her rosary. A moment of silence. The King touches the piles of money,*
> *moving them around ... The Queen, her prayer finished, places her rosary on the*
> *table.*
> QUEEN: Sir, let's take the money, and drive out the Jews
>   Anyway. I can't accept to have them as subjects.
> *The King raises his head. The Queen insists.*
>   Let's expel the Jews, and keep their money.
> KING: Yes, I thought of that.
>   But that might discourage other ransoms.
> QUEEN (*staring at the money*):
>   Thirty thousand golden crowns! In your hands ...
> KING: In yours.

QUEEN: Could we ask for more?
KING: Later.   (2, 2, 4)

Hugo's rhetorically biased representation of Ferdinand and Isabella as pious misers, religious hypocrites, and political double-dealers ready to break their solemn pledges to their subjects contradicts his earlier quoted remarks about his treatment of historical figures. Far from being seen only 'in profile,' as he wrote to Albert Lacroix, their Christian Majesties here display in the full view of spectators his version of the cynicism governing their *Realpolitik*.

Hugo increases the pathos of the Jews' plight by contrasting, in another eloquent stage direction, the humility of the representatives of the subject people and the arrogance of the royal couple:

> *Through the wide-open upstage door comes a frightened, ragged crowd between two lines of soldiers carrying halberds and pikes. They are the representatives of the Jews: men, women, children, all covered with dust and dressed in rags, barefoot, with ropes around their necks; some, mutilated and made infirm by torture, drag themselves along on crutches or on their stumps; others, whose eyes have been put out, are led along by children. At their head is the Chief Rabbi, Moses Ben Habib. All wear the yellow disc on their torn clothes. At a certain distance from the table, the rabbi stops and falls down on his knees. All those behind him prostrate themselves. The old people strike the ground with their foreheads. Neither the King nor the Queen looks at them. They stare fixedly away into the distance over the heads.* (2, 2, 3) [10]

Ferdinand and Isabella remain silent and distant throughout the rabbi's pleas, ignoring even his final, climactic appeal: 'King, Queen, have pity!' (2, 2, 4) Once again Hugo's stage direction establishes the royal reaction: '*A moment of silence. Absolute immobility on the part of Ferdinand and Isabella. Neither the King nor the Queen turn their eyes [towards the Jews].*' The inhumanity shown by King and Queen makes it easy for Torquemada, by threatening to turn the Inquisition against the royal couple, to get his way: one hundred Jewish men will be burnt the next day and all unbaptized Jews will be banished forthwith from Spain.

Modern critics point, naturally, to Hugo's prescience in foreseeing events in our own century. And indeed, the tragic fate of the Jews in *Torquemada* reduces the horror spectators might feel at other shocking events or speeches in the play: the Pope speaking in favour of incest (1, 2, 3), for example, or even the sado-masochistic hallucinations of Torquemada himself. These occur as he contemplates in imagination the mass burnings of the victims of decrees promulgated by the Holy Office. However, when Hugo insists on representing such events, as in a detailed stage direction to

Part 2, Act 2, scene 5, the effect in a performance accompanied by special visual and sound effects could not be less than devastating:

TORQUEMADA: – Look.

He descends three steps, goes over to the upstage gallery and violently drags the curtain aside.

Night is beginning to fall. – *The upstage gallery is an enormous wide-open grating showing in the dusk Tablada Square covered with people. In the centre of the square is the* quemadero, *a colossal structure, belching flame, filled with stakes and funeral pyres and with prisoners undergoing torture in* sanbenitos *glimpsed through the smoke. Barrels of pitch and burning bitumen, hooked onto the top of the stakes, pour down flaming debris on the heads of the condemned. Tied to iron stakes, women, stripped by the flames, blaze. Screaming can be heard clearly. At the four corners of the* quemadero, *the four gigantic statues, called the Four Evangelists, look like coals glowing red hot. There are holes and cracks in them through which can be seen yelling faces and waving arms that look like living firebrands. An immense vision of torture and fire.* – *The King and Queen look in terror. Gucho, under the table, stretches his neck, trying to see.* – *Torquemada feasts his eyes, contemplating the* quemadero.[11]

TORQUEMADA: O feast, O glory, O joy!

Clemency, terrible and superb, is blazing!

Eternal Deliverance! May the Damned be absolved!

The earthly pyre extinguishes hellfire beneath.   (2, 2, 5)

The sight (and sound) of such an Apocalypse render virtually insignificant remarks on the evident sado-masochistic nature of Torquemada's enjoyment at and subsequent rhetorical celebration of the *auto-da-fé* he has arranged.

More meaningful might be questions concerning the performability of such a scene. Hugo's warning against religious fanaticism is of little use if it cannot be staged. *Torquemada* did in fact have to wait until 7 May 1936 for its first performance, by the Nouvelle Comédie, directed by Henri Lesieur. Then in 1971 Denis Lorca produced the drama within the walls of the medieval castle at Carcassonne. The Théâtre du Midi troupe apparently included in the latter performances many historical and modern elements, suggesting parallels with the Holocaust. This was once again the formula adopted in 1976 by Jean Kerschbron when he presented Hugo's last drama on French TV (Channel 2). Roger Maria, reviewing the production in *L'Humanité*, after declaring 'Shakespearean' the power of Hugo's drama, concluded that TV is probably the medium best adapted to solve the physical and practical problems presented by the play. 'Jean Kerchbron [he wrote], "opened it out" superbly, filming most of the scenes in exteriors exactly suited to the subject, notably in the austere setting of Les Baux in

Provence.'[12] The deliberately spectacular nature of Hugo's Romantic dramas lends itself, of course, to televisual or cinematic treatment.

After 1869 Hugo wrote no more dramas, reducing his theatrical activity to supervising rehearsals for, or simply attending, Parisian revivals of his plays. In 1872, for instance, he attended several rehearsals for what was to be Sarah Bernhardt's triumph in the revival of *Ruy Blas* at the Odéon. Later on, how- ever, he contented himself with merely being present to acknowledge the applause of the spectators of his dramas. Victor Hugo died in Paris on 22 May 1885. After a National Funeral, his remains were interred in the Panthéon.

10. Conclusion: The Romantic Drama after Victor Hugo

As we have already seen, Fernand Baldensperger, writing in 1929, declared that Hugo's Romantic manifesto, the Preface to *Cromwell*, changed 'forever' the history of the theatre in France by 'liberating' it once and for all from the neo-classical rules governing the genres forming literary theatre.[1] Clearly, Hugo's rhetorical presentation of the theory of dramatic genres proved convincing and its influence has lasted into our own day. But Hugo's Romantic dramas themselves, as we have also seen, did not always find a public, at the State-funded theatres or elsewhere, 'grateful' for this liberation. Because they were ahead of their time, in both symbolic complexity and advanced staging techniques, Hugo's dramas needed time to find acceptance by the French theatre-going public. By 1867, however, we already find Gautier reporting that, on the revival of *Hernani* at the Comédie-Française, the new public fully realized Hugo's confident optimism by taking in their stride innovations which in 1830 had caused a scandal:

> When you attend a performance of *Hernani* nowadays, [Gautier wrote], as you follow the actors on an old copy that [in 1830] you marked in the margin with your finger nail in order to record those audiences' interruptions, outcries, and whistles ..., you [now] feel a surprise not easy to express and one that the present-day public, whom our valiant efforts succeeded in ridding of such nonsense, will never be able to fully understand. How can one imagine that a line such as: 'What time is it? – Midnight soon,' could have provoked such stormy scenes, and that we would have had to fight for three days for its first half? [In 1830] it was declared trivial, familiar, improper. A

King asks the time like any bourgeois, and he receives the answer 'Midnight,' as if he were some bumpkin. That's well done. It would have been
'polite' if he had used some fine periphrasis like: 'The hour/Will soon
attain its final resting place.' As well as wanting to exclude precise, concrete
terms from verse, [previous audiences] tolerated just as impatiently any
epithet, metaphor, or simile, in fact any poetic expression at all – in a word,
lyricism itself.[2]

In fact, the history of the Romantic drama after Hugo begins with the
growing acceptance that his plays provided the alternative aesthetic norm
to the neo-classical model that had until 1830 governed the production
and reception of dramatic works in France.

But opposition to the Romantic drama and to Romanticism itself did not
die out as more and more dramas of mixed generic makeup appeared and
as, after Ponsard, neo-classical imitations entirely dried up. Opposition to,
or espousal of, Hugo's theatre often reflected the political affiliations of his
critics, friendly and unfriendly. In France, where aesthetic questions soon
become openly politicized, the history of the reception of Hugo's dramas
since his death displays the ever-present dialectic between right-wing and
left-wing French critics. From the 1920s on, the most striking example
of the political oppositions underlying the criticism of his dramas found
expression when the extreme Right, represented by Maurras and the
Action Française, came into conflict with the Surrealists whose sympathies
were Marxist. In 1923 Eugène Marsan, writing in *Paris-Journal* on the first
production of Hugo's *Les Deux Trouvailles de Gallus*, revealed that ideological bias lay at the base of his criticisms both of Hugo and of Romanticism:

In the matter of Victor Hugo, I must be suspect on several counts. In fact, I
belong to the critical school, founded by Charles Maurras, which has not
ceased over the last 20 years in its attacks against Romanticism in general,
and against the enormous errors of Victor Hugo in particular.

As is well known, our attacks have not been in vain. Not long ago, the epithet 'Romantic' was currently understood as a term of praise, synonymous
with poetic, lyrical, even generous and magnanimous. Today all that has
changed; the same epithet has gradually taken on a pejorative sense so
marked and clear that anyone called Romantic nowadays no longer feels
flattered. That is our work. Our analyses, our definitions have won the day.
Who nowadays remains unconvinced of the psychological inanity of *Romanticism?* ... Romanticism = lies, puerility, bombast. (*PF*, 275)

Obviously, no rhetoric, by any writer of a liberal or left-wing persuasion
could hope to convince such a dramatic critic for, as Aristotle reminds us,

in order to persuade, an orator must appeal to the generally accepted beliefs of his public.[3]

Thirty years later, Louis Aragon, eminent Surrealist poet, Resistance hero and uncontested Communist leader of intellectual France at that time, writing after a 1952 performance of *Hernani* at the Comédie-Française, during which the well-heeled audience had misbehaved, also chose to couch his condemnation in socio-political rather than in literary or aesthetic terms: 'A public that calls itself *le Tout-Paris* (Everybody who is Anybody in Paris) and that remains unknown to Parisians, and which, being composed of a few cretins and their ladies, dares to call itself 'Society,' had the indecency to celebrate France's greatest poet with its sniggering' (*PF*, 278). And the same year, Paul Éluard, another Resistance hero and also a principal Surrealist poet, speaking at a meeting celebrating International Communism in Moscow, declared:

> I read, understood, and loved Victor Hugo at 13 ... Hugo was for me at 13, the illumination of poetry and I might say of the world ... La Fontaine taught me to read, as it were, but Hugo taught me to speak ...
>
> What will best preserve Hugo's works from time's assaults is the vulgarity with which the 'enlightened' have reproached him. Is Victor Hugo vulgar? Yes, if to be vulgar is to reveal his emotion without doubting that of others. Yes, if it is to assert boldly the exclusive importance of Good (over Evil). Yes, if it means not fearing any single word, be it the rarest or most banal ... How also could one excuse the bad taste he showed in celebrating the poor, better and more highly than anyone else, in words sparkling with truth and generosity. (*PF*, 336)

It is only to be expected that Aragon and Éluard would, as Marxist poets, respond so severely against the intellectual snobbery of a self-declared Right-wing élite and, equally, that they would favour the passion for social justice that forms, as we have seen, one of the principal rhetorical appeals made in Hugo's works, notably his Romantic dramas.

Such ideological squabbling in the world comprising literary Paris did nothing, however, to reduce the place Hugo's Romantic dramas carved out for themselves in the canon of performed works in France. His dramas have occupied the stage at the Comédie-Française much more frequently than the works of any other Romantic dramatist. In her 1979 history of France's premier theatre, Sylvie Chevalley provided statistics which, for instance, establish that out of thirty-three authors whose works have been featured at the Comédie-Française 'at least 1000 times between 25 August 1680 and 31 December 1978,' Victor Hugo stood in twelfth place, with 2,685 performances. Further, out of seventy 'plays featured at least

500 times' between the same dates, *Hernani* and *Ruy Blas* were in twenty-ninth and thirtieth place with 979 and 957 performances, respectively. Their only 'Romantic' rival was Rostand's affectionate caricature of a Romantic hero, *Cyrano de Bergerac*, in thirty-fifth place, with 854 performances. Finally, Chevalley shows that out of forty-nine 'plays featured at least 100 times in the 25 years between 1 January 1954 and 31 December 1978,' *Ruy Blas* with 150 performances took twenty-eighth place. Only in this more recent period do plays – other than Rostand's – that show the influence of the Romantic drama begin to appear: *Cyrano* is notable in second place with 438 per-formances, but there are others. Montherlant's three historical dramas, set in Portugal, Spain, and France in the seventeenth century (*Port-Royal, La Reine morte*, and *Le Cardinal d'Espagne*) take twelfth, twenty-sixth, and fortieth places, with 325, 155, and 119 performances respectively in the 25 years. Also in the list is Anouilh's historical confrontation between Henry II and his Archbishop of Canterbury, *Becket ou l'Honneur de Dieu* (forty-fourth place, 110 performances) and, for the first time, we find the only Romantic drama comparable to Hugo's in scope and dramatic effect, Musset's *Lorenzaccio* (in forty-seventh place with 102 performances).[4] Strikingly absent from the list are the Romantic dramas of Alexandre Dumas and Alfred de Vigny.

But this empirical, statistical proof of Hugo's success as a dramatist is contradicted by the relative failure of his plays in the Anglo-Saxon world. In fact, outside the francophone world, *Lorenzaccio* may well be better known than any of Hugo's dramas, given their infrequent performance. (It is fair to say that, as the twentieth century draws to an end, the musical version of Hugo's great novel, *Les Misérables*, represents almost the only 'dramatic' work by Victor Hugo occupying stages outside France.)[5] Nowadays in England and North America, Hugo's plays find themselves in something like the void to which Shakespeare's plays were banished in France in the seventeenth and early eighteenth centuries. Lacking adequate translations, and without exciting productions, they have failed to attract the attention of Anglo-Saxon theatrical directors or audiences. Until 1996 the only French Romantic drama to have played successfully since the 1960s in London, at Stratford, Ontario, and on Broadway was Musset's *Lorenzaccio*, partly, perhaps, because of the tradition – since Sarah Bernhardt created the role in 1896 – that its eponymous (and androgynous) hero has usually been played by a woman. Richard Eyre's 1996 production at London's Royal National Theatre of Hugo's *Le Roi s'amuse*, as adapted by Tony Harrison, has set a powerful precedent for future directors.

Hugo's Romantic dramas would seem obvious candidates for any of the four principal kinds of production that Ralph Berry sees as characterizing

modern productions of Shakespeare.[6] Whether played in the sets and costumes appropriate to their historical period, or in modern dress, or in
what Berry calls the 'Period Analogue' style, that is, with 'elegant and
appealing' costumes and sets and serving some overriding 'concept,' aesthetic, political or historical in nature, or finally in some 'eclectic' or metaphorical version, Hugo's dramas have been adapted to fit such categories
much less frequently, even in France, than have those of Shakespeare
throughout the world. While one can think easily and quickly of many
examples of Shakespeare's plays fitting into all four of Berry's categories,
even Ubersfeld, the great specialist on Hugo's Romantic dramas both in
their written form and in performance, admits that for about a hundred
years, from 1850 to 1950, the only kind of performances Hugo's dramas
received were strictly of what she calls the 'commemorative' kind, content
merely to repeat the style of previous successful productions.

Only with Jean Vilar in the 1950s did Hugo's dramas begin to receive
in France the kind of dramatic treatment likely to attract modern audiences. With stars like Gérard Philippe and Maria Casarès, *Ruy Blas* and
Marie Tudor achieved, on the vast sets provided by the Courtyard of the
Palais des Papes in Avignon or at the Palais de Chaillot in Paris, the kind
of popular success in France that Shakespeare's plays have found the
world over. Later, modern productions came from French directors like
Hubert Gignoux (*Mille Francs*), Antoine Vitez (*Les Burgraves*, 1977; *Hernani*, 1985), and Jean-Louis Barrault (*Angelo*, 1984). Most recently, the
Comédie-Française presented within the single 1994–5 season both
Lucrèce Borgia, in a powerful *mise en scène* by Jean-Luc Boutté which leant
towards the 'Period Analogue' approach and *Mille Francs de récompense*,
finally admitted to the canonical repertoire. In all cases, modern theories
and practice of theatrical production have revealed new dimensions in
Hugo's Romantic dramas.

Finally, Hugo's dramas have successfully made the transition to other
media: radio, film and television have extended the possibilities for displaying the spectacular effects that Hugo wrote into his dramas. On TV, for
instance, the striking visual effects and sequences in *Marie Tudor, Torquemada, Les Burgraves*, have all, by their ability to enhance the performance of
Hugo's dramas, tempted directors working for the small screen (*PF*, 377–
80). And for decades, all of Hugo's dramas have been fairly regularly presented on French radio, with some of them being issued on disk or cassette
(ibid., 369–71). But it is in the cinema that Hugo's dramas have found their
most frequent modern medium. In its first hundred years, the French cinema, as well as producing versions of Hugo's novels – *Notre-Dame de Paris*
and *Les Misérables* being the most popular – has produced (sometimes several) versions, faithful or otherwise, of *Lucrèce Borgia, Le Roi s'amuse, Ruy*

Blas, Hernani, Marion de Lorme, Marie Tudor, and even *Cromwell* (*PF,* 372–6). We may confidently expect that in the twenty-first century such transfers will extend to other media – both videodisc and CD-ROM readily suggest themselves. It is to be hoped that the increasing accessibility that such media transfers make possible will introduce Hugo's Romantic dramas to a wider international audience.

Chronology of Hugo's Life and Writings

POLITICAL EVENTS/ GOVERNMENT & THEATRE	VICTOR HUGO: LIFE	PRINCIPAL WORKS (Dramatic works in bold)	FRENCH ROMANTIC DRAMA
			1769–1962 Ducis translates Shakespeare
			1771 Diderot, *Le Fils naturel* at Comédie-Française
			1778–83 Le Tourneur translates Shakespeare
			1783 L.S. Mercier, *La Mort de Louis XI*
			1784 Beaumarchais, *Le Mariage de Figaro*
			1785 French translation of Schiller's *Brigands*
1789 Fall of the Bastille			

POLITICAL EVENTS/ GOVERNMENT & THEATRE	VICTOR HUGO: LIFE	PRINCIPAL WORKS (Dramatic works in bold)	FRENCH ROMANTIC DRAMA
1791 National Assembly proclaims freedom of theatres			
1793 Louis XVI executed. Convention establishes free performances 'for and by the people'	**1797** Léopold Hugo marries Sophie Trébuchet in Paris		**1797** Pixérécourt's melodramas: *Le Château des Apennins* and *Le Fantôme vivant*
1798 18 Brumaire, coup d'état. Bonaparte 1st Consul			**1800** Lemercier, *Pinto ou la Journée d'une conspiration*;
1802 Bonaparte Consul for Life	**1802** Birth in Besançon of Victor Marie Hugo		Pixérécourt, *Coelina ou l'Enfant du mystère*
	1802–18 During the disunion and infidelities of his parents, Victor sides with his mother		
1804 Duke d'Enghien executed. Napoleon Emperor			
1807 Imperial Decree limits to 7 the no. of theatres in Paris			
1809 Decree authorizes re-opening of Porte-St-Martin Theatre, the 'People's Opera'			**1809** Constant adapts Schiller's *Wallenstein* and adds an important Preface

POLITICAL EVENTS/ GOVERNMENT & THEATRE	VICTOR HUGO: LIFE	PRINCIPAL WORKS (Dramatic works in bold)	FRENCH ROMANTIC DRAMA
			1810 Ciceri appointed chief set designer at the Opéra. G. de Staël, *De l'Allemagne*. Pixérécourt, *Les Ruines de Babylone*
1812 Moscow campaign. Decree reorganizes Comédie-Française	**1811–12** Victor, his mother and brothers in Spain to visit General Hugo	**1812 Le Château du diable**, 3-act melodrama; **L'Enfer sur terre**, 1-act comedy	
		1814 Improvises plays for puppet theatre	
1815 Napoleon defeated at Waterloo. Louis XVIII's Second Restoration in Paris			**1815** Pixérécourt, *Christophe Colomb*
		1816 Irtamène, 5-act tragedy	**1816** Odéon Theatre opens. *Hamlet* played as 'pantomime with music'
		1817 Athélie ou les Scandinaves, unfinished tragedy (2 acts completed)	
		A.Q.C.H.E.B., comic opera	
	1818 Léopold and Sophie separate. Eugène's first signs of mental imbalance	**1818–21** Hugo theatre critic for *Le Conservateur Littéraire*	
		1819 Inez de Castro, melodrama in 2 acts and 2 interludes	**1819** C. Delavigne, *Les Vêpres siciliennes*
	1820 Victor's secret promise to marry Adèle Foucher ignored by Sophie		**1820** P. Lebrun, *Marie Stuart*
	1821 Death of Sophie		**1821** New translation by Le Tourneur of Shakespeare, with Guizot's *Vie de Shakespeare* as Preface

POLITICAL EVENTS/ GOVERNMENT & THEATRE	VICTOR HUGO: LIFE	PRINCIPAL WORKS (Dramatic works in bold)	FRENCH ROMANTIC DRAMA
	1822 12 Oct. Hugo marries Adèle Foucher. Eugène's mental breakdown follows	**1822** *Les Odes et poésies diverses* **1822–6** *Bug-Jargal*, novel **1822–7 Amy Robsart**, 5-act drama	**1822** English troupe plays Shakespeare in Paris provoking a riot. Opéra stage lit with gas for first time **1823** Frédérick Lemaître as Robert Macaire; Stendhal, *Racine et Shakespeare* (1)
1824 Death of Louis XVIII	**1824** Birth of Léopoldine Hugo		**1824** Mérimée, *Le Théâtre de Clara Gazul*
1825 Charles X crowned. Baron Taylor at Comédie-Française	**1825** Hugo chevalier de la Légion d'honneur. Attends coronation of Charles X		**1825** Stendhal, *Racine et Shakespeare* (2). Ciceri uses a 'cyclorama' in Opéra production
	1826 Birth of Charles Hugo	**1826–7 Cromwell**, drama, and Preface	**1826** Death of Talma **1827–8** Triumphant Parisian season of English actors
	1828 Death of Léopold Hugo. François-Victor, Hugo's second son, born	**1828 Amy Robsart** has one performance at Odéon. *Odes et ballades*	**1828** Mérimée, *La Jacquerie*. Lemaître plays Mephisto in Stapfer's adaptation of Goethe's *Faust*
1829 Polignac's right-wing Ministry bans *Marion de Lorme*		**1829** 1–30 June, writes **Marion de Lorme**; July, accepted by Comédie-Française. *Les Orientales*, poems. *Le Dernier Jour d'un condamné à mort*, novel	**1829** A. Dumas, *Henri III et sa cour*. A. de Vigny, *Le More de Venise*. B. Constant, *Réflexions sur la tragédie*. Ciceri invents the 'mobile cyclorama'

POLITICAL EVENTS/ GOVERNMENT & THEATRE	VICTOR HUGO: LIFE	PRINCIPAL WORKS (Dramatic works in bold)	FRENCH ROMANTIC DRAMA
1830 Revolution. Louis-Philippe King	**1830** Hugo refuses Charles X's offer of seat on Council of State. Sainte-Beuve declares his love for Mme Hugo. Birth of Adèle, Hugo's daughter	**1830** 25 Feb. Premiere of **Hernani** at Comédie-Française; 'battle' continues for 39 performances	**1830** Dumas, *Christine*. A. de Musset, *La Nuit vénitienne* flops at Odéon
		1831 Marion de Lorme performed at Porte-Saint-Martin Theatre; *Notre-Dame de Paris,* novel; *Les Feuilles d'automne,* poems	**1831** Dumas, *Charles VII chez ses grands vassaux; Antony; Napoléon Bonaparte; Richard Darlington*
		1832 22 Nov. **Le Roi s'amuse**; after one performance, taken off by order of the censor	**1832** Dumas, *Térésa; La Tour de Nesles*; Musset, *Un Spectacle dans un fauteuil*
	1833 Hugo begins liaison with Juliette Drouet	**1833** 2 Feb. **Lucrèce Borgia**; 6 Nov. **Marie Tudor** (Porte-Saint-Martin)	
		1834 *Littérature et philosophie mêlées,* essays; *Les Chants du crépuscule,* poems	**1834** Dumas, *Catherine Howard*. Pixérécourt, *Latude ou Trente-Cinq Ans de captivité*
1835 Censorship restored		**1835** 28 April. **Angelo, tyran de Padoue** Comédie-Française	**1835** Delavigne, *Don Juan d'Autriche*. Vigny, *Chatterton*
		1836 Hugo fails twice to gain election to the Académie française	**1836** Dumas, *Kean*
	1837 Eugène dies at Charenton	**1837** *Les Voix intérieures,* poems	**1837** Dumas' tragedy, *Caligula,* flops at Comédie-Française

POLITICAL EVENTS/ GOVERNMENT & THEATRE	VICTOR HUGO: LIFE	PRINCIPAL WORKS (**Dramatic works in bold**)	FRENCH ROMANTIC DRAMA
		1838 8 Nov. **Ruy Blas**	**1838** Rachel débuts at Comédie-Française
	1839–40 Hugo and Juliette visit the Rhineland. He fails again to become an Academician	**1839** Writes 3 acts of **Les Jumeaux**	**1839** Dumas, *L'Alchimiste*. G. de Nerval, *Léo Burckhardt*
	1841 Hugo elected to the Academy	**1840** *Les Rayons et les ombres*, poems; *Le Retour de l'empereur*, poem	
		1842 *Le Rhin, lettres à un ami*	**1842** E. Scribe, *Le Fils de Cromwell*
	1843 Léopoldine marries Charles Vacquerie; both drown at Villequier	**1843** 7 March. **Les Burgraves**	**1843** Ponsard, *Lucrèce*
	1845 Hugo appointed Peer of France		
1848 February. Revolution ends the monarchy. Second Republic; Louis Napoleon President	**1848** Hugo refuses Ministry of Education, offered by Lamartine		
	1849 Hugo elected to Legislative Assembly. President of the International Peace Conference		
1850 Theatre censorship restored			
1851 Louis Napoleon Bonaparte's coup d'état.	**1851** Hugo a member of the committee resisting coup d'état. 11 Dec. begins his exile from France		

POLITICAL EVENTS/ GOVERNMENT & THEATRE	VICTOR HUGO: LIFE	PRINCIPAL WORKS (Dramatic works in bold)	FRENCH ROMANTIC DRAMA
1852 Press censorship legalized. 2 Dec. Second Empire established	**1852–5** Hugo at Marine Terrace, Jersey; expelled	**1852** *Napoléon le petit*, political polemic	
		1853 *Oeuvres oratoires*	
		1854 *Les Châtiments*, poems. **La Forêt**	
	1856 Buys Hauteville House, Guernsey. Juliette settles nearby	**mouillée**	
	1858 Mme Hugo returns to Paris. François-Victor publishes translation of Shakespeare. Hugo suffers nearly fatal bout of anthrax		
	1859 Refuses political amnesty offered by Napoleon III. Tries to save the life of John Brown	**1859** *La Légende des siècles*, epic poetry	
	1862 Hugo establishes, at his expense, a weekly meal for poor children in Guernsey	**1862** *Les Misérables*, novel	
	1863 *Victor Hugo raconté par un témoin de sa vie*. Daughter Adèle leaves for Halifax, Nova Scotia, in pursuit of Albert Pinson		
1864 Musset's *Lorenzaccio* banned by Imperial censor		**1864** *William Shakespeare*, criticism	

POLITICAL EVENTS/ GOVERNMENT & THEATRE	VICTOR HUGO: LIFE	PRINCIPAL WORKS (Dramatic works in bold)	FRENCH ROMANTIC DRAMA
		1865 **La Grand'mère**; *Les Chansons des rues et des bois*, poems	
	1866 Adèle follows Pinson, now married, to Barbados	1866 **Mille Francs de récompense; L'Intervention**	
		1867 **Mangeront-ils?**	
	1868 Death of Mme Hugo		
		1869 **Margarita; L'Épée; Esca; Torquemada**; *L'Homme qui rit*, novel	
1870 Franco-Prussian War. End of Second Empire	1870 Hugo returns to Paris and national acclaim		
1871 Paris Commune. Third Republic	1871 Elected to National Assembly. Resigns. Charles Hugo dies. In Brussels, Hugo offers asylum to members of the Paris Commune. Expelled from Belgium, he and Juliette take refuge in Vianden		
	1872 Adèle brought back from Barbados to an asylum in Saint-Mandé	1872 *L'Année terrible*, poems 1872–6 *Actes et paroles*, essays	
	1873 Death of François-Victor	1873 **Sur la lisière d'un bois**	
	1876 Hugo elected Senator	1874 *Quatre-vingt-treize*, novel	

POLITICAL EVENTS/ GOVERNMENT & THEATRE	VICTOR HUGO: LIFE	PRINCIPAL WORKS (Dramatic works in bold)	FRENCH ROMANTIC DRAMA
		1877 *La Légende des siècles, nouvelle série*; *L'Art d'être grand-père*, poems	
		1877–8 *Histoire d'un crime*, political polemic	
	1878 June. Hugo suffers stroke. Convalesces in Guernsey with Juliette	**1878** *Le Pape*; *L'Âne*, philosophic poems	
	1881 Paris celebrates Hugo's 80th year	**1881** *Les Quatre Vents de l'esprit*, poems	
	1882 Hugo re-elected Senator		
	1883 Death of Juliette Drouet	**1883** *La Légende des siècles, série complémentaire*	
	1885 22 May. Death of Victor Hugo. National funeral, burial in the Panthéon		

Notes

INTRODUCTION

1 Bill Alexander, Associate Director of the Royal Shakepeare Company, in *On Directing Shakespeare*, ed. Ralph Berry (London: Hamilton 1989), 177.

2 Ruth L. Doyle, *Victor Hugo's Dramas. An Annotated Bibliography, 1900–1980* (Westport, Conn.: Greenwood Press 1981), 3. Meanwhile, Michel Butor offers the following summary of critical attitudes towards Hugo's plays, before going on to contradict it: 'One is tempted to say: Victor Hugo's poetry is exciting, his novels are exciting, his critical and political works are all exciting. Let's then allow his theatre to sleep in peace, let's forgive him for [having written] it. But that would only be possible if his theatre represented in his works something subsidiary, a detour from his fundamental path; well, even the most cursory examination reveals that the reality is quite different' (*Nouvelle Revue Française* [1964], quoted in *PF*, 335).

3 Joanna Richardson, *Victor Hugo* (New York: St. Martin's Press 1976). Hugo's most recent biographer, Graham Robb, in describing as follows the ideological prejudices shaping Richardson's account, points also to the faults in her scholarship: 'Nourished by lies long since disproved, it briefly describes a self-serving, ignorant megalomaniac inexplicably adored by the French as their greatest poet. It is in part an unacknowledged paraphrase of other biographies. The plot summaries, also unattributed, are lifted, with minute changes, from the old *Oxford Companion to French Literature*, ed. Sir Paul Harvey and J.E. Heseltine (Oxford: Clarendon Press 1959). Each borrowed passage is followed by a judgment from the biographer's own pen: "cumbersome plot," "the plot and characters do not bear analysis," "has long since become unreadable," etc. Works –

even major works – not described by the *Companion* are not mentioned in the
biography' (*Victor Hugo* [London: Picador 1997], xvii).

4 Victor Hugo / Tony Harrison, *Le Roi s'amuse / The Prince's Play* (London: Faber
& Faber 1996). Harrison adapted, rather than translated, Hugo's drama into
English rhyming couplets. See below, Chapter 5.

5 In *Classical Literary Criticism. Aristotle, On the Art of Poetry, Horace, On the Art of
Poetry, Longinus: On the Sublime*, trans. T.S. Dorsch (Harmondsworth: Penguin
Books 1965) 34.

6 *Hamlet* 2, 2, 398–400, in William Shakespeare, *The Complete Works*, ed. Stanley
Wells and Gary Taylor (Oxford: The Clarendon Press 1988), 667.

7 Michel Lioure, *Le Drame de Diderot à Ionesco* (Paris: Armand Colin 1963) 8. All
translations from texts in French are mine, unless otherwise stated.

8 Ibid.; emphasis in the original.

9 See Chaim Perelman and Lucie Olbrechts-Tyteca, *The New Rhetoric: A Treatise on
Argumentation*, trans. J. Wilkinson and P. Weaver (Notre Dame: University of
Notre Dame Press 1969), 266, 273–4.

CHAPTER 1

1 Jacques Derrida, *L'Écriture et la différence* (Paris: Seuil, 'Points' 1979), 340.

2 'During the wars of Empire, while their husbands and brothers were in Germany, anguished mothers had given birth to a generation at once fiery-spirited,
pale and nervous. Conceived between battles, educated in colleges to the beat
of the drum, thousands of boys watched each other darkly, all the while testing
their puny muscles ... They breathed the air of a pure sky, brilliant with glory
shining on so much military armour, fully aware that their fate was a mass grave
... [But] death itself was so fine, so great, so splendid in funereal purple ... The
boys left college and, seeing no longer either sabres or armour, infantry or cav-
alry, in their turn asked after their fathers. But answer came that the war was
over, that Caesar was dead, and the portraits of Wellington and Blücher hung in
the anterooms of consulates and embassies, bearing underneath them two
words: *Salvatoribus mundi.*

'Then upon a world in ruins settled a careworn young generation. All of these
children were drops of the hot blood that had flooded the earth; born in the
midst of war, for war. For fifteen years they had dreamed of Moscow's snows and
of the sun over the Pyramids. They had never left behind their native towns, but
they had been told that, from every gate of such towns they would go to capture
the capitals of Europe. In their heads they had carried a whole world. But now,
they looked at earth, sky, streets and byways and found all empty, and only the
bells of their parish churches rang in the distance.' (*La Confession d'un enfant du
siècle*, in *Oeuvres complètes en prose*, [Paris: Gallimard, '*Bibliothèque de la Pléiade*'
1960], 65–7.)

3 Since I intend to follow the chronological indications established for Hugo's works by the editors of the Massin edition of his *Complete Works*, it is only fair to point out when they allow that some chronological uncertainties still remain. They give, as the date of both these plays, '1812 (?).' In her presentation of them, Éliette Vasseur argues in favour of this date, but is unable to offer any convincing proof. See *OC*, 1, i–iv.

4 It may be significant, in this regard, that the play the Hugo family had seen previous to *The Ruins of Babylon* was Molière's *La Comtesse d'Escarbagnas*, in which a female protagonist is taught a salutary lesson in love.

5 Maurice Lever, *Sade: A Biography*, trans. Arthur Goldhammer (New York: Farrar, Straus & Giroux 1993), 61.

6 Quoted in Hazard Adams, *Critical Theory since Plato* (New York: Harcourt, Brace, Jovanovich 1971), 265–6.

7 *Hamlet* 3, 1, 77–8; Voltaire, *Lettres philosophiques* (Oxford: Blackwell 1958), 71. Stendhal quotes an amusing example of the idiocies made necessary by the '*style noble*': 'What is anti-Romantic is M. Legouvé in his tragedy [*The Death of*] *Henry IV*, being unable to reproduce the finest sentence of that patriotic king: "I would like the poorest peasant in my realm to have at least a chicken in the pot on Sundays." This truly French saying would have given the least of Shakespeare's emulators a touching scene. *Racinianesque* tragedy says it much more nobly:

> I wish finally that on the day marked for rest,
> That the laborious host in his modest hamlet
> May have on his humble table, through my benevolence,
> Some of those dishes reserved for the well-to-do classes.' (Act 4; *RS*, 65–6)

8 *Art poétique* quoted in Adams, *Critical Theory*, 267.

9 Barbara Cooper sees this idealization of Louis XVIII as part of the pervasive propaganda campaign organized by Bourbon sympathizers who, for instance, also compared Louis to Henri IV, with whom he shared no more than their common Bourbon ancestry. See Cooper, '"Il faut suivre votre modèle": Theatre and Society in Early Nineteenth-Century France,' *French Literature Series*, vol. 15, ed. A. Maynor Hardee (Columbia: University of South Carolina Press 1988), 95–108.

10 *Dictionnaire de Victor Hugo* (Paris: Larousse 1970), 54.

11 *Poetics*, Chapter 16. On *anagnorisis*, see Terence Cave, *Recognitions: A Study in Poetics* (Oxford: Clarendon Press 1990), passim.

12 Gérard Genette, 'Vraisemblance et motivation,' *Figures II* (Paris: Seuil 1969), 97–8.

13 *VHR*, 362. As the annotators to this passage point out, it is perfectly possible to reverse cause and effect. So, rather than seeing Victor's success as triggering Eugène's mental disturbance, one may well believe that it was the disease which

triggered his violent emotional and physical reactions. I suspect that the choice of explanation will depend upon one's like or dislike of Victor Hugo and/or his works, dramatic or otherwise.

CHAPTER 2

1 See Sylvie Chevalley, *La Comédie-Française, hier et aujourd'hui* (Paris: Didier 1979), 33.
2 Quoted in Robert Baldick, *The Life and Times of Frédérick Lemaître* (London: Hamish Hamilton 1959), 36.
3 We shall discuss repressive censorship in France within the context of Hugo's battle against it. For a more general study, see F.W.J. Hemmings, *Theatre and State in France, 1760–1905* (Cambridge: Cambridge University Press 1994), Chapter 14.
4 Lekain is famous also for disencumbering, in 1759, the Comédie's stage of the seats and frequently disruptive spectators it had tolerated since its foundation in 1680 by Louis XIV.
5 Problems of memorization and reliance on prompters continued at the Comédie-Française throughout the last century and into ours, for we find Sarah Bernhardt complaining in her manual for future actors, written at the end of her life: '[T]he dramatic artist must have a good memory, otherwise he must hum and haw, waiting for the prompter, which is odious – really only in France does the prompter still exist with his evil little box which blocks the spectators' view and is generally out of place on the set' (Sarah Bernhardt, *L'Art du théâtre* [1923; Monaco: Éditions Sauret 1993], 31).
6 *Le Courrier Français*, 13 September 1827 (*SG*, 98).
7 According to Mme Hugo, after Victor read to the great actor scenes from his unfinished drama, Talma cried: 'Those are the kind of lines I need! The whole scene suits me. Finish your play, Monsieur Hugo, and I'll act it straight away!' (*VHR*, 412)
8 Without quoting him directly, Descotes gives Gustave Planche as the source of this judgment: 'G. Planche, *Revue des Deux Mondes* (1836), VIII, 120 et. sq.'
9 Alexandre Dumas, *Mes Mémoires* (Paris: Plon 1986), 355.
10 Baldick, *Lemaître*, 37–8.
11 Quoted in Jean Gaudon, *Hugo dramaturge* (Paris: L'Arche 1955), 153.
12 Jules Janin, *Histoire de la littérature dramatique* (Paris: Michel Lévy 1853–8), VI, 156, trans. R. Baldick, *Lemaître*, 54.
13 F.W.J. Hemmings, *The Theatre Industry in Nineteenth-Century France* (Cambridge: Cambridge University Press 1993), 101.
14 Ibid., 115–16.
15 'Essai sur le genre dramatique sérieux' in *Théâtre complet* (Paris: Gallimard, 'Bibliothèque de la Pléiade' 1957), 12.

16 See Denis Diderot, *Paradoxe sur le comédien* (Paris: Garnier-Flammarion 1981), 126–9.

17 Diderot, 'Entretiens sur Le Fils naturel,' in *Oeuvres esthétiques*, ed. Paul Vernière (Paris: Éditions Garnier 1968), 78.

18 Ibid., 152.

19 Benjamin Constant, *Wallenstein, tragédie en cinq actes et en vers, précédée de quelques réflexions sur le théâtre allemand*, ed. J.-R. Derré (Paris: Perrin 1965), 57.

20 See August Wilhelm Schlegel, *Vorlesungen über dramatische Kunst und Literatur* (1809), Lesson 11.

21 Mme de Staël, *De l'Allemagne* (Paris: Garnier-Flammarion 1968), Part 2, Chapter 15, 255.

22 F. Guizot, 'Vie de Shakespeare,' in Shakespeare, *Oeuvres complètes*, trans. P. Le Tourneur (Paris: Ladvocat 1821), cli.

23 Quoted by Gaudon, *Hugo dramaturge*, 27–8.

24 J.L. Smith, *Melodrama* (London: Methuen 1973), 65.

CHAPTER 3

1 V. Hugo, Preface to *Les Rayons et les ombres*, *OC*, 6, 19.

2 On different treatments of the Inez legend, from the seventeenth to the twentieth century, see Martin Nozick, 'The Inez de Castro Theme in European literature,' *Comparative Literature* 3 (Fall 1951), 330–41. The most recent version, James MacMillan's opera, *Inès de Castro*, premiered during the Edinburgh Festival in 1996.

3 In the Preface to *Cromwell*, Hugo insisted that the nineteenth-century poet must free himself from the imitation of existing forms: 'Let the poet especially beware of imitating anyone, no more Shakespeare than Molière, no more Schiller than Corneille' (*OC*, 3, 68–9).

4 See, for instance, Maurice Descotes, *L'Obsession de Napoléon dans le 'Cromwell' de Victor Hugo* (Paris: Minard, 'Archives des lettres modernes' 1967).

5 *Cromwell* was finally staged, in a shortened form, in July 1956 in the *Cour Carrée* (Square Courtyard) of the Louvre where, in the opinion of some contemporary critics, the setting distracted from the play.

6 Hugo's views on Scott's 'dramatic novels' appeared in his review of Scott's *Quentin Durward*: '*Quentin Durward ou l'Écossais à la cour de Louis XI*, par sir Walter Scott,' *La Muse Française*, (July 1823), in *OC*, 2, 431–8.

7 Mikhail Bakhtin, *The Dialogic Imagination. Four Essays*, ed. Michael Holquist, trans. Caryl Emerson and Michael Holquist (Austin: University of Texas Press 1981), 68–82.

8 Longinus, 'On the Sublime,' in *Classical Literary Criticism*, trans. T.S. Dorsch, 100.

9 Pierre Grosclaude in Victor Hugo, *Préface de Cromwell*, (Paris: Larousse 1949) 12.

10 V. Hugo, 'Lettre-préface aux *Poésies de feu Charles Dovalle,*' *OC,* 3, 1085; Hugo reprinted the passage in the Preface to *Hernani;* see *OC,* 3, 922. Nothing, perhaps, better confirms the essentially social nature of Hugo's literary values than this kind of definition. Thirty-four years later, forced into exile and having moved further to the Left, Hugo's definition of the same concept shows the ideology that gave rise to *Les Misérables:* 'The Revolution closed one century and opened another. An agitation in people's minds prepared an actual upheaval; that was the eighteenth century. After the political revolution, a literary and social revolution took place. That is the nineteenth [century]. Romanticism and socialism, it has been said with hostility, but with accuracy, are the same thing' (*William Shakespeare* [1864], *OC,* 12, 305).

11 See Stendhal, *Romans et contes* (Paris: Gallimard 'Bibliothèque de la Pléiade' 1983) 1, 557.

12 On Hugo's exploitation of stage illusion, see also Frederick Burwick, 'Stage Illusion and the Stage Designs of Goethe and Hugo,' *Word & Image,* 4, nos. 3 and 4 (July-December 1988), 692–718.

13 The twelve plays so identified include, in verse: *Cromwell, Hernani, Marion de Lorme, Le Roi s'amuse, Ruy Blas, Les Burgraves, Torquemada,* and *L'Épée, drame en 5 scènes* in *Le Théâtre en liberté.* The prose dramas are: *Lucrèce Borgia, Marie Tudor, Angelo, tyran de Padoue,* and *Mille Francs de récompense.*

14 *Histoire du romantisme* (Paris: Charpentier 1874), 5.

15 Adèle Hugo, *Victor Hugo raconté par un témoin de sa vie* (Paris: Nelson 1936), 2, 278, 280.

16 Maurice Souriau, *La Préface de 'Cromwell,' Introduction, texte, et notes* (Paris: Boivin 1897), 157.

17 'Les Années 1827–28 en France et au dehors,' *Revue des Cours et Conférences,* (30 June 1929), 529.

CHAPTER 4

1 Michel Butor, 'Le Théâtre de Victor Hugo,' *Nouvelle Revue Française* (December 1964), 862.

2 For the details of *Marion*'s censorship, see *OC,* 3, 1496–7.

3 The relevant passages in the correspondence between Hugo and Sainte-Beuve may be consulted in *OC,* 3, 1010–87.

4 See A. Dumas, *Mes Mémoires,* 446–55.

5 Maloeuvre's engraving is reproduced in *RH,* 42.

6 See E. Starkie, *Petrus Borel, the Lycanthrope* (London: Faber & Faber 1954), 30–41.

7 Ibid., 37.

8 Hugo's list of annotations to the lines that were hissed or which drew catcalls appears in Jean Gaudon, 'Sur *Hernani,*' *Cahiers de l'Association Internationale des Études Françaises* (May 1983), 101–20, 278–80.

9 Ubersfeld applies Bakhtin's notion of 'carnival' to Hugo's dramatic output in *RB*, 461–506.

10 See Massin, 'Présentation,' *OC*, 3, 919ff. One of the most frequently quoted modern sources for recent psycho-analytical critics of Hugo remains Charles Mauron's, 'Les Personnages de Victor Hugo, étude psychocritique,' ibid., 2, i–xlii. More directly relevant because restricted to the characters in his plays is Hermann Hugi's, *Les Drames de Victor Hugo expliqués par la psychanalyse* (Berne: Buch und Kunstdruckerei 1930). *RB* also contains psycho-critical analyses of Hugo's dramas.

11 Burwick, 'Stage Illusion,' 692–3.

12 Ibid., 693–4.

13 In speaking of the 'dramatic elements that have been used by almost all play-wrights,' namely, 'spectacle, character, plot, diction, song, and thought,' Aristotle continues: 'Of these elements the most important is the plot, the ordering of the incidents' (*Poetics*, 6, 50a, 14–15, in Aristotle, Horace, Longinus, *Classical Literary Criticism*, 39).

14 For a discussion of the generic differences between *Hernani* and contemporary melodrama, see Jean-Marie Thomasseau, 'Dialogues avec tableaux à ressorts,' *Europe*, nos. 703–4 (November–December 1987), 61–70.

15 On the dangers to the audience's suspension of disbelief caused by the 'overmotivation' of such devices, see G. Genette, 'Vraisemblance et motivation,' 71–99.

16 'Victor Hugo and Poe,' *Revue de Littérature Comparée*, 42 (October–December 1968), 494–519.

17 Fernande Bassan offers a brief overview of the history of the receptions accorded *Hernani* between 1830 and 1974 in 'La Réception critique d'*Hernani* de Victor Hugo,' *Revue d'Histoire du Théâtre* (1984), 69–77.

18 For details concerning Hugo's receipts, see *PVH*, 32.

19 Barbara C. Cooper studies parodies of Hugo's dramas in 'Parodying Hugo,' *European Romantic Review* (1991), 23–38.

20 Text reproduced by Maurice Rostand, 'La Gloire de Victor Hugo,' *Lettres Françaises* (21 February, 1952), 1.

21 François, duc de La Rochefoucauld, *Réflexions, ou Sentences et maximes morales. Réflexions diverses*, ed. Dominique Secretan (Genève: Droz 1967), 9 (maxime 8).

CHAPTER 5

1 V. Hugo, *OC*, 3, 1272–3, 1270–1.

2 Basing her remarks on her study of Hugo's manuscripts, Ubersfeld explains as follows his speed of composition: 'He does not usually begin to write a theatrical text until everything is already complete, until the whole play is constructed in his head' (*RB*, 90). This does not mean, of course, that he completed all the projects he began, as we shall see in discussing *Les Jumeaux*.

3 For evidence of the receptions given the play on its revivals in 1882, 1911, and 1965, see *PVH*, 78, *DR*, 150, 168, and *PF*, 270–1.

4 By most, perhaps, but not all. Among the unfavourable reviews of Francesco Piave's libretto, one anonymous writer criticized the historical allusion inevitable in the change of names, as Verdi's biographer, Mary Jane Phillips-Matz tells us. Writing in a Venetian newspaper, *Il Vaglio*, on 15 March 1851, the reviewer accused Piave of wishing to 'make a gift to the honourable house of the Dukes of Gonzaga' by making their ancestor 'a new Don Giovanni,' before going on to remind him that members of the Gonzaga family still lived in Venice. See *Verdi, A Biography* (New York, Oxford University Press 1996), 285.

5 Charles Spencer, review of *The Prince's Play*, *Daily Telegraph* (22 April 1996), cited in *Theatre Record*, 16, issue 8 (13 May, 1996), 495.

6 V. Hugo / Tony Harrison, *Le Roi s'amuse / The Prince's Play*, 24, 78.

7 Ibid., 116.

8 See, for instance, Benedict Nightingale in *The Times* of 22 April 1996, John Gross in the *Sunday Telegraph* of 28 April, cited in *Theatre Record*, 495, 496.

9 Victor Hugo, ms. 13371, folio 96, dated 1 July [probably] 1832; see *RB*, 160. The following historical summary by Arnaud Laster may help to explain Hugo's remark: 'Alexander Borgia, at first married to the Roman Vanozza Catanei (a more than easy lady) became Pope as Alexander VI, in 1492. He had four children, the eldest Juan di Gandía (Hugo calls him Jean), murdered by his younger brother, Cesare, Duke of Valentinois; Lucrezia, and finally Jofré. Lucrezia was married four times: her first husband is unknown; the second (Giovanni Sforza) had to divorce her; the third, Alfonso of Aragon, whom she seems to have loved, was murdered by Cesare. The fourth was Alfonso d'Este. Hugo uses two probably legendary rumours: she is said to have slept with both of her brothers, Cesare and the eldest Juan, by whom she is said to have had a child' *(VHTL*, 1, 1423, n18). Hugo's parallel between the Borgias and the House of Atreus, 'virtually unrivalled in antiquity for complexity and corruption' *(Encyclopedia Britannica* [1974], 1, 680) underlines his treatment of Lucrezia as myth.

10 Baldick, *Lemaître*, 118.

11 Ibid., 119.

12 G. Sand, *Correspondance* (Paris: Éditions Garnier 1986), 21, 806.

13 The three endings fall neatly into two of Aristotle's types of *anagnorisis*: recognition in the first two depends upon the interpretation of 'acquired' (rather than hereditary) signs, i.e., his mother's letters; the third arises from the logic of the incidents themselves. Aristotle adds, in reference to the latter case, the adverb 'plausibly': clearly, the decision on the plausibility of such events belongs to the spectator. See T. Cave, *Recognitions: A Study in Poetics* (Oxford: Clarendon Press 1988), 38.

14 Quoted in *RB*, 182.

CHAPTER 6

1 V. Hugo, ms. folio 137 (112e cote / 63e pièce). Ubersfeld, who cites this note, adds that Hugo wrote it 'after 1848 (?)' (*RB*, 195, n34).

2 For Dumas' letter and Hugo's reply, see *OC*, 4, 1115–16. Granier de Cassagnac did declare that Hugo had nothing to do with the letter, which, he said, was conceived and written entirely by himself.

3 Quoted by A. Laster, *PF*, 378. Laster notes that Gance's admission helps to prove Ubersfeld's thesis that Hugo, by breaking with the principal conventions of melodrama, while keeping its 'tools' (poison, masks, secret rooms, etc.) produced anti-melodrama.

4 *Hamlet*, 4, 5, 122.

5 Carlson quotes as his source the Promptbook for *Angelo* in the Association des Régisseurs collection. See M. Carlson, 'French Stage Composition from Hugo to Zola,' *Educational Theatre Journal* (December 1971), 364, n4.

6 Ibid., 365. The incident occurs in *Angelo* 2, 5.

7 Burwick, 'Stage Illusion,' 693, 706.

8 For details, see *RB*, 294. For Hugo's letters to Védel, see *OC*, 5, 1132–3, 1136.

CHAPTER 7

1 J.-F. Merle in *La Quotidienne*, 22 November 1838, quoted in *RB*, 341.

2 Burwick, 'Stage Illusion,' 694.

3 In his funeral oration over the tomb of the dead actor in 1876, Hugo himself stated his view that Lemaître was the people incarnate: 'No other actor was his equal, because no one *could* equal him. Other actors before him portrayed kings, pontiffs, or captains, what are normally called heroes, or gods; he, thanks to the times in which he lived, *was* the people. (*Agitation* [among the mourners].) [There is] no richer, no higher role. Because he was the people, he became the drama; he possessed all the faculties, strength and grace of the people; he was indomitable, vigorous, pathetic, tempestuous, and charming. Like the people, he *was* tragedy and he *was* comedy. Hence his total command, for fear and pity are all the more tragic when they include the poignant irony of the human condition. Aristophanes complements Aeschylus; and what moves a crowd most completely is terror combined with laughter. Frédérick Lemaître possessed this gift of duality, which is why, of all the dramatic artists of his time, he was the supreme actor' (*OC*, 15, 1372).

4 *Revue des Deux Mondes* (December 1838), quoted in *RB*, 347.

5 Burwick, 'Stage Illusion,' 705.

6 In fact, Hugo uses the conditional mood: 'Ruy Blas *would be* the people.' But he does so because he begins the sentence with the 'topic of modesty' ('If the author had succeeded in bringing off the part of his idea'), so as to protect him-

self against the criticism that he is overstating the importance, or the value, philosophical or otherwise, of his drama.

7 The fact that Hugo did not begin *Ruy Blas* with this confrontation, choosing rather to show the action prior to it, rather than to have recourse to 'flashbacks' in the form of narratives by 'messengers' or eye-witnesses to unstaged action, confirms that this is his last fully-realized Romantic drama before *Torquemada* thirty years later. Both his epic melodrama, *Les Burgraves* and *Mille Francs de récompense* rely extensively on the reporting of events represented as occurring many years before the action dramatized onstage.

8 Quoted by Ubersfeld, *RB*, 329.

9 For explanations of rhetorical figures of vehemence and vituperation such as those mentioned: *ara, cataplexis, categoria, insultatio,* and *ominatio,* see Bernard Dupriez, *A Dictionary of Literary Devices: Gradus, A–Z,* trans. A.W. Halsall (Toronto: University of Toronto Press 1991). For a discussion of these figures in Hugo's novels, see A.W. Halsall, *Victor Hugo et l'art de convaincre* (Montréal: Éditions Balzac, 'L'Univers du discours' 1995).

CHAPTER 8

1 *Timber, or Discoveries Made upon Men and Matter* (1641) in *Ben Jonson,* ed. Ian Donaldson (Oxford; New York: Oxford University Press 1985), 539.

2 Although staged in 1836, two years before *Ruy Blas, La Esmeralda* belongs to the beginning of the period under discussion here, when Hugo's difficulties with the composition and reception of his plays would eventually discourage him from seeking to have them performed in Parisian theatres.

3 *The Memoirs of Hector Berlioz,* trans. and ed. David Cairns (London: Panther 1970), 292.

4 The mummers' booth before which gathers an audience to whom Guillou–Gorju and Tagus perform represents the meta-theatrical, or theatre-in-the-theatre device beloved of post-modernist literary theory. See Burwick, 'Stage Illusion,' 707–8.

5 'Chronique de la quinzaine,' *Revue des Deux Mondes* (30 April 1841) cited by Olga W. Russell, *Étude historique et critique des 'Burgraves' de Victor Hugo* (Paris: Nizet 1962), 45.

6 Quoted by Russell, *Étude historique et critique des 'Burgraves,'* 235.

7 In fact, he entitled the three parts 'The Ancestor,' 'The Beggar,' and 'The Lost Vault.'

CHAPTER 9

1 These fragments may be consulted in *OC,* 9 (1853–5), 879–1013; 10 (1856–60), 1025–1146; 12 (1860–5), 993–1051.

2 In April 1866, when it looked as if *Mille Francs* might be performed in Paris, Hugo referred to the play as a 'drama' in letters to his son, François-Victor, to Marc Fournier, Director of the Porte-Saint-Martin Theatre, and to Auguste Vacquerie. See *OC,* 13, 786–7.

3 'I'm an outsider,' he says (4, 6).

4 Examples include, as we have seen, Saverny in *Marion de Lorme* and Don César in *Ruy Blas.*

5 On Hugo's use of asides, see Samia Chahine, *La Dramaturgie de Victor Hugo* (Paris: Nizet 1971), 239–40. Other examples of the cinematic use of the address to the camera, and therefore directly to the spectator, include: Michael Caine's *Alfie,* as well as both Laurence Olivier's and Ian McKellen's versions of Shakespeare's *Richard III;* and in the TV dramatization of three novels by Michael Dobbs that included, *House of Cards, To Play the King,* and *Final Cut,* Ian Richardson, in his portrayal of the evil British Prime Minister Francis Urquhart, used the same clearly rhetorical technique in a (largely successful) attempt to persuade TV audiences to see things from his point of view, as it were, and as a result to reduce their antipathy to him.

6 Quoted in V. Hugo, *Théâtre complet* (Paris: Gallimard, 'Bibliothèque de la Pléiade' 1963), 2, 1908.

7 The others are, along with the date each one entered the repertoire: *Hernani* (1830), *Le Roi s'amuse* (1832), *Angelo* (1835), *Marion de Lorme* (1838), *Les Burgraves* (1843), *Ruy Blas* (1879), *Lucrèce Borgia* (1918), *Mangeront-ils?* (1919), *Esca* (1923), *Margarita* (1923), *La Forêt mouillée* (1930), and *La Grand'mère* (1931). See Laster, *PF,* 284.

8 The *Encyclopedia Britannica* (1974), for example, gives the figure 2,000 as the number of his victims; article 'Torquemada' (11, 855).

9 Aristotle: 'The difference [between the historian and the poet] is that the one tells of what has happened, the other of the kinds of things that might happen,' 'On the Art of Poetry,' in *Classical Literary Criticism,* 43 (Chapter 9).

10 In his critical edition of *Torquemada* (New York: University Press of America 1989), xiv–xv), John J. Janc points out that on 27 April 1881, the year before Hugo wrote his drama, a pogrom occurred in Elisabethgrad, in central Russia, during which Jews were slaughtered and driven out of the city and surrounding countryside. Hugo furiously denounced the pogrom in *Le Rappel* of 19 June 1882. His drama appeared one week later on 26 June. Hugo's fury at the Russian massacre seems to inform his powerful denunciation of the Spanish monarchy's refusal to save Sephardic Jews from Torquemada's fanaticism.

11 Hugo's historical source for his rhetorically heightened *hypotyposis* representing this all but incredible scene of massacre by fire is Jean-Antoine Lhorente's *Histoire critique de l'inquisition espagnole, depuis l'époque de son établissement par Ferdinand V, jusqu'au règne de Ferdinand VII,* trans. Alexis Pellier (Paris: Treuttel and Würtz 1917). See *Torquemada,* ed. Janc, 209, 223.

12 *L'Humanité*, 30 May 1976, 7.

CHAPTER 10

1 Fernand Baldensperger, 'Les Années 1827–28 en France et au dehors,' *Revue des Cours et Conférences*, 30 June 1929, 529.
2 Quoted in V. Hugo, *Théâtre complet* (Pléiade edition), 1, 1766.
3 Aristotle, *On Rhetoric: A Theory of Civic Discourse*, Book 1, Chapter 2, 1356b, 33–4; trans. George A. Kennedy (New York: Oxford University Press 1991), 41.
4 Chevalley, *La Comédie-Française, hier et aujourd'hui*, 83–6.
5 Richard Eyre's 1996 production at London's Royal National Theatre of *Le Roi s'amuse* in Tony Harrison's translation / adaptation, entitled *The Prince's Play* is a notable exception.
6 Berry, ed., *On Directing Shakespeare*, 14–23.

Works Consulted

Hugo, Victor, *Oeuvres complètes*. Ed. Jean Massin. 18 vols. Paris: Le Club Français du Livre 1967–70.
- *Cromwell*. Ed. Anne Ubersfeld. Paris: Garnier-Flammarion 1968.
- *Les Deux Trouvailles de Gallus*. Ed. John J. Janc. New York: University Press of America 1983.
- *Mangeront-ils?* Ed. René Journet and Guy Robert. Paris: Flammarion 1970.
- *Préface de 'Cromwell.'* Ed. Pierre Grosclaude. Paris: Larousse 1949.
- *Ruy Blas*. Ed. Anne Ubersfeld. 2 vols. Paris: Les Belles Lettres 1971–2.
- *Théâtre complet*. 2 vols. Paris: Gallimard, 'Bibliothèque de la Pléiade' 1963.
- *Théâtre*. 2 vols. Paris: Robert Laffont 1985.
- *Torquemada*. Ed. John J. Janc. New York: University Press of America 1989.
V. Hugo / Tony Harrison. *Le Roi s'amuse / The Prince's Play*. London: Faber & Faber 1996.

ON VICTOR HUGO AND HIS DRAMAS

Affron, Charles. *A Stage for Poets: Studies in the Theatre of Hugo and Musset*. Princeton NJ: Princeton University Press 1971.
L'Avant-scène-théâtre, nos. 767–8, Spécial 'Victor Hugo,' 1–15 April 1985.
Bassan, Fernande. 'La Réception critique d'*Hernani* de Victor Hugo,' *Revue d'Histoire du Théâtre* (1984), 69–77.
Burwick, Frederick. 'Stage Illusion and the Stage Designs of Goethe and Hugo,' *Word & Image*, 4, nos. 3 & 4, (July-December 1988), 692–718.
Butor, Michel. 'La Voix qui sort de l'ombre et le poison qui transpire à travers les murs.' In *Répertoire III*. Paris: Les Éditions de minuit 1968, 185–213.

Carlson, Marvin. '*Hernani*'s Revolt from the Tradition of French Stage Composition,' *Theatre Survey*, 13, no. 1 (May 1972), 1–27.

Chahine, Samia. *La Dramaturgie de Victor Hugo (1816–1843)*. Paris: Nizet 1971.

Cooper, Barbara C. 'Parodying Hugo,' *European Romantic Review* (1991), 23–38.

Delalande, Jean. *Victor Hugo à Hauteville House*. Paris: Éditions Albin Michel 1947.

Descotes, Maurice. *L'Obsession de Napoléon dans le 'Cromwell' de Victor Hugo*. Paris: Minard, Collection 'Archives des lettres modernes' 1967.

Doyle, Ruth L. *Victor Hugo's Dramas. An Annotated Bibliography, 1900–1980*. Westport CT: Greenwood Press 1981.

Duchet, Claude. 'Victor Hugo et l'âge d'homme (*Cromwell* et sa Préface).' In *OC*, 3, 5–37.

Gaudon, Jean. *Victor Hugo dramaturge*. Paris: L'Arche 1955.

– 'Sur *Hernani*,' *Cahiers de l'Association Internationale des Études Françaises* (May 1983), 101–20.

– *Victor Hugo et le théâtre : stratégie et dramaturgie*. Paris: Suger 1985.

– 'En Marge de la bataille d'Hernani,' *Europe* (March 1985), 116–27.

Gohin, Yves. *Victor Hugo*. Paris: Presses Universitaires de France 1987.

Guillemin, Henri. *Hugo*. Paris: Seuil, Collection 'Écrivains de toujours' 1951.

Hugo, Adèle [Mme V.H.]. *Victor Hugo raconté par Adèle Hugo*. Paris: Plon 1985.

– *Victor Hugo raconté par un témoin de sa vie*. 2 vols. Paris: Nelson 1936.

Laster, Arnaud. *Pleins Feux sur Victor Hugo*. Paris: Comédie-Française 1981.

– *Victor Hugo*. Paris: Pierre Belfond 1984.

Lyonnet, Henri. *Les 'Premières' de Victor Hugo*. Paris: Delagrave 1930.

Maurois, André. *Olympio*. New York: Pyramid Books 1968.

Murphy, Bernardette L. '*Cromwell*, ou les Avatars de la royauté,' *Symposium*, 43, no. 1 (Spring 1989), 56–72.

– 'Jeux et enjeux de la théâtralité dans *Cromwell*,' *Nineteenth-Century French Studies*, 16, no. 3 (Spring 1988), 223–44.

Pollin, Burton R. 'Victor Hugo and Poe,' *Revue de Littérature Comparée*, 42 (October–December 1968), 494–519.

Richardson, Joanna. *Victor Hugo*. New York: St. Martin's Press 1976.

Robb, Graham. *Victor Hugo*. London: Picador 1997.

Rostand, Maurice. 'La Gloire de Victor Hugo,' *Lettres Françaises* (21 February 1952), 1–2.

Russell, Olga Wester. *Étude historique et critique des 'Burgraves' de Victor Hugo*. Paris: Nizet 1962.

Shayer, David. *Victor Hugo in Guernsey*. Guernsey, CI: Toucan Press 1987.

Smith Dow, Leslie. *Adèle Hugo – la misérable*. Fredericton, NB: Goose Lane Editions 1993.

Theatre Record, 16, issue 8 (13 May 1996), 494–8.

Thomasseau, Jean-Marie. 'Pour une analyse du para-texte théâtral. Quelques éléments du para-texte hugolien,' *Littérature* (February 1984), 79–103.

– 'Dialogues avec tableaux à ressorts,' *Europe*, (November-December 1987), 61–70.

Tieghem, Philippe van. *Dictionnaire de Victor Hugo*. Paris: Larousse 1970.

Ubersfeld, Anne. 'Le Carnaval de *Cromwell*,' *Romantisme* 1–2 (1971), 80–93.

– *Le Roi et le bouffon*. Paris: Corti 1974.

– *Le Roman d'Hernani*. Paris: Comédie-Française-Mercure de France 1985.

Vitez, Antoine, Yannis Kokkos, and Éloi Recoing. *Le Livre de 'Lucrèce Borgia' drame de Victor Hugo*. Arles: Actes Sud 1985.

Ward, Patrica A., Bernardette Lintz Murphy, and Michel Grimaud. 'Victor Hugo : oeuvres et critique 1981–1983,' *Revue des Lettres Modernes*, 1992.

ON FRENCH THEATRE

Allévy, Marie-Antoinette. *La Mise en scène en France dans la première moitié du dix-neuvième siècle*. Paris: E. Droz 1938.

Ambrière, Francis. *Mademoiselle Mars et Marie Dorval*. Paris: Seuil 1992.

Baldick, Robert. *The Life and Times of Frédérick Lemaître*. London: Hamish Hamilton 1959.

Becker, Colette. *Les Hauts Lieux du romantisme*. Paris: Bordas 1991.

Bernhardt, Sarah. *L'Art du théâtre*. Monaco: Éditions Sauret 1993.

Berthier, Patrick. *Le Théâtre au dix-neuvième siècle*. Paris: Presses Universitaires de France, Collection 'Que sais-je?' 1986.

Bony, Jacques. *Lire le romantisme*. Paris: Dunod 1992.

Boudet, Micheline. *Mademoiselle Mars, l'inimitable*. Paris: Perrin 1987.

Brownstein, Rachel M. *Tragic Muse: Rachel of the Comédie-Française*. New York: Alfred A. Knopf 1993.

Carlson, Marvin. 'French Stage Composition from Hugo to Zola,' *Educational Stage Journal* (December 1971), 363–78.

– *The French Stage in the Nineteenth Century*. Metuchen NJ: The Scarecrow Press 1972.

Chahine, Samia. *La Dramaturgie de Victor Hugo (1816–1843)*. Paris: Nizet 1971.

Chevalley, Sylvie. *La Comédie-Française hier et aujourd'hui*. Paris: Didier 1979.

Constant, Benjamin. *Wallenstein, tragédie en cinq actes et en vers, précédée de quelques réflexions sur le théâtre allemand*. Ed. J.-R. Derré. Paris: Perrin 1965.

Cooper, Barbara C. '"Il faut suivre votre modèle": Theatre and Society in Early Nineteenth-Century France.' In *French Literature Series*, Vol. 15. Ed. A. Maynor Hardee. Columbia: University of South Carolina 1988, 95–108.

Cox, Jeffrey N. *In the Shadows of Romance: Romantic Tragedy in Germany, England, and France*. Athens OH: Ohio University Press 1987.

Descotes, Maurice. *Le Drame romantique et ses grands créateurs*. Paris: Presses Universitaires de France 1955.

Devaux, Patrick. *La Comédie-Française*. Paris: Presses Universitaires de France, Collection 'Que sais-je?' 1993.

Dumas, Alexandre. *Mes Mémoires*. Paris: Plon 1986.

Gautier, Théophile. *Histoire de l'art dramatique en France depuis vingt-cinq ans.* 6 vols. Paris: Hetzel 1858–9.

Hemmings, F.W.J. *The Theatre Industry in Nineteenth-Century France.* Cambridge: Cambridge University Press 1993.

– *Theatre and State in France, 1760–1905.* Cambridge: Cambridge University Press 1994.

Howarth, W.D. *Sublime and Grotesque: a Study of French Romantic Drama.* London: Harrap 1975.

Hubert, Marie-Claude. *Le Théâtre.* Paris: Armand Colin 1988.

Janin, Jules. *Histoire de la littérature dramatique.* 6 vols. Paris: Michel Lévy 1853–8.

Jomaron, Jacqueline de, ed. *Le Théâtre en France.* Paris: Armand Colin 1992.

Krokovitch, Odile. *Hugo censuré. La Liberté au théâtre au XIXe siècle.* Paris: Calmann-Lévy 1985.

Le Hir, Marie-Pierre. *Le Romantisme aux enchères : Ducange, Pixérécourt, Hugo.* Amsterdam/Philadelphia: John Benjamins 1992.

Lioure, Michel. *Le Drame.* Paris: Armand Colin 1963.

– *Le Drame de Diderot à Ionesco.* Paris: Armand Colin 1968.

Marcoux, J. Paul. *Guilbert de Pixérécourt.* New York: Peter Lang 1992.

Oliver, A. Richard. 'Romanticism and Opera,' *Symposium* (Fall-Winter 1969), 325–31.

Pavis, Patrice. *Dictionnaire du théâtre.* Paris: Éditions sociales 1980.

Przyboś, Julia. *L'Entreprise mélodramatique.* Paris: Corti 1987.

Roubine, Jean-Jacques. 'La Grande Magie.' In Jomaron, ed., *Le Théâtre en France,* 597–675.

– *Introduction aux grandes théories du théâtre.* Paris: Bordas 1990.

Smith, James L. *Melodrama.* London: Methuen 1973.

Souriau, Étienne. *Les Deux Cent Mille Situations dramatiques.* Paris: Flammarion 1950.

Souriau, Maurice. *De la convention dans la tragédie classique et dans le drame romantique.* Paris: Hachette 1885.

– *La Préface de 'Cromwell,' Introduction, texte, et notes.* 2 vols. Paris: Boivin 1897.

Steiner, George. *The Death of Tragedy.* London: Faber & Faber 1963.

Thomassau, Jean-Marie. *Le Mélodrame.* Paris: Presses Universitaires de France 1984.

Thomson, Philip. *The Grotesque.* London: Methuen 1972.

Ubersfeld, Anne. *Le Drame romantique.* Paris: Éditions Belin 1993.

– 'L'Ère du spectacle en France (1815–1887).' In Jomaron, ed., *Le Théâtre en France,* 534–96.

CRITICAL WORKS

Adams, Hazard. *Critical Theory since Plato.* New York: Harcourt, Brace, Jovanovich 1971.

Aristotle, *On Rhetoric: A Theory of Civic Discourse.* Trans. George A. Kennedy. New York: Oxford University Press 1991.

Aristotle, Horace, Longinus. *Literary Criticism.* Trans. T.S. Dorsch. Harmondsworth: Penguin 1965.

Bakhtin, Mikhail. *The Dialogic Imagination. Four Essays.* Ed. Michael Holquist, trans. Caryl Emerson and Michael Holquist. Austin: University of Texas Press 1981.

Baldensperger, Fernand. 'Les Années 1827–28 en France et au dehors,' *Revue des Cours et Conférences* (30 June 1929), 528–42.

Berlioz, Hector. *The Memoirs of Hector Berlioz.* Trans. and ed. David Cairns. London: Panther 1970.

Booth, Wayne C. *A Rhetoric of Irony.* Chicago: University of Chicago Press 1974.

Cave, Terence. *Recognitions: A Study in Poetics.* Oxford: Clarendon Press 1990.

Derrida, Jacques. *L'Écriture et la différence.* Paris: Seuil, Collection 'Points' 1979.

Diderot, Denis. 'Entretiens sur *Le Fils naturel.*' In *Oeuvres esthétiques,* ed. Paul Vernière. Paris: Éditions Garnier 1968.

Dupriez, Bernard. *A Dictionary of Literary Devices: Gradus, A-Z.* Trans. A.W. Halsall. Toronto: University of Toronto Press 1991.

Encyclopedia Britannica. 15th edition. Chicago: University of Chicago 1974.

Gautier, Théophile. *Histoire du romantisme.* Paris: Charpentier 1874.

Genette, Gérard. 'Vraisemblance et motivation.' *Figures II.* Paris: Seuil 1969, 71–99.

Guizot, François. 'Vie de Shakespeare.' In Shakespeare, *Oeuvres complètes.* Trans. P. Le Tourneur. Paris: Ladvocat 1821.

Halsall, Albert W. *Victor Hugo et l'art de convaincre. Le récit hugolien : rhétorique, argumentation, persuasion.* Montréal: Éditions Balzac, 'L'univers du discours' 1995.

Lacey, Alexander. *Pixérécourt and the French Romantic Drama.* Toronto: University of Toronto Press 1928.

Lever, Maurice. *Sade: A Biography.* Trans. Arthur Goldhammer. New York: Farrar, Straus & Giroux 1993.

Muecke, D. C. *The Compass of Irony.* London: Methuen 1969.

Nozick, Martin. 'The Inez de Castro Theme in European literature,' *Comparative Literature* 3 (Fall 1951), 330–41.

Perelman, Chaim and Lucie Olbrechts-Tyteca. *The New Rhetoric: A Treatise on Argumentation.* Trans. J. Wilkinson and P. Weaver. Notre Dame: University of Notre Dame Press 1969.

Phillips-Matz, Mary Jane. *Verdi, A Biography.* New York: Oxford University Press 1996.

Sand, George [Aurore Dupin]. *Correspondance,* vol. 21. Paris: Éditions Garnier 1986.

Shakespeare, William. *The Complete Works.* Ed. Stanley Wells and Gary Taylor. Oxford: The Clarendon Press 1988.

Staël, G. de. *De l'Allemagne.* Ed. S. Balayé. Paris: Garnier-Flammarion 1968.

Starkie, Enid. *Petrus Borel, the Lycanthrope.* London: Faber & Faber 1954.

Stendhal [M.H. Beyle]. *Racine et Shakespeare.* Paris: J.-J. Pauvert 1965.

– *Romans et contes.* 2 vols. Paris: Gallimard: 'Bibliothèque de la Pléiade' 1983.

Index